THE
CAVALIER
MR.
THOMPSON

A SAM HILL NOVEL
SAM'S EARLY DAYS: 1924

BY RICH TOMMASO

THE CAVALIER

MR.

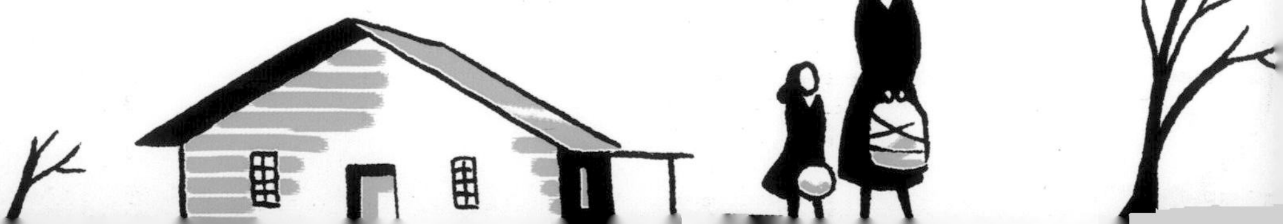

A SAM HILL NOVEL
SAM'S EARLY DAYS: 1924
THOMPSON

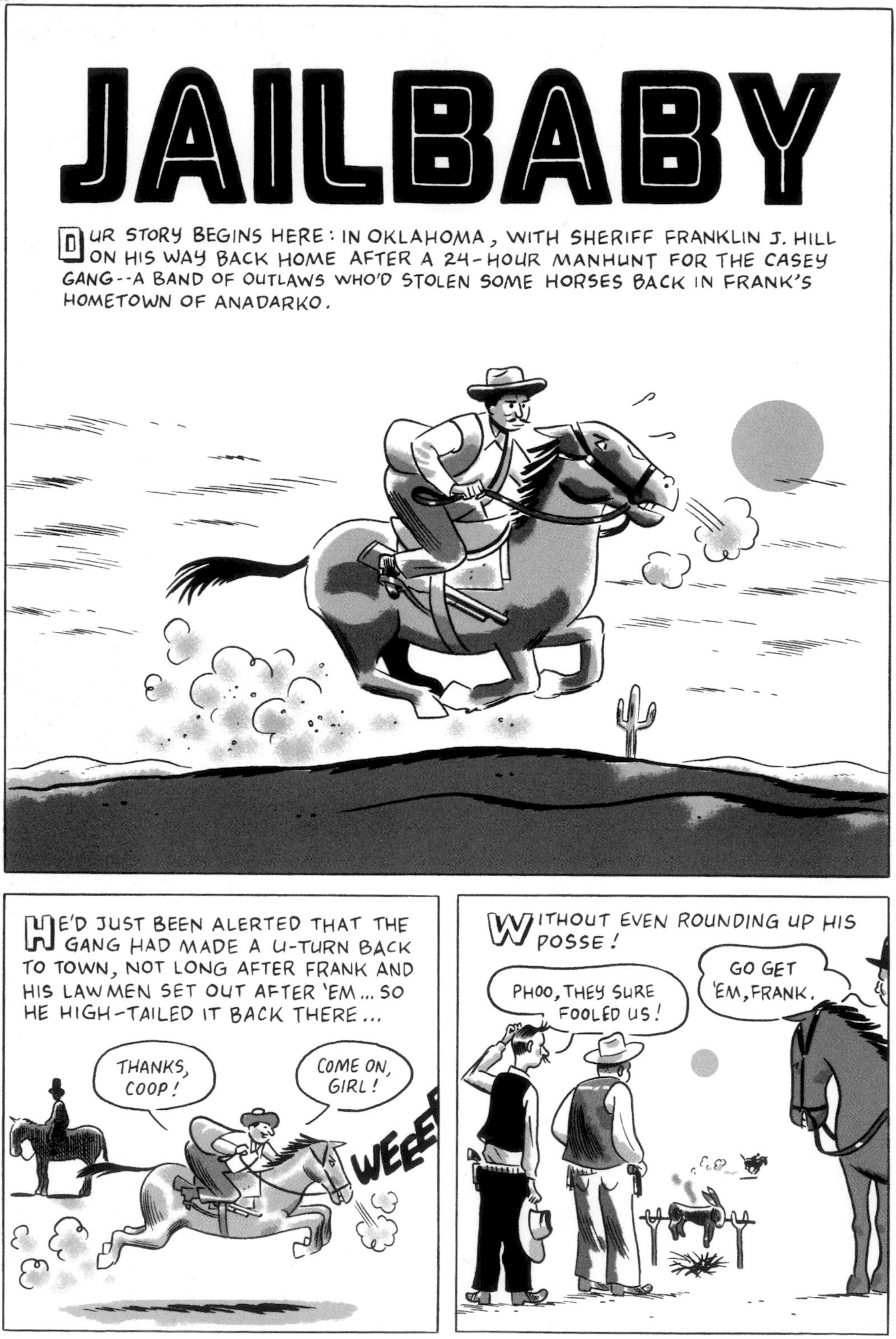
JAILBABY
OUR STORY BEGINS HERE: IN OKLAHOMA, WITH SHERIFF FRANKLIN J. HILL ON HIS WAY BACK HOME AFTER A 24-HOUR MANHUNT FOR THE CASEY GANG--A BAND OF OUTLAWS WHO'D STOLEN SOME HORSES BACK IN FRANK'S HOMETOWN OF ANADARKO.
HE'D JUST BEEN ALERTED THAT THE GANG HAD MADE A U-TURN BACK TO TOWN, NOT LONG AFTER FRANK AND HIS LAWMEN SET OUT AFTER 'EM... SO HE HIGH-TAILED IT BACK THERE...
THANKS, COOP!
COME ON, GIRL!
WEEE
WITHOUT EVEN ROUNDING UP HIS POSSE!
PHOO, THEY SURE FOOLED US!
GO GET 'EM, FRANK.

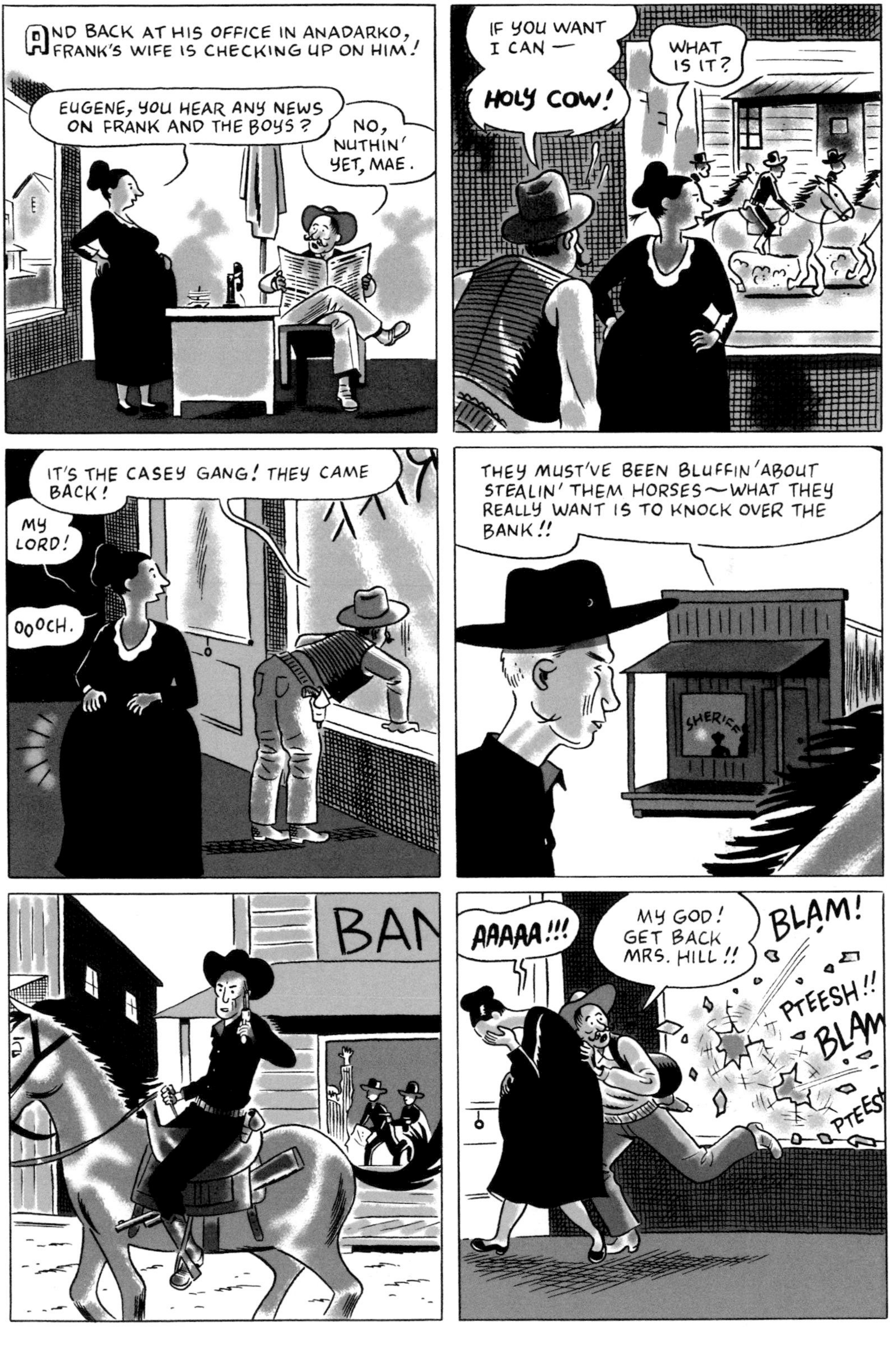
AND BACK AT HIS OFFICE IN ANADARKO, FRANK'S WIFE IS CHECKING UP ON HIM!
EUGENE, YOU HEAR ANY NEWS ON FRANK AND THE BOYS?
NO, NUTHIN' YET, MAE.
IF YOU WANT I CAN —
HOLY COW!
WHAT IS IT?
IT'S THE CASEY GANG! THEY CAME BACK!
MY LORD!
OOOCH.
THEY MUST'VE BEEN BLUFFIN' ABOUT STEALIN' THEM HORSES — WHAT THEY REALLY WANT IS TO KNOCK OVER THE BANK!!
SHERIFF
BAN
AAAAA!!!
MY GOD! GET BACK MRS. HILL!!
BLAM!
PTEESH!!
BLAM
PTEESH

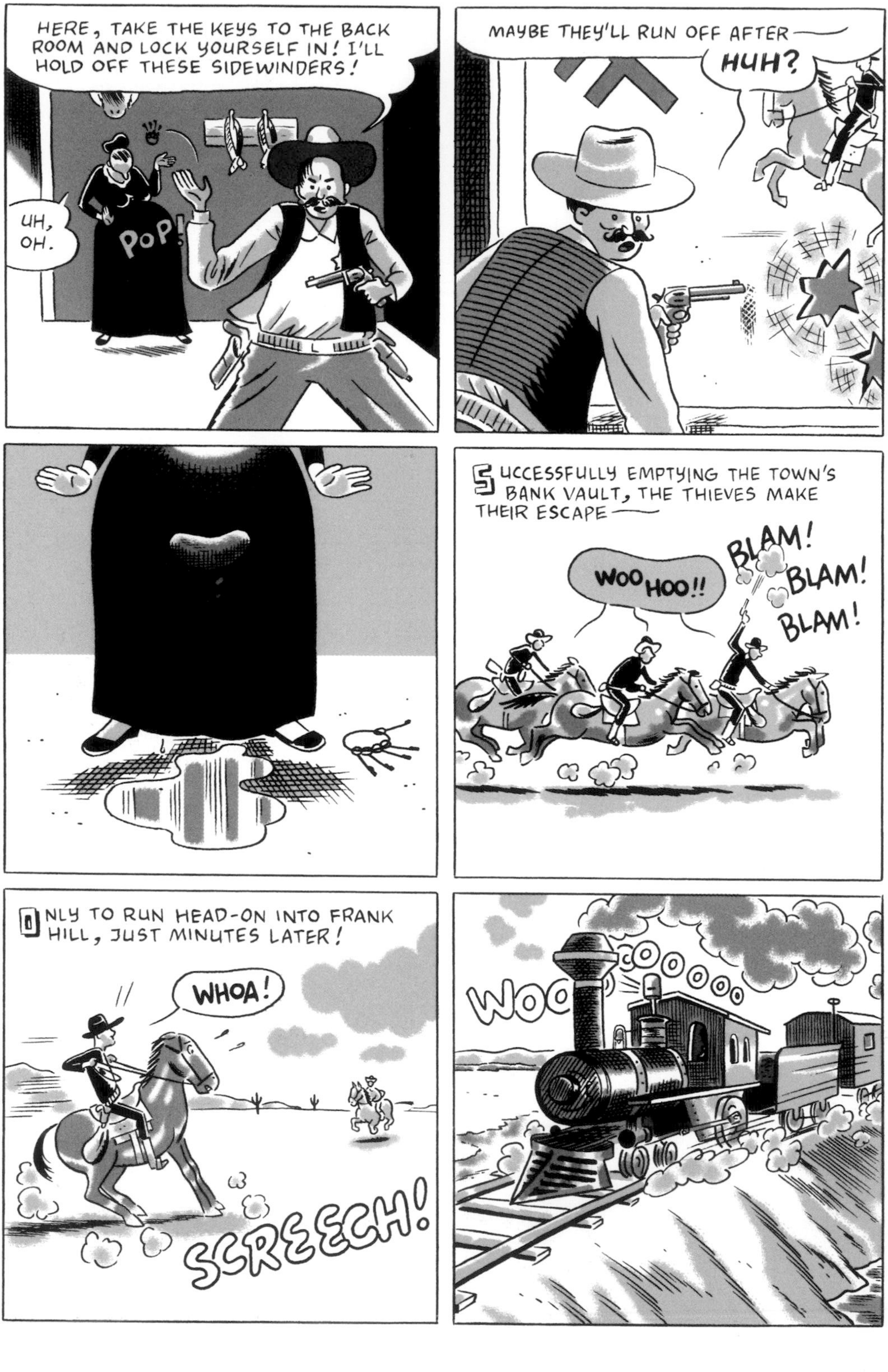
HERE, TAKE THE KEYS TO THE BACK ROOM AND LOCK YOURSELF IN! I'LL HOLD OFF THESE SIDEWINDERS!
UH, OH.
POP!
MAYBE THEY'LL RUN OFF AFTER—
HUH?
SUCCESSFULLY EMPTYING THE TOWN'S BANK VAULT, THE THIEVES MAKE THEIR ESCAPE—
WOO HOO!!
BLAM!
BLAM!
BLAM!
ONLY TO RUN HEAD-ON INTO FRANK HILL, JUST MINUTES LATER!
WHOA!
SCREECH!
WOOOOOOOO

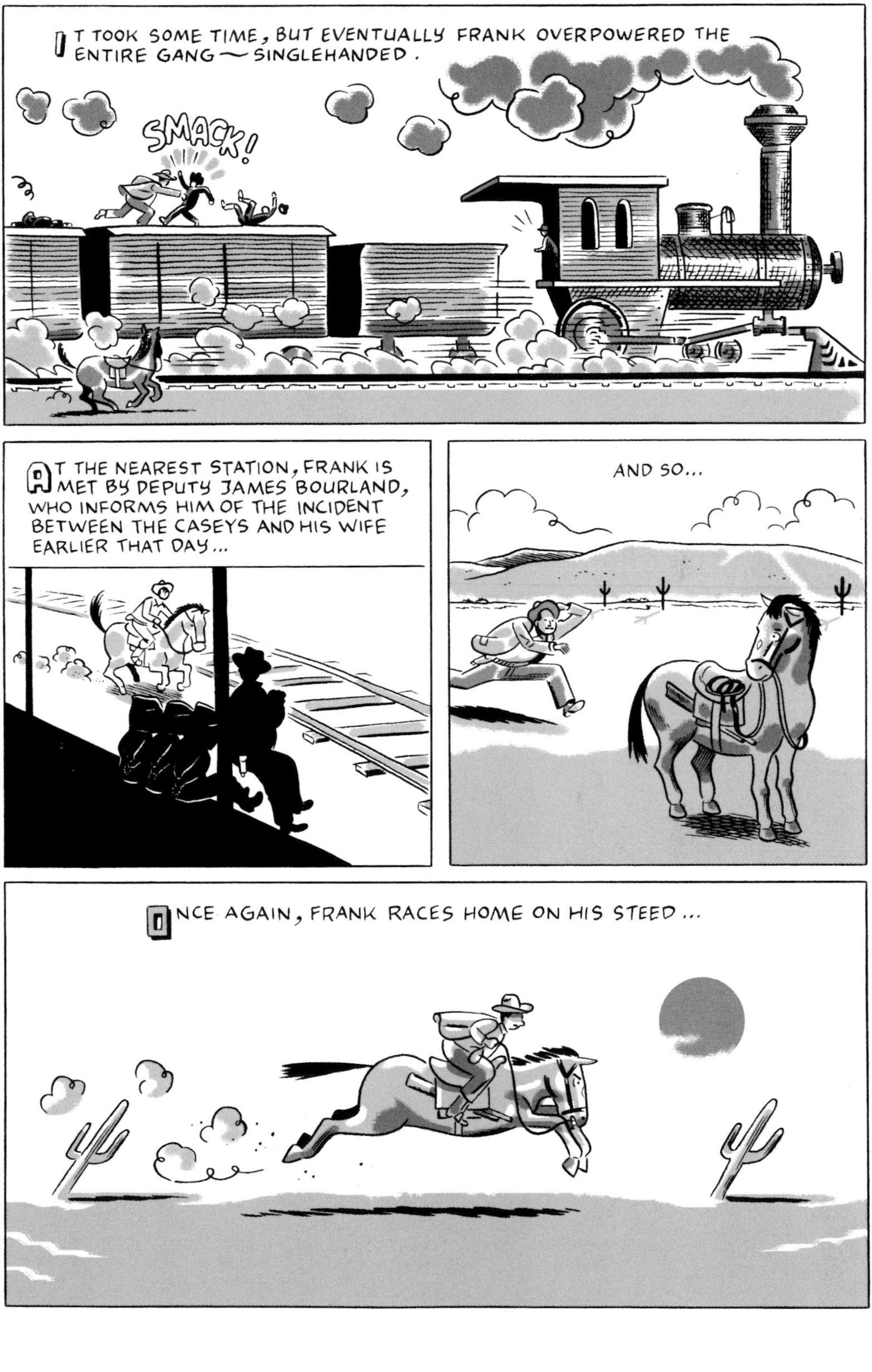
IT TOOK SOME TIME, BUT EVENTUALLY FRANK OVERPOWERED THE ENTIRE GANG — SINGLEHANDED.
SMACK!
AT THE NEAREST STATION, FRANK IS MET BY DEPUTY JAMES BOURLAND, WHO INFORMS HIM OF THE INCIDENT BETWEEN THE CASEYS AND HIS WIFE EARLIER THAT DAY...
AND SO...
ONCE AGAIN, FRANK RACES HOME ON HIS STEED...

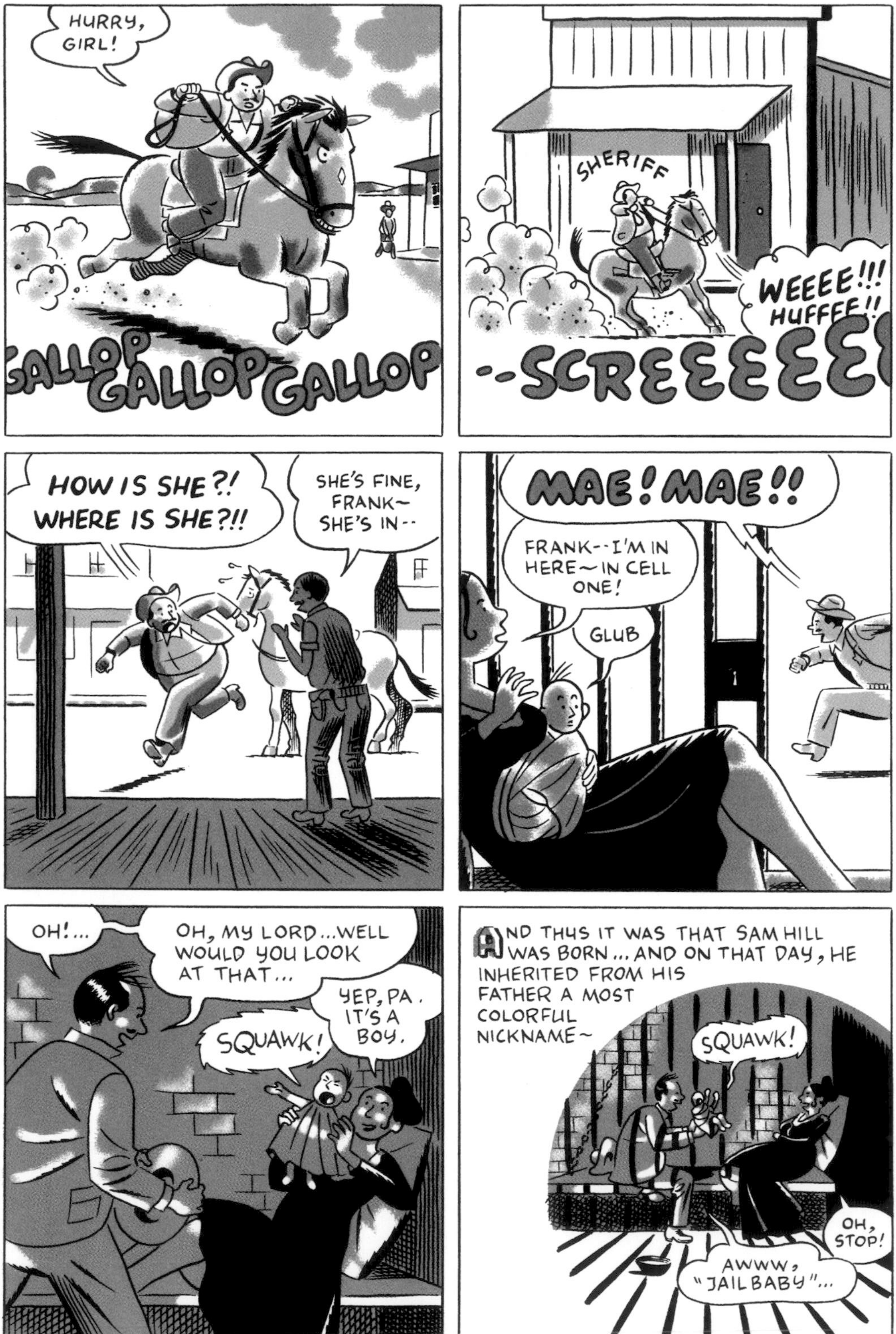
HURRY, GIRL!
GALLOP GALLOP GALLOP
SHERIFF
WEEEE!!! HUFFFF!!
--SCREEEEEE
HOW IS SHE?! WHERE IS SHE?!!
SHE'S FINE, FRANK~ SHE'S IN--
MAE! MAE!!
FRANK--I'M IN HERE~IN CELL ONE!
GLUB
OH!...
OH, MY LORD...WELL WOULD YOU LOOK AT THAT...
YEP, PA. IT'S A BOY.
SQUAWK!
AND THUS IT WAS THAT SAM HILL WAS BORN... AND ON THAT DAY, HE INHERITED FROM HIS FATHER A MOST COLORFUL NICKNAME~
SQUAWK!
OH, STOP!
AWWW, "JAIL BABY"...

1924
THE BOXER

OUR STORY NOW MOVES A LITTLE FURTHER SOUTH TO... WEST TEXAS!

AT THE CAVALIER HOTEL, WHERE ~AFTER MANY YEARS OF "WILDCATTING" ACROSS THE SOUTHWEST, SEEKING OUT AND BURNING THROUGH EVERY BUSINESS VENTURE OF HIS PASSING FANCY ~FRANK HAS FINALLY SETTLED DOWN WITH HIS FAMILY... WELL, NOT HIS _ENTIRE_ FAMILY...

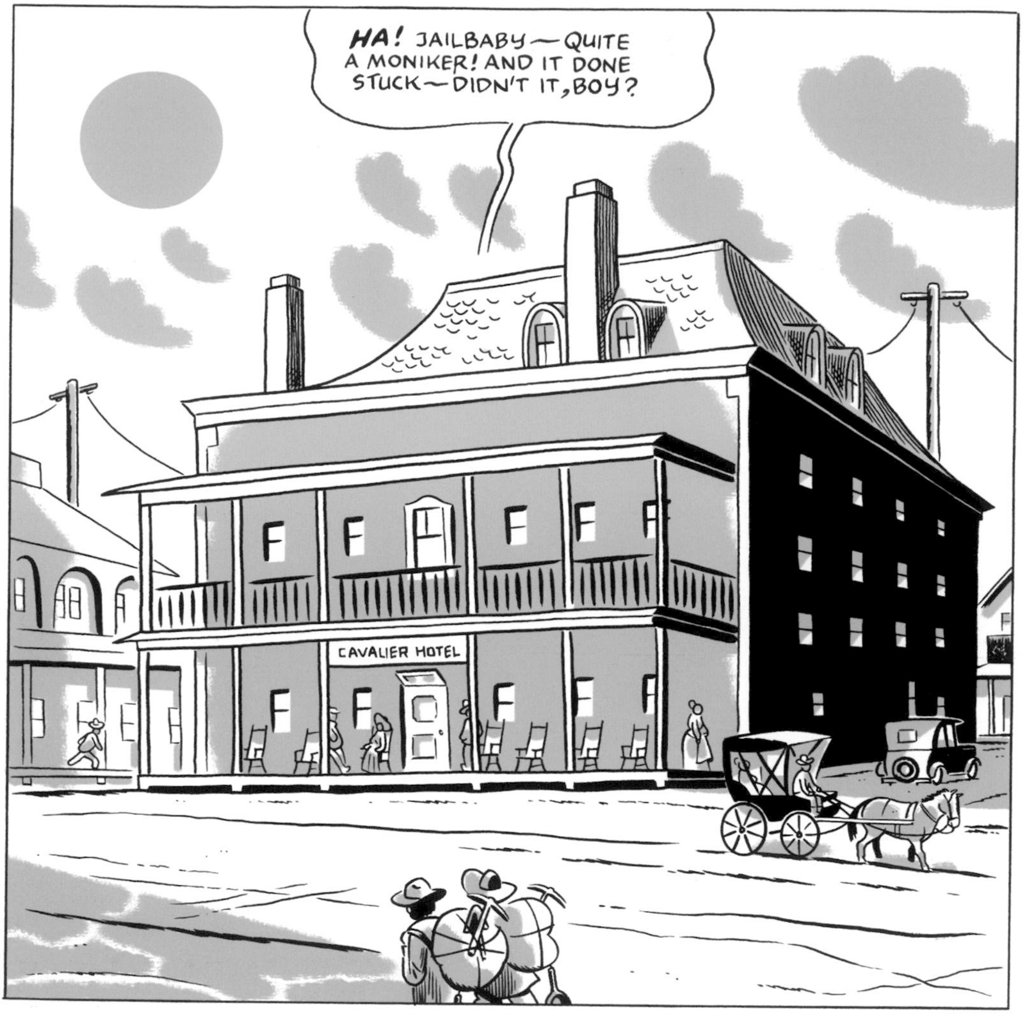
HA! JAILBABY — QUITE A MONIKER! AND IT DONE STUCK — DIDN'T IT, BOY?
CAVALIER HOTEL

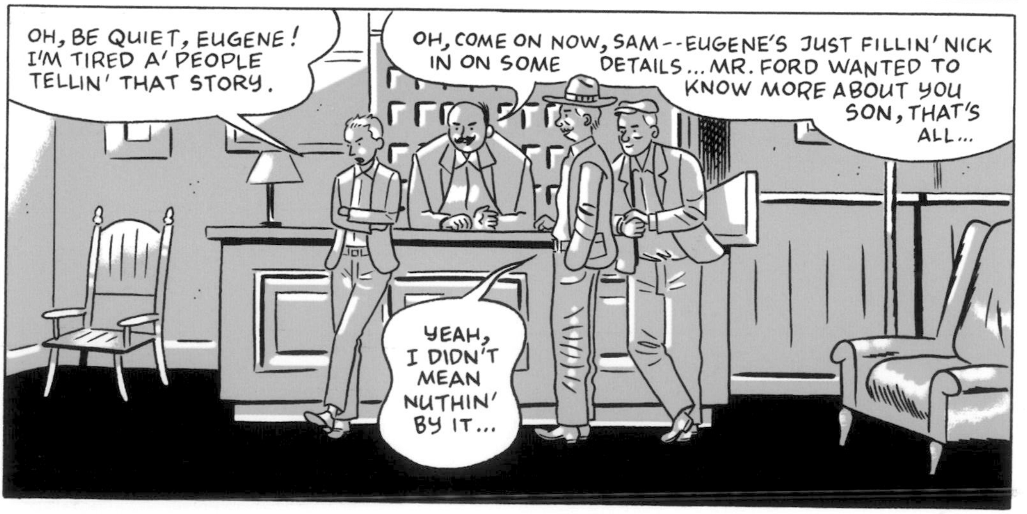
OH, BE QUIET, EUGENE! I'M TIRED A' PEOPLE TELLIN' THAT STORY.
OH, COME ON NOW, SAM--EUGENE'S JUST FILLIN' NICK IN ON SOME DETAILS... MR. FORD WANTED TO KNOW MORE ABOUT YOU SON, THAT'S ALL...
YEAH, I DIDN'T MEAN NUTHIN' BY IT...

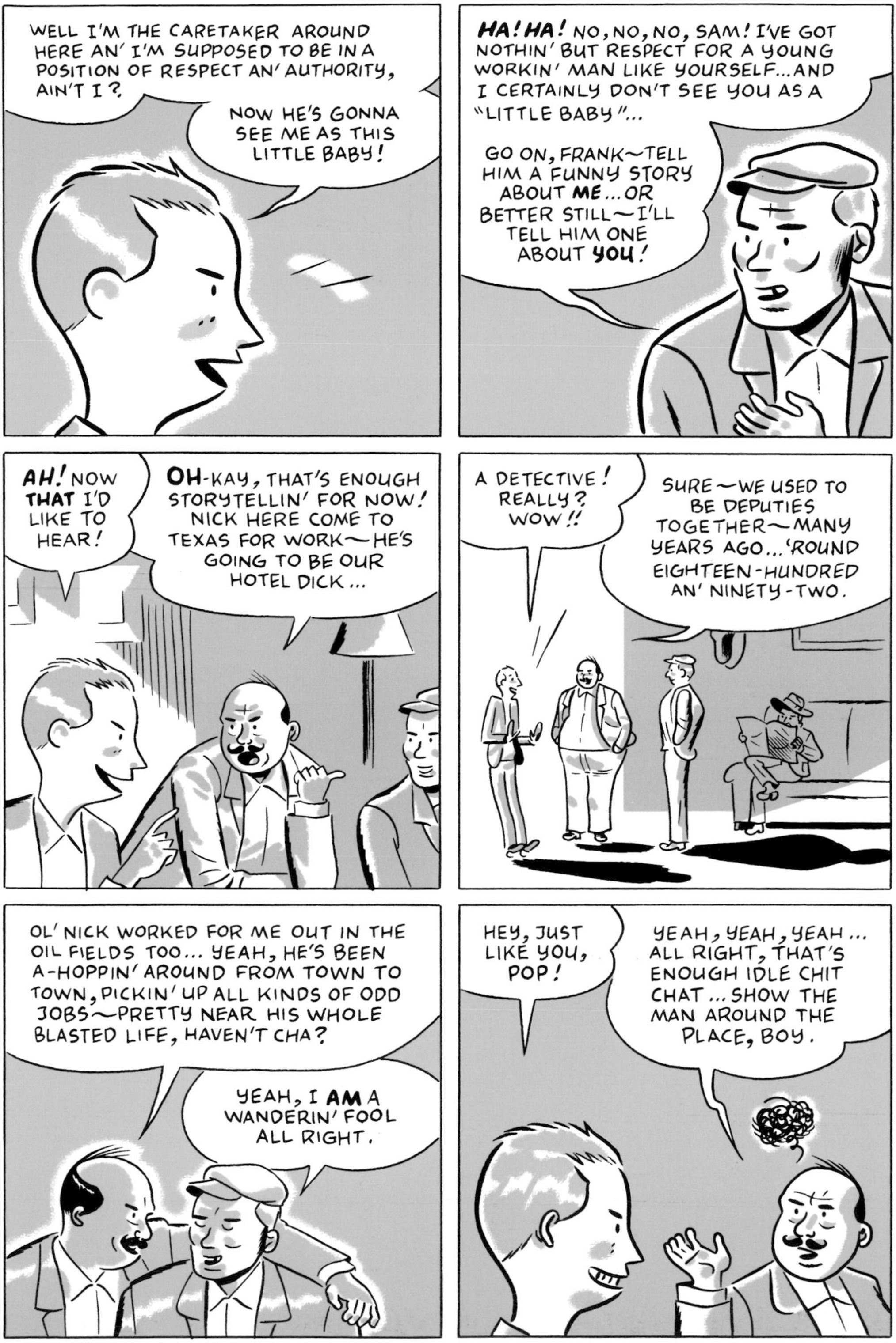
WELL I'M THE CARETAKER AROUND HERE AN' I'M SUPPOSED TO BE IN A POSITION OF RESPECT AN' AUTHORITY, AIN'T I?
NOW HE'S GONNA SEE ME AS THIS LITTLE BABY!
HA! HA! NO, NO, NO, SAM! I'VE GOT NOTHIN' BUT RESPECT FOR A YOUNG WORKIN' MAN LIKE YOURSELF... AND I CERTAINLY DON'T SEE YOU AS A "LITTLE BABY"...
GO ON, FRANK~TELL HIM A FUNNY STORY ABOUT ME... OR BETTER STILL~I'LL TELL HIM ONE ABOUT YOU!
AH! NOW THAT I'D LIKE TO HEAR!
OH-KAY, THAT'S ENOUGH STORYTELLIN' FOR NOW! NICK HERE COME TO TEXAS FOR WORK~HE'S GOING TO BE OUR HOTEL DICK...
A DETECTIVE! REALLY? WOW!!
SURE~WE USED TO BE DEPUTIES TOGETHER~MANY YEARS AGO... 'ROUND EIGHTEEN-HUNDRED AN' NINETY-TWO.
OL' NICK WORKED FOR ME OUT IN THE OIL FIELDS TOO... YEAH, HE'S BEEN A-HOPPIN' AROUND FROM TOWN TO TOWN, PICKIN' UP ALL KINDS OF ODD JOBS~PRETTY NEAR HIS WHOLE BLASTED LIFE, HAVEN'T CHA?
YEAH, I AM A WANDERIN' FOOL ALL RIGHT.
HEY, JUST LIKE YOU, POP!
YEAH, YEAH, YEAH... ALL RIGHT, THAT'S ENOUGH IDLE CHIT CHAT... SHOW THE MAN AROUND THE PLACE, BOY.

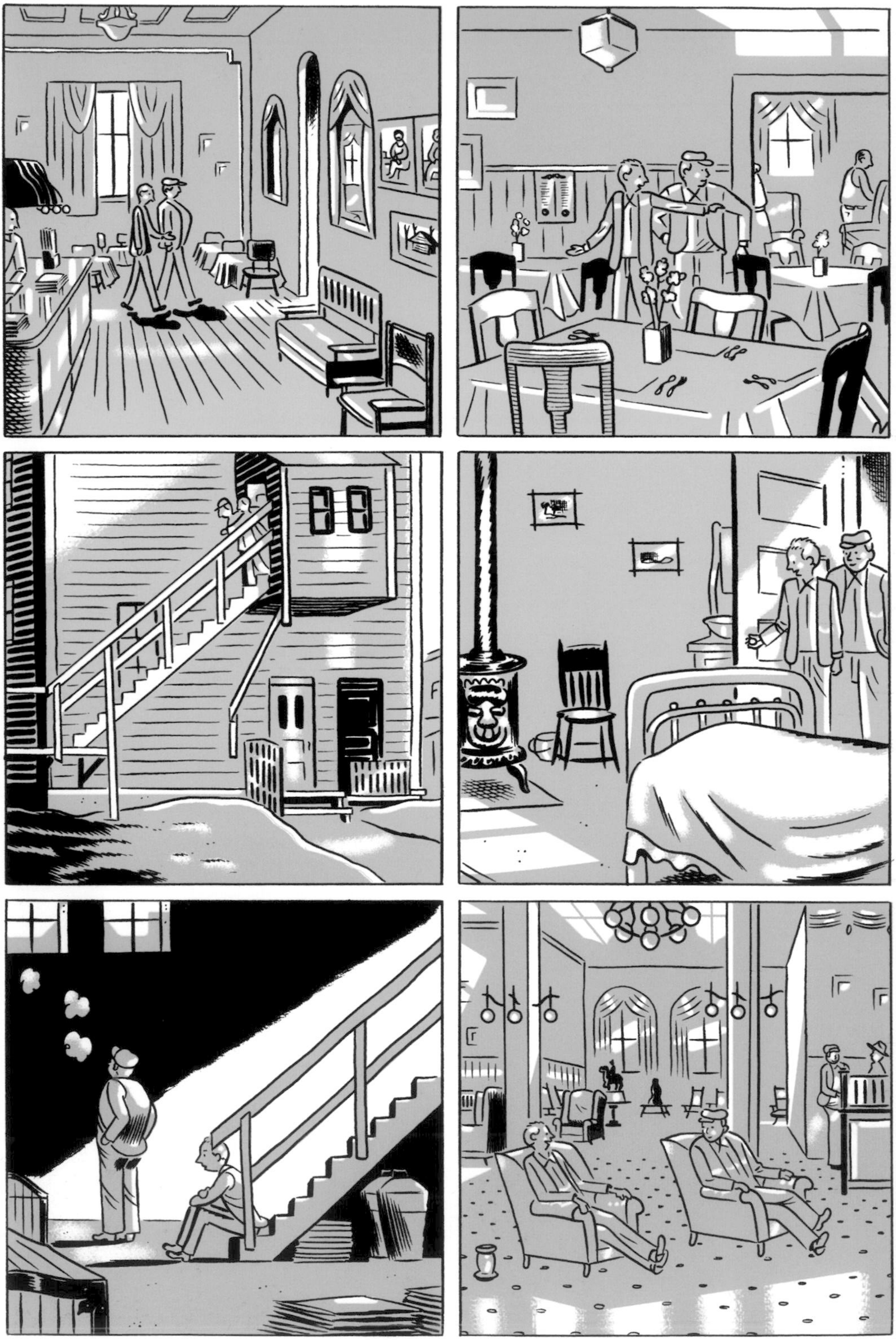

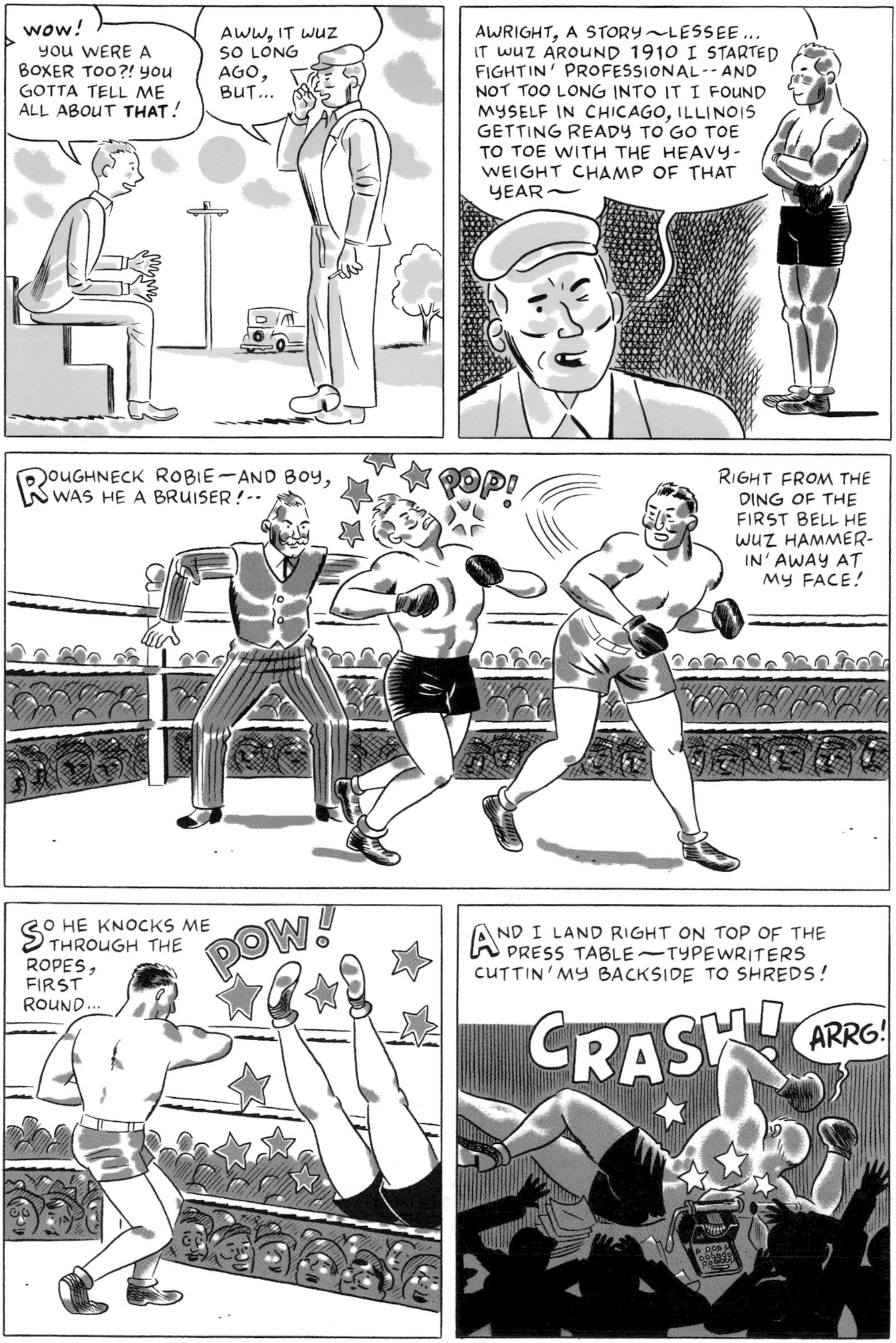
WOW! YOU WERE A BOXER TOO?! YOU GOTTA TELL ME ALL ABOUT THAT!
AWW, IT WUZ SO LONG AGO, BUT...
AWRIGHT, A STORY ~ LESSEE... IT WUZ AROUND 1910 I STARTED FIGHTIN' PROFESSIONAL--AND NOT TOO LONG INTO IT I FOUND MYSELF IN CHICAGO, ILLINOIS GETTING READY TO GO TOE TO TOE WITH THE HEAVY-WEIGHT CHAMP OF THAT YEAR ~
ROUGHNECK ROBIE — AND BOY, WAS HE A BRUISER!--
POP!
RIGHT FROM THE DING OF THE FIRST BELL HE WUZ HAMMER-IN' AWAY AT MY FACE!
SO HE KNOCKS ME THROUGH THE ROPES, FIRST ROUND...
POW!
AND I LAND RIGHT ON TOP OF THE PRESS TABLE — TYPEWRITERS CUTTIN' MY BACKSIDE TO SHREDS!
CRASH!
ARRG!

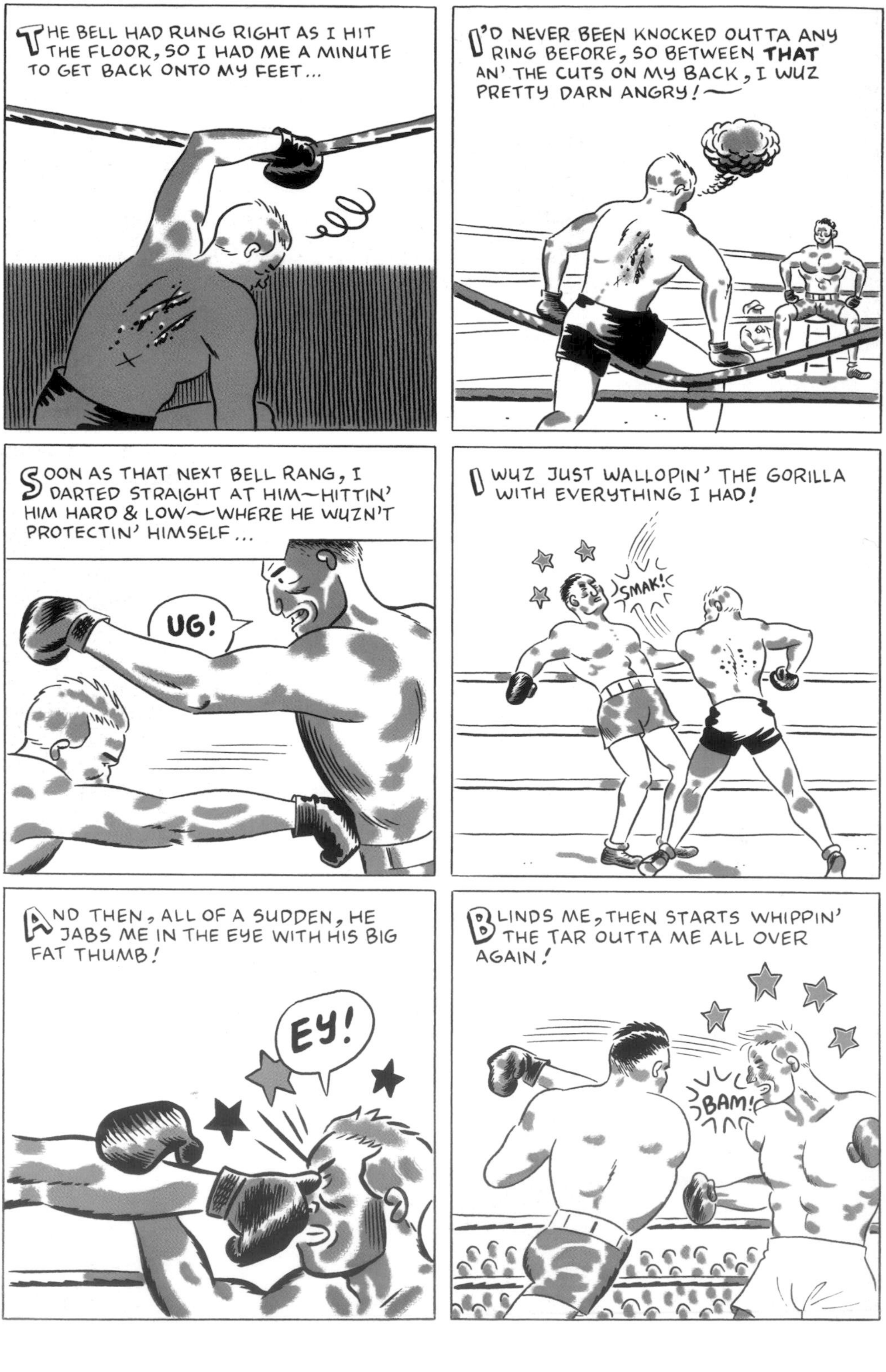
THE BELL HAD RUNG RIGHT AS I HIT THE FLOOR, SO I HAD ME A MINUTE TO GET BACK ONTO MY FEET...
I'D NEVER BEEN KNOCKED OUTTA ANY RING BEFORE, SO BETWEEN THAT AN' THE CUTS ON MY BACK, I WUZ PRETTY DARN ANGRY!~
SOON AS THAT NEXT BELL RANG, I DARTED STRAIGHT AT HIM~HITTIN' HIM HARD & LOW~WHERE HE WUZN'T PROTECTIN' HIMSELF...
UG!
I WUZ JUST WALLOPIN' THE GORILLA WITH EVERYTHING I HAD!
SMAK!
AND THEN, ALL OF A SUDDEN, HE JABS ME IN THE EYE WITH HIS BIG FAT THUMB!
EY!
BLINDS ME, THEN STARTS WHIPPIN' THE TAR OUTTA ME ALL OVER AGAIN!
BAM!

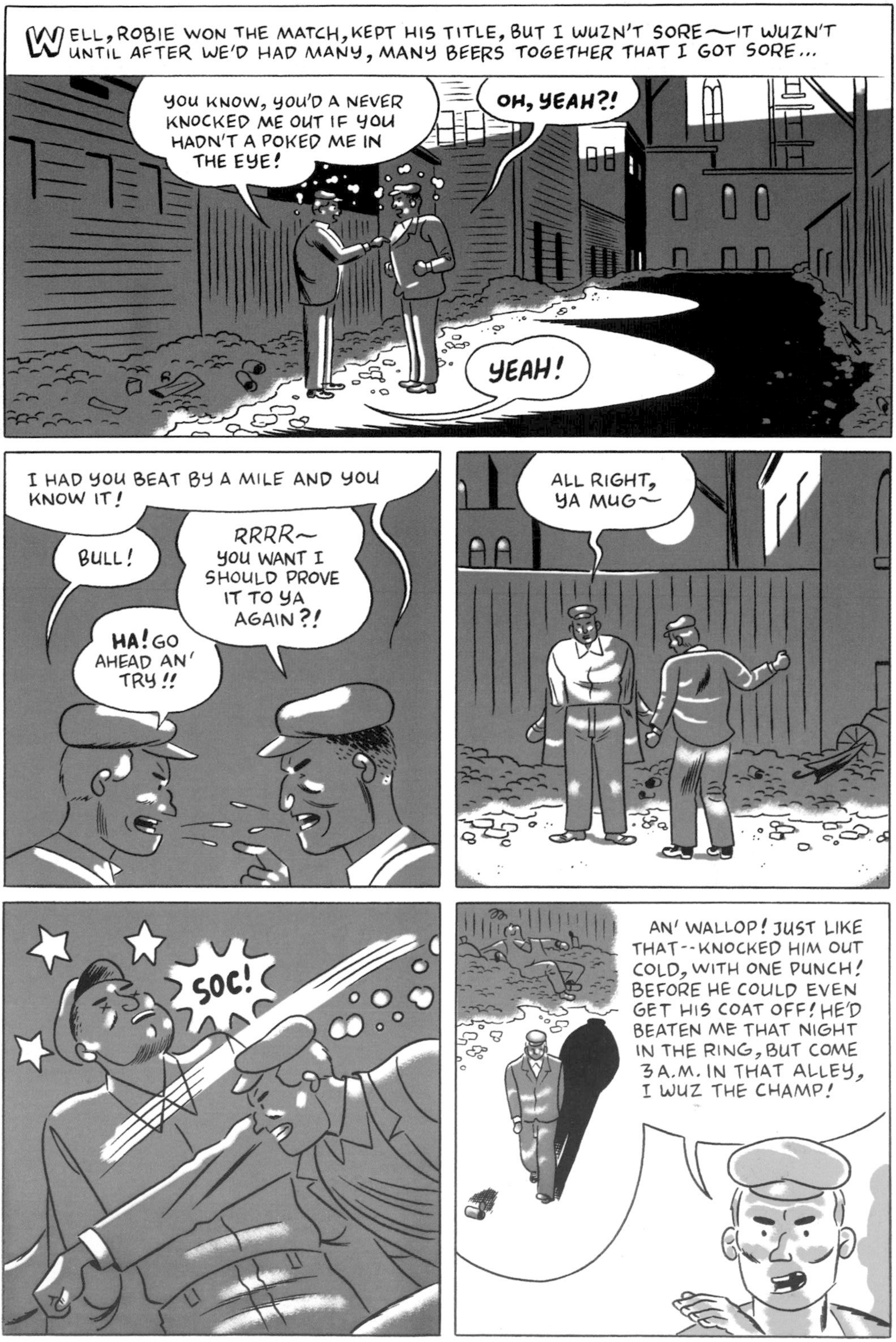
WELL, ROBIE WON THE MATCH, KEPT HIS TITLE, BUT I WUZN'T SORE — IT WUZN'T UNTIL AFTER WE'D HAD MANY, MANY BEERS TOGETHER THAT I GOT SORE...
YOU KNOW, YOU'D A NEVER KNOCKED ME OUT IF YOU HADN'T A POKED ME IN THE EYE!
OH, YEAH?!
YEAH!
I HAD YOU BEAT BY A MILE AND YOU KNOW IT!
BULL!
RRRR~ YOU WANT I SHOULD PROVE IT TO YA AGAIN?!
HA! GO AHEAD AN' TRY!!
ALL RIGHT, YA MUG~
SOC!
AN' WALLOP! JUST LIKE THAT--KNOCKED HIM OUT COLD, WITH ONE PUNCH! BEFORE HE COULD EVEN GET HIS COAT OFF! HE'D BEATEN ME THAT NIGHT IN THE RING, BUT COME 3 A.M. IN THAT ALLEY, I WUZ THE CHAMP!

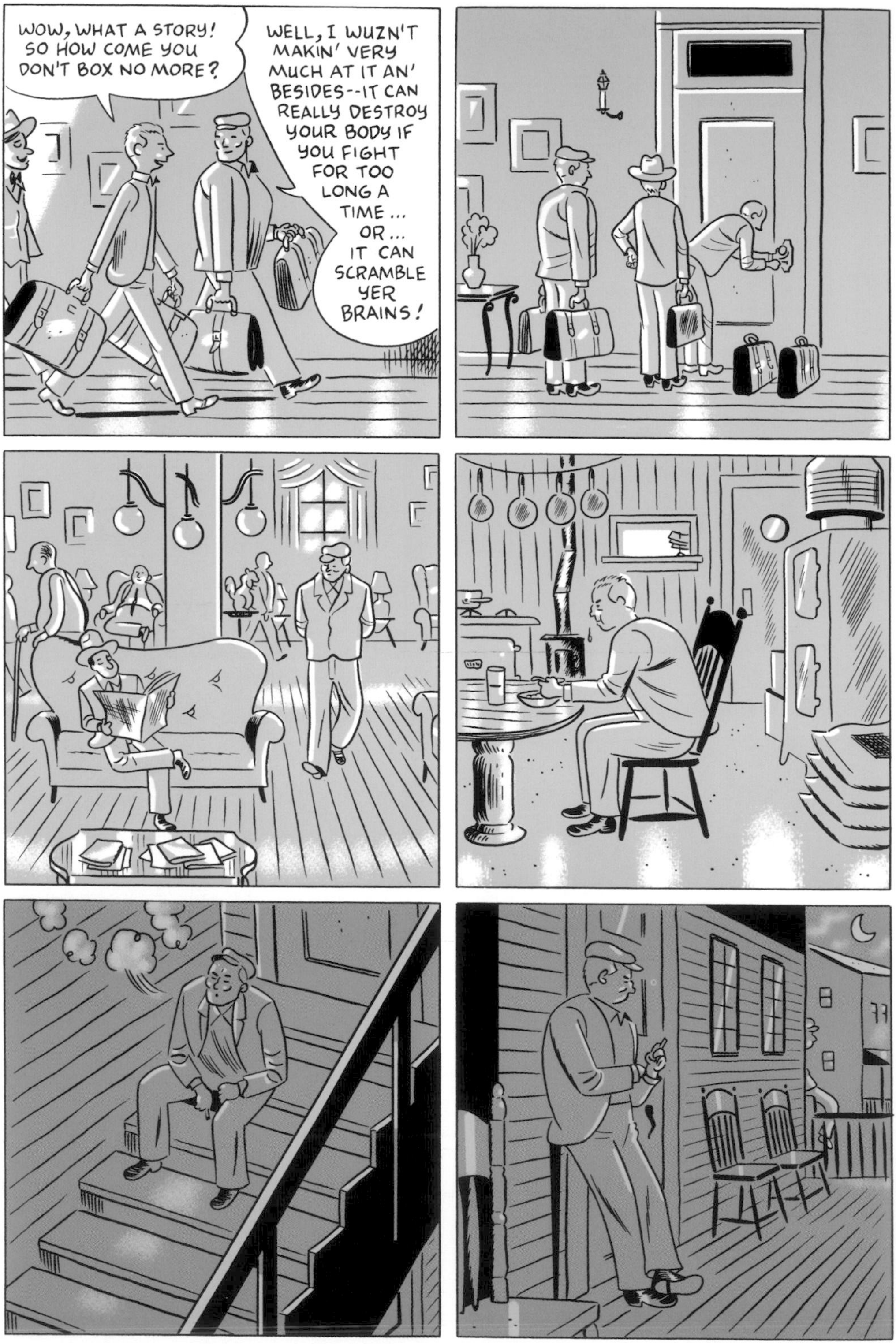
WOW, WHAT A STORY! SO HOW COME YOU DON'T BOX NO MORE?
WELL, I WUZN'T MAKIN' VERY MUCH AT IT AN' BESIDES--IT CAN REALLY DESTROY YOUR BODY IF YOU FIGHT FOR TOO LONG A TIME ... OR ... IT CAN SCRAMBLE YER BRAINS!

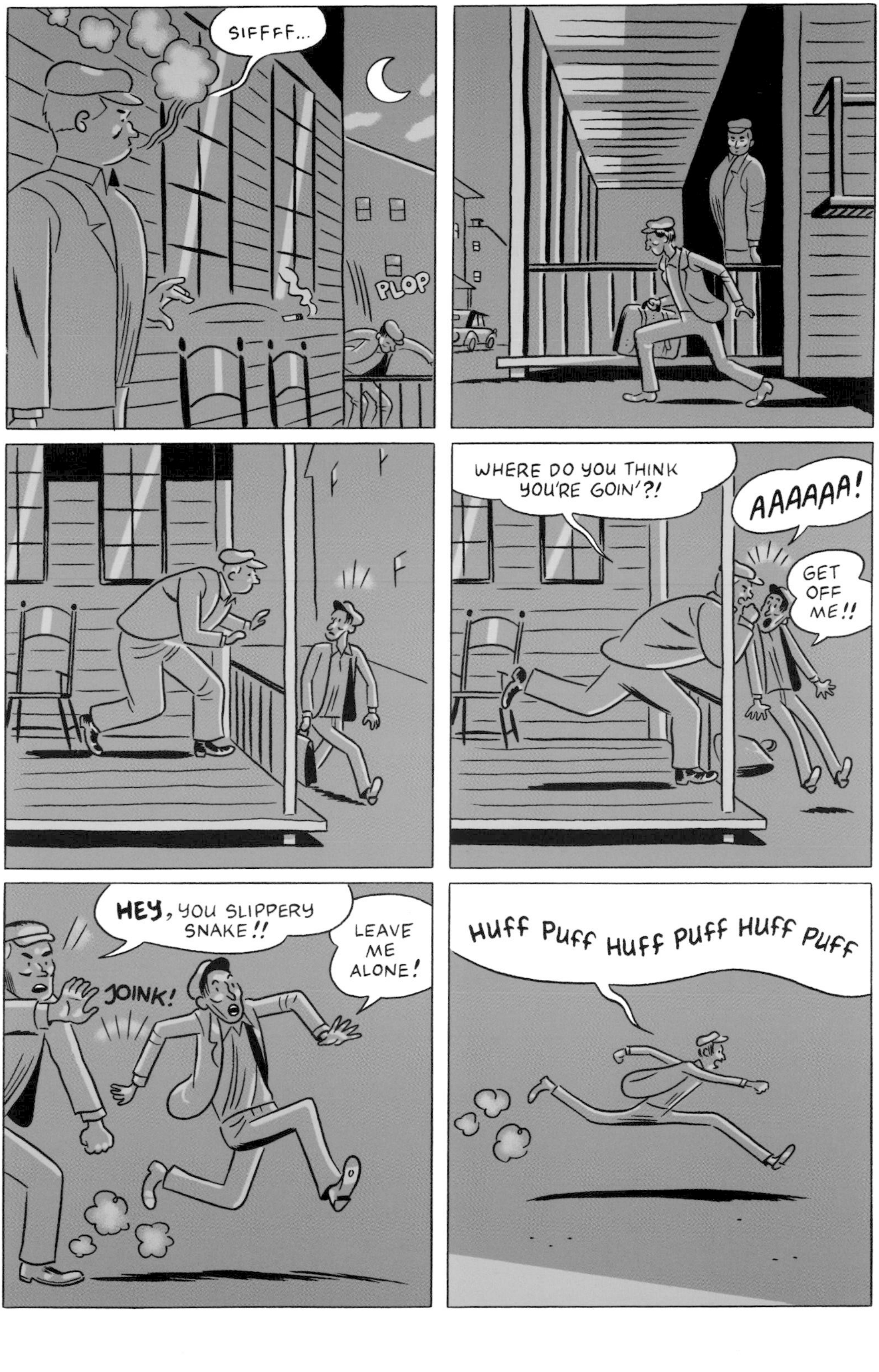
SIFFFF...
PLOP
WHERE DO YOU THINK YOU'RE GOIN'?!
AAAAAA!
GET OFF ME!!
HEY, YOU SLIPPERY SNAKE!!
JOINK!
LEAVE ME ALONE!
HUFF PUFF HUFF PUFF HUFF PUFF

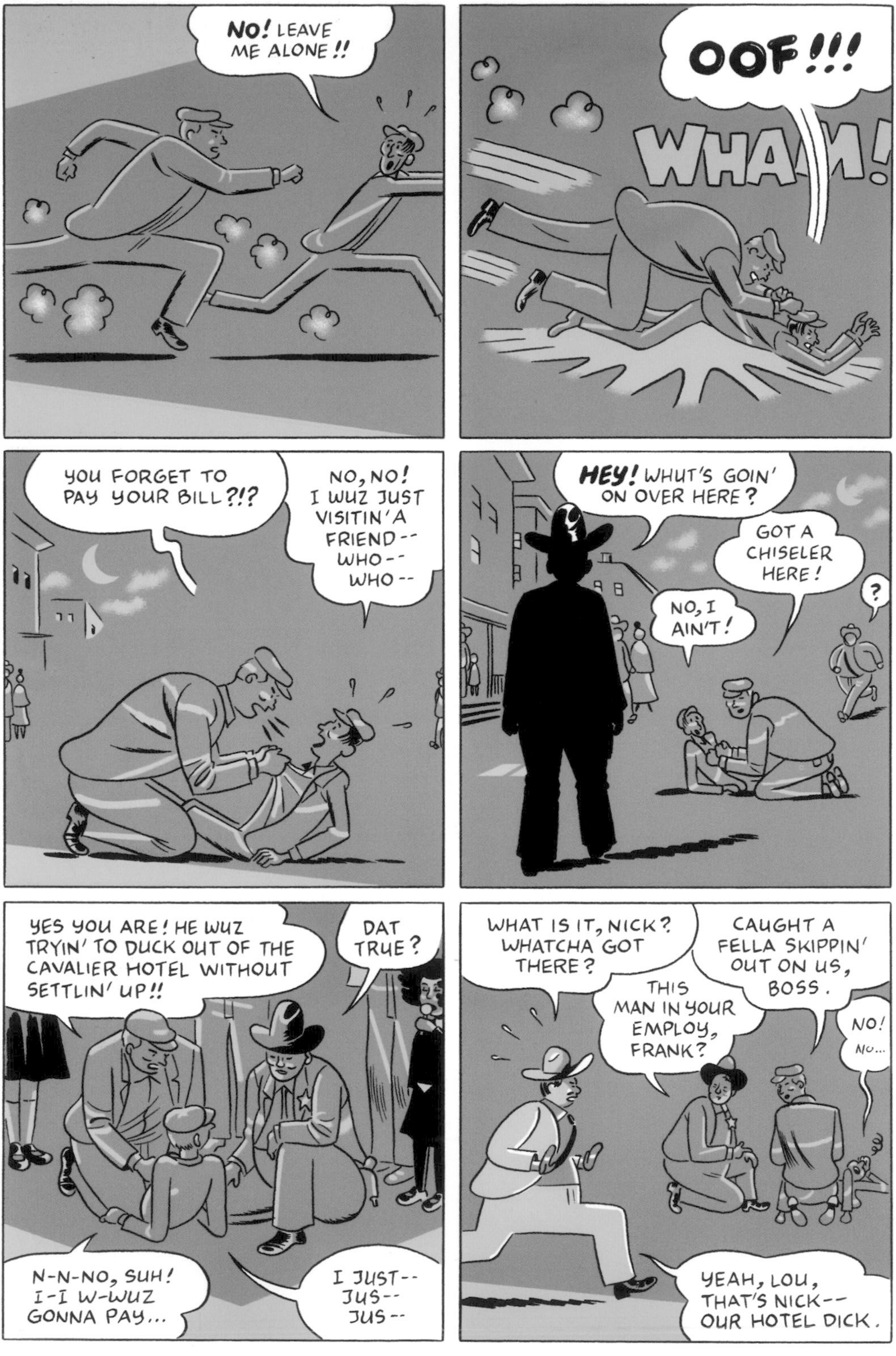
NO! LEAVE ME ALONE!!
OOF!!!
WHAM!
YOU FORGET TO PAY YOUR BILL?!?
NO, NO! I WUZ JUST VISITIN' A FRIEND-- WHO-- WHO--
HEY! WHUT'S GOIN' ON OVER HERE?
GOT A CHISELER HERE!
NO, I AIN'T!
?
YES YOU ARE! HE WUZ TRYIN' TO DUCK OUT OF THE CAVALIER HOTEL WITHOUT SETTLIN' UP!!
DAT TRUE?
N-N-NO, SUH! I-I W-WUZ GONNA PAY...
I JUST-- JUS-- JUS--
WHAT IS IT, NICK? WHATCHA GOT THERE?
THIS MAN IN YOUR EMPLOY, FRANK?
CAUGHT A FELLA SKIPPIN' OUT ON US, BOSS.
NO! NO...
YEAH, LOU, THAT'S NICK-- OUR HOTEL DICK.

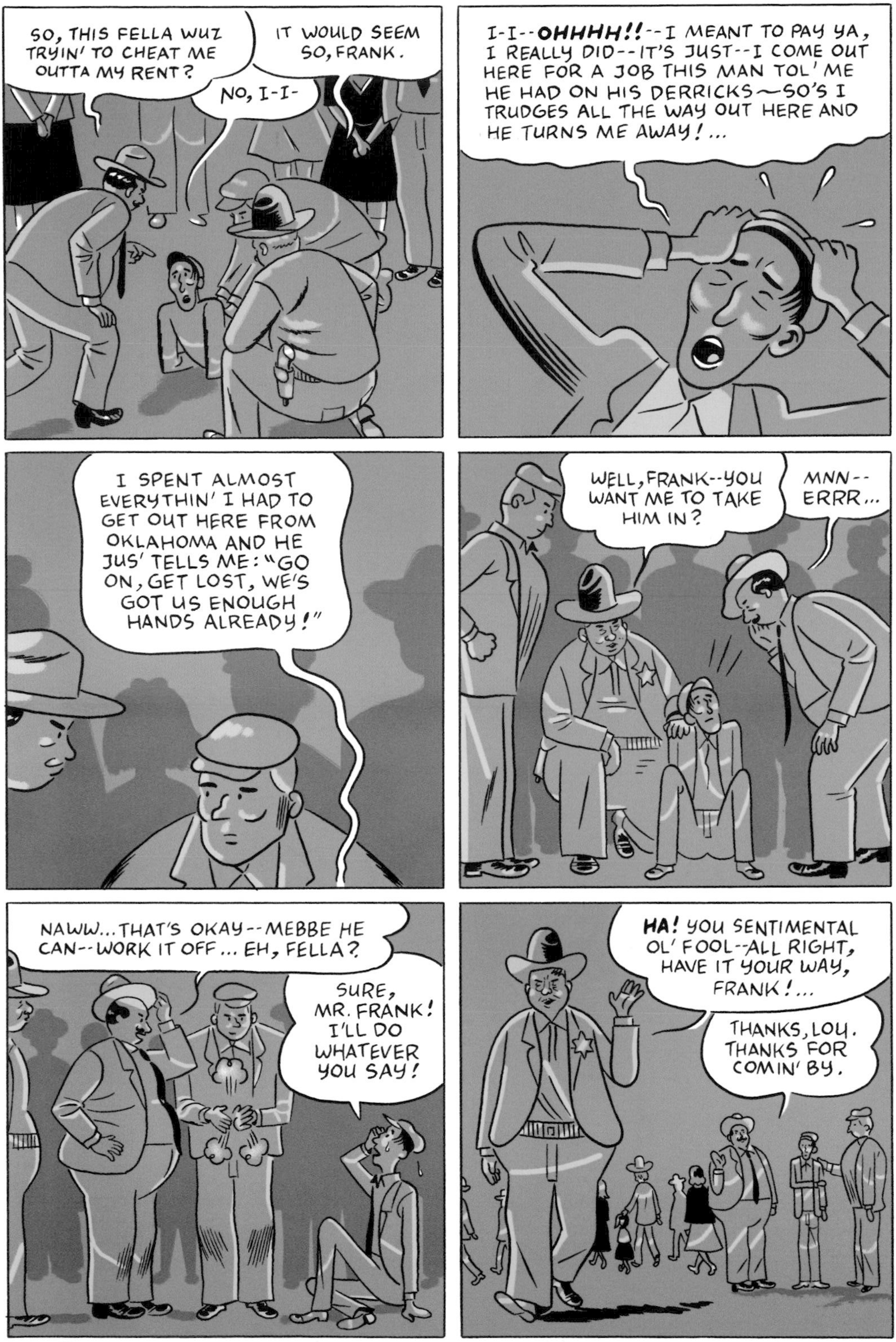
SO, THIS FELLA WUZ TRYIN' TO CHEAT ME OUTTA MY RENT?
IT WOULD SEEM SO, FRANK.
NO, I-I-
I-I--**OHHHH!!**--I MEANT TO PAY YA, I REALLY DID--IT'S JUST--I COME OUT HERE FOR A JOB THIS MAN TOL' ME HE HAD ON HIS DERRICKS~SO'S I TRUDGES ALL THE WAY OUT HERE AND HE TURNS ME AWAY!...
I SPENT ALMOST EVERYTHIN' I HAD TO GET OUT HERE FROM OKLAHOMA AND HE JUS' TELLS ME: "GO ON, GET LOST, WE'S GOT US ENOUGH HANDS ALREADY!"
WELL, FRANK--YOU WANT ME TO TAKE HIM IN?
MNN--ERRR...
NAWW...THAT'S OKAY--MEBBE HE CAN--WORK IT OFF... EH, FELLA?
SURE, MR. FRANK! I'LL DO WHATEVER YOU SAY!
HA! YOU SENTIMENTAL OL' FOOL--ALL RIGHT, HAVE IT YOUR WAY, FRANK!...
THANKS, LOU. THANKS FOR COMIN' BY.

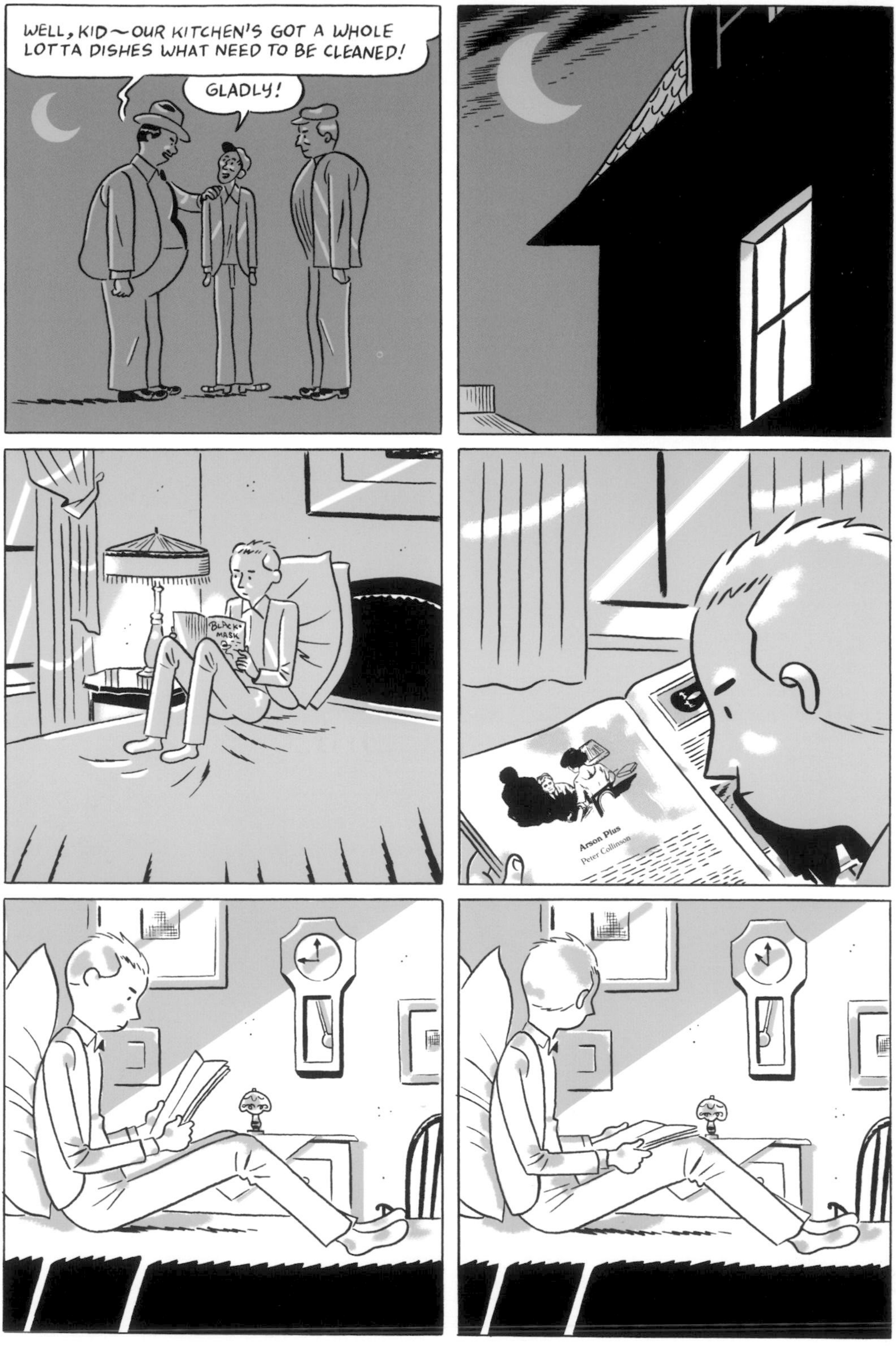
WELL, KID~OUR KITCHEN'S GOT A WHOLE LOTTA DISHES WHAT NEED TO BE CLEANED!
GLADLY!
BLACK MASK
Arson Plus
Peter Collinson

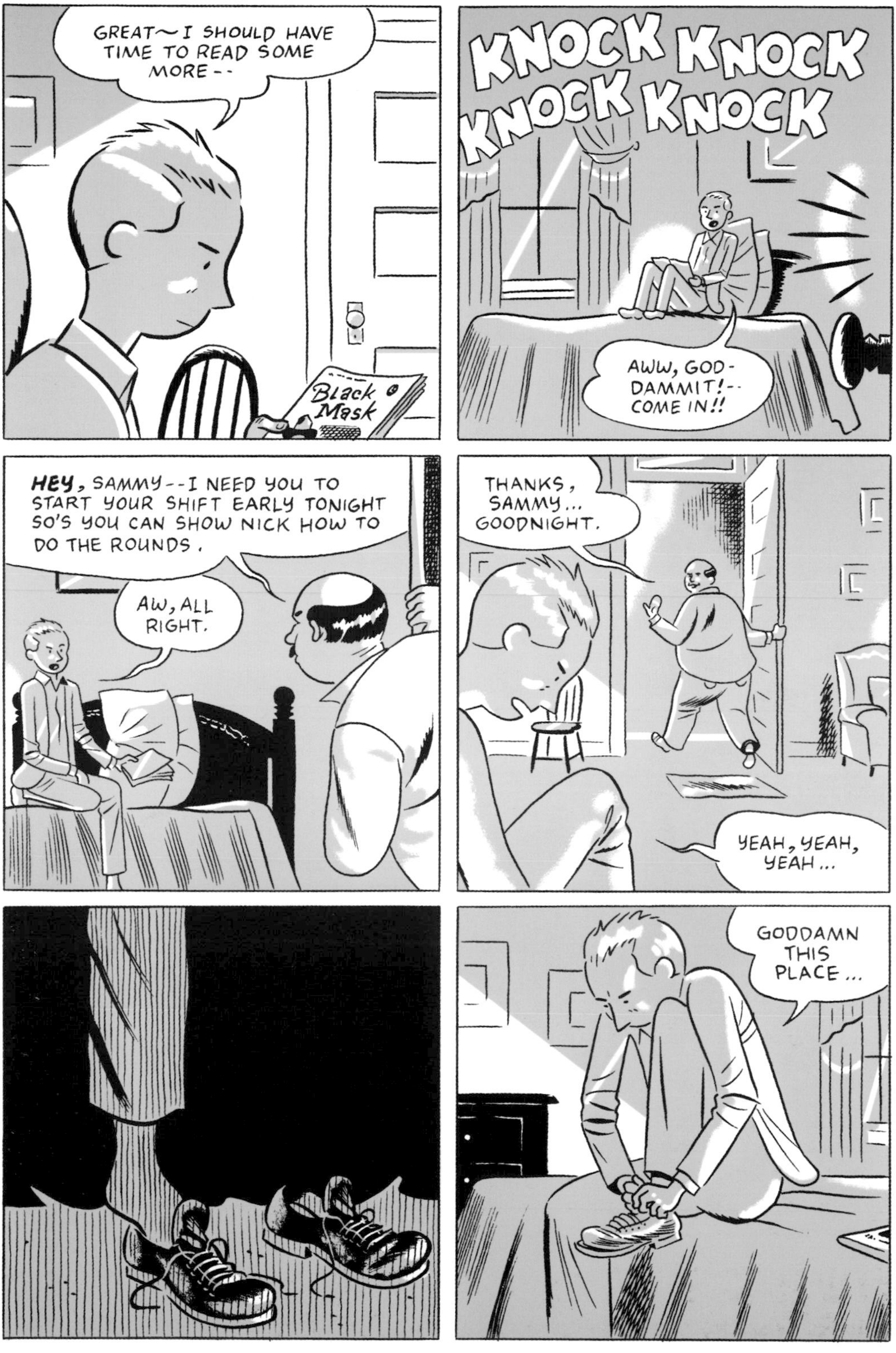

GREAT~I SHOULD HAVE TIME TO READ SOME MORE--
Black Mask
KNOCK KNOCK KNOCK KNOCK
AWW, GOD-DAMMIT!--COME IN!!
HEY, SAMMY--I NEED YOU TO START YOUR SHIFT EARLY TONIGHT SO'S YOU CAN SHOW NICK HOW TO DO THE ROUNDS.
AW, ALL RIGHT.
THANKS, SAMMY... GOODNIGHT.
YEAH, YEAH, YEAH...
GODDAMN THIS PLACE...

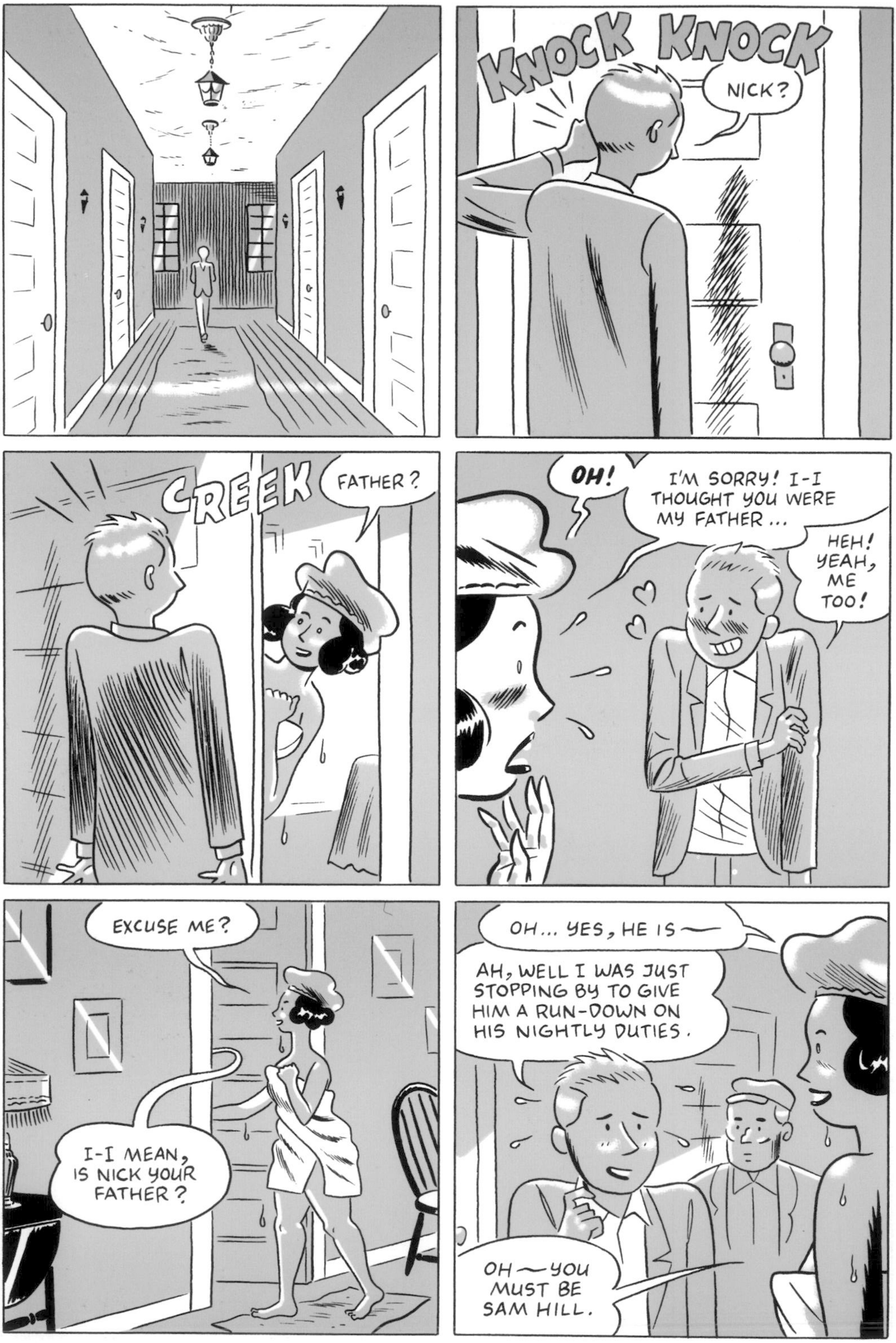
KNOCK KNOCK
NICK?
CREEK
FATHER?
OH!
I'M SORRY! I-I THOUGHT YOU WERE MY FATHER...
HEH! YEAH, ME TOO!
EXCUSE ME?
I-I MEAN, IS NICK YOUR FATHER?
OH... YES, HE IS—
AH, WELL I WAS JUST STOPPING BY TO GIVE HIM A RUN-DOWN ON HIS NIGHTLY DUTIES.
OH—YOU MUST BE SAM HILL.

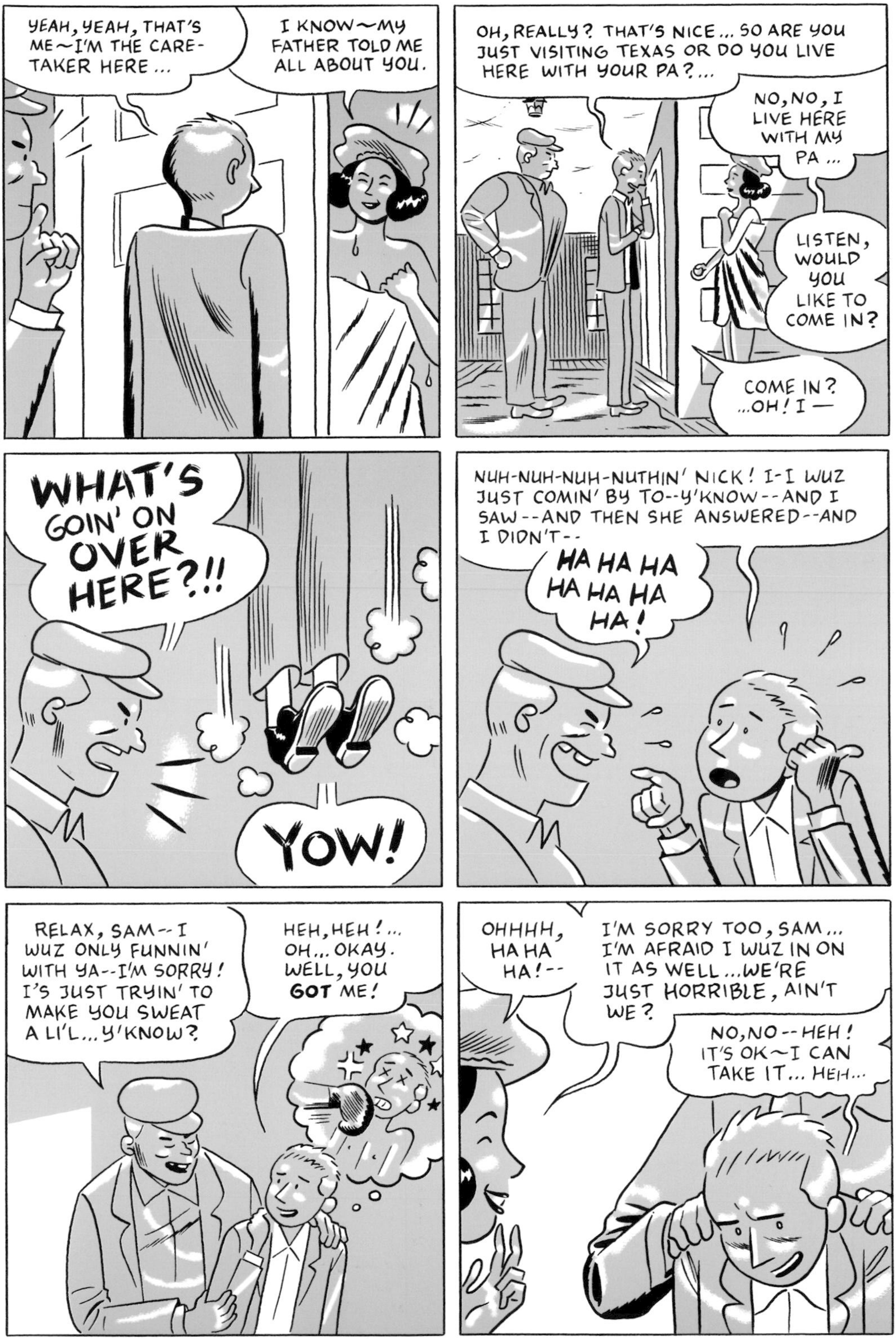
YEAH, YEAH, THAT'S ME~I'M THE CARE-TAKER HERE...
I KNOW~MY FATHER TOLD ME ALL ABOUT YOU.
OH, REALLY? THAT'S NICE... SO ARE YOU JUST VISITING TEXAS OR DO YOU LIVE HERE WITH YOUR PA?...
NO, NO, I LIVE HERE WITH MY PA...
LISTEN, WOULD YOU LIKE TO COME IN?
COME IN? ...OH! I —
WHAT'S GOIN' ON OVER HERE?!!
YOW!
NUH-NUH-NUH-NUTHIN' NICK! I-I WUZ JUST COMIN' BY TO--Y'KNOW--AND I SAW--AND THEN SHE ANSWERED--AND I DIDN'T--
HA HA HA HA HA HA HA!
RELAX, SAM--I WUZ ONLY FUNNIN' WITH YA--I'M SORRY! I'S JUST TRYIN' TO MAKE YOU SWEAT A LI'L... Y'KNOW?
HEH, HEH!... OH... OKAY. WELL, YOU GOT ME!
OHHHH, HA HA HA!--
I'M SORRY TOO, SAM... I'M AFRAID I WUZ IN ON IT AS WELL... WE'RE JUST HORRIBLE, AIN'T WE?
NO, NO--HEH! IT'S OK~I CAN TAKE IT... HEH...

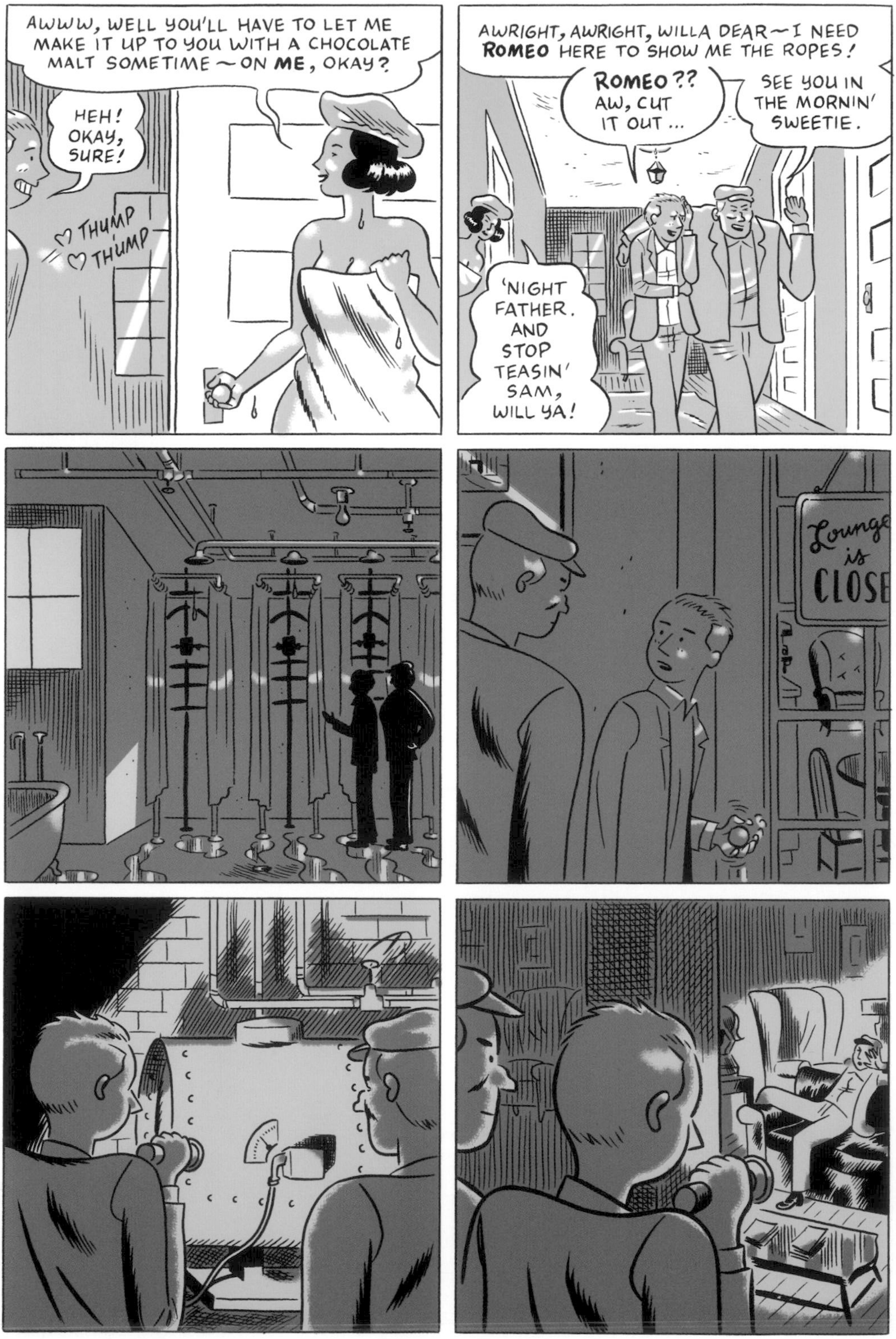
AWWW, WELL YOU'LL HAVE TO LET ME MAKE IT UP TO YOU WITH A CHOCOLATE MALT SOMETIME ~ ON **ME**, OKAY?
HEH! OKAY, SURE!
♡ THUMP ♡ THUMP
AWRIGHT, AWRIGHT, WILLA DEAR ~ I NEED **ROMEO** HERE TO SHOW ME THE ROPES!
ROMEO?? AW, CUT IT OUT...
SEE YOU IN THE MORNIN' SWEETIE.
'NIGHT FATHER. AND STOP TEASIN' SAM, WILL YA!
Lounge is CLOSE

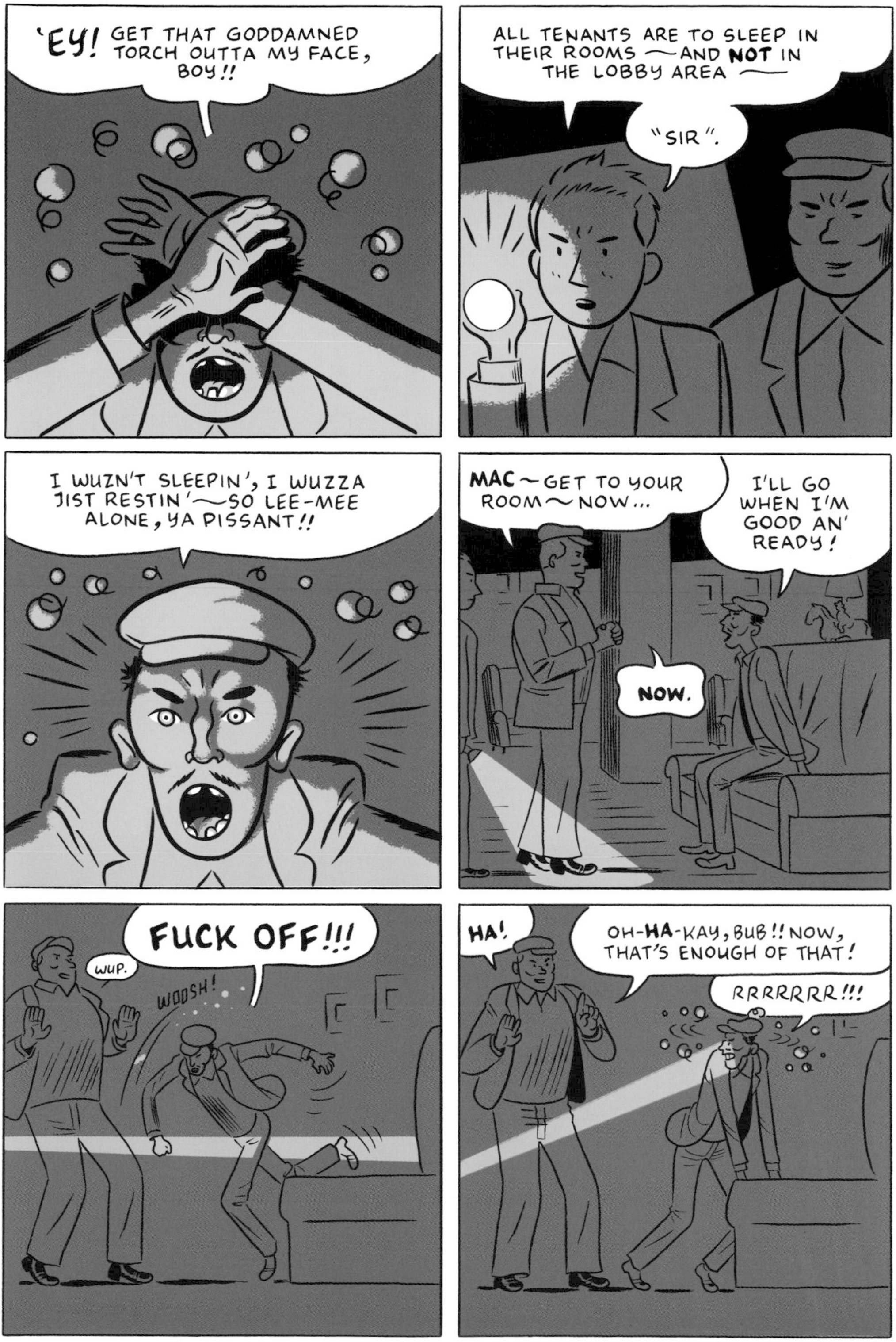
'EY! GET THAT GODDAMNED TORCH OUTTA MY FACE, BOY!!
ALL TENANTS ARE TO SLEEP IN THEIR ROOMS — AND NOT IN THE LOBBY AREA —
"SIR".
I WUZN'T SLEEPIN', I WUZZA JIST RESTIN' — SO LEE-MEE ALONE, YA PISSANT!!
MAC ~ GET TO YOUR ROOM ~ NOW...
I'LL GO WHEN I'M GOOD AN' READY!
NOW.
FUCK OFF!!!
WUP.
WOOSH!
HA!
OH-HA-KAY, BUB!! NOW, THAT'S ENOUGH OF THAT!
RRRRRRR!!!

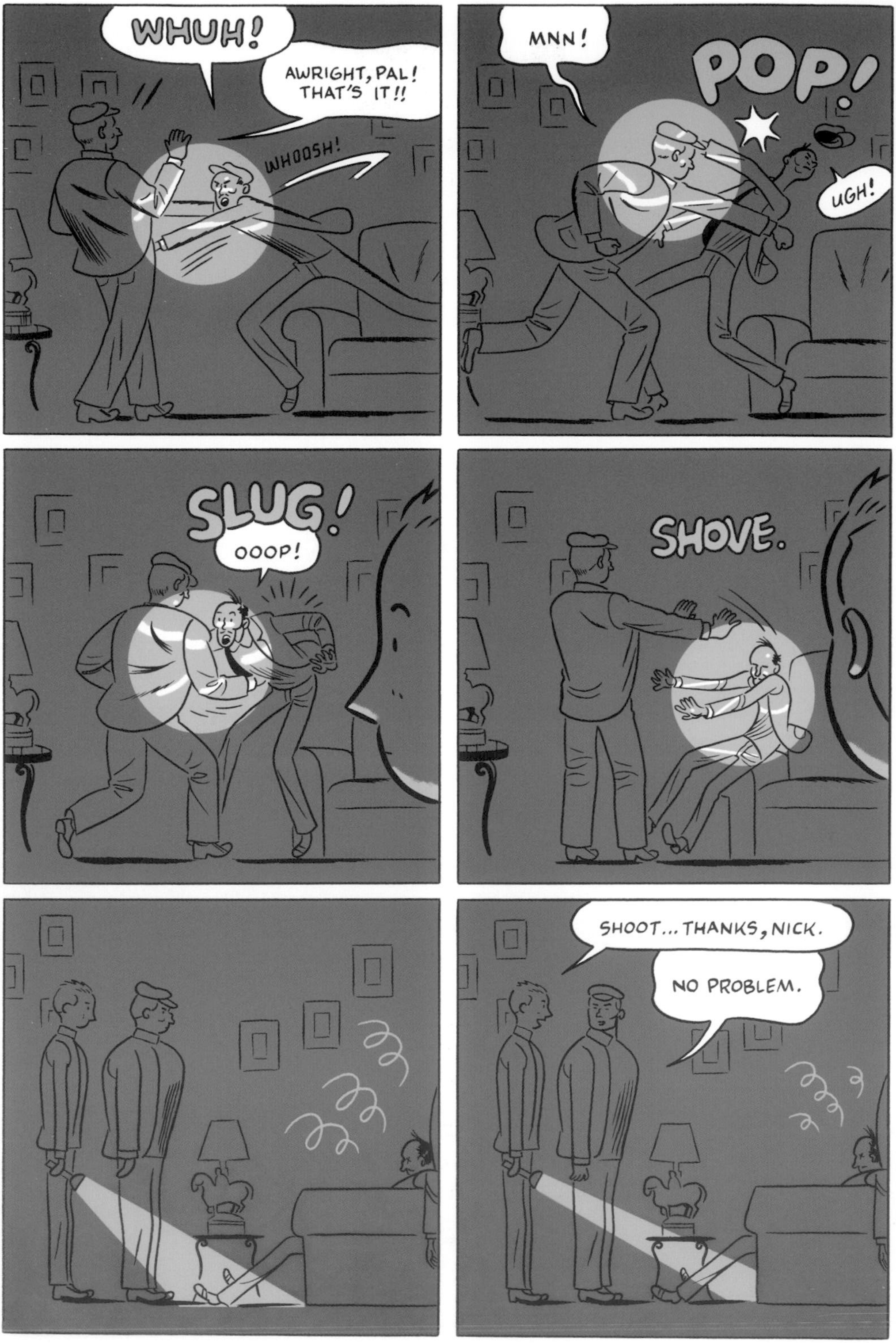
WHUH!
AWRIGHT, PAL! THAT'S IT!!
WHOOSH!
MNN!
POP!
UGH!
SLUG!
OOOP!
SHOVE.
SHOOT... THANKS, NICK.
NO PROBLEM.

THE GRIFTER

L ET US LIFT OUR GAZE NORTHWARD FOR A MOMENT, TO A RAILROAD STATION IN THE CITY OF CHICAGO...

W HERE WE FIND OUR STORY'S TITULAR CHARACTER, MR. THOMPSON — MR. **ROSS** THOMPSON... A STOUT FELLOW, FOURTY-TWO YEARS OF AGE, WITH LITTLE TO NO SCRUPLES... A DEGENERATE CON-MAN, SKILLFUL AT GRAFTING BOTH THE PITIFULLY NAIVE TO THE SAVVY ELITE OF AMERICA'S URBAN POPULATION.

H OWEVER, AT **THIS** VERY MOMENT, HE IS HASTILY MAKING HIS WAY SOUTH-BOUND — **OUT** OF THE WINDY CITY...

...AND FOR **GOOD**.

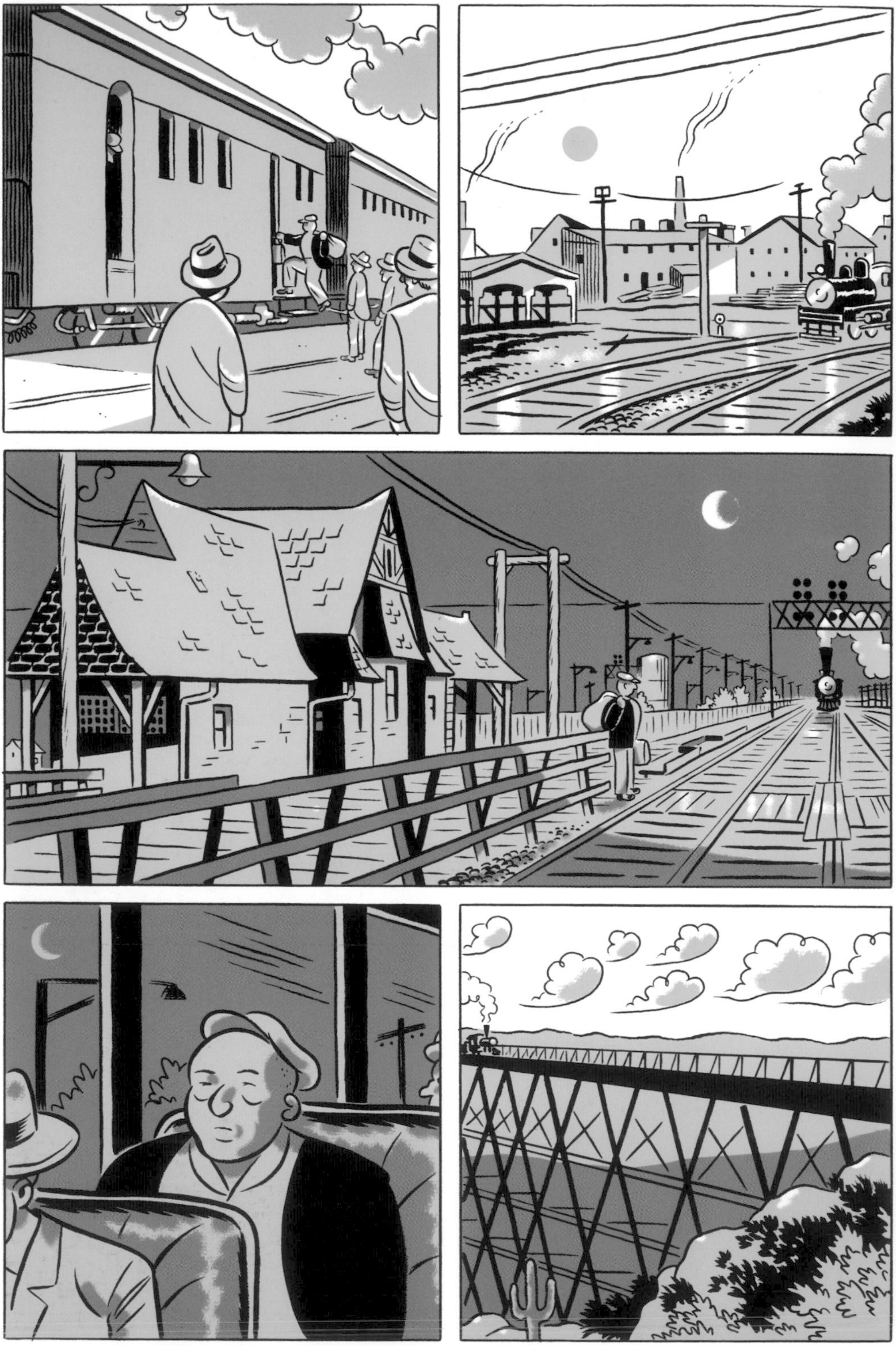

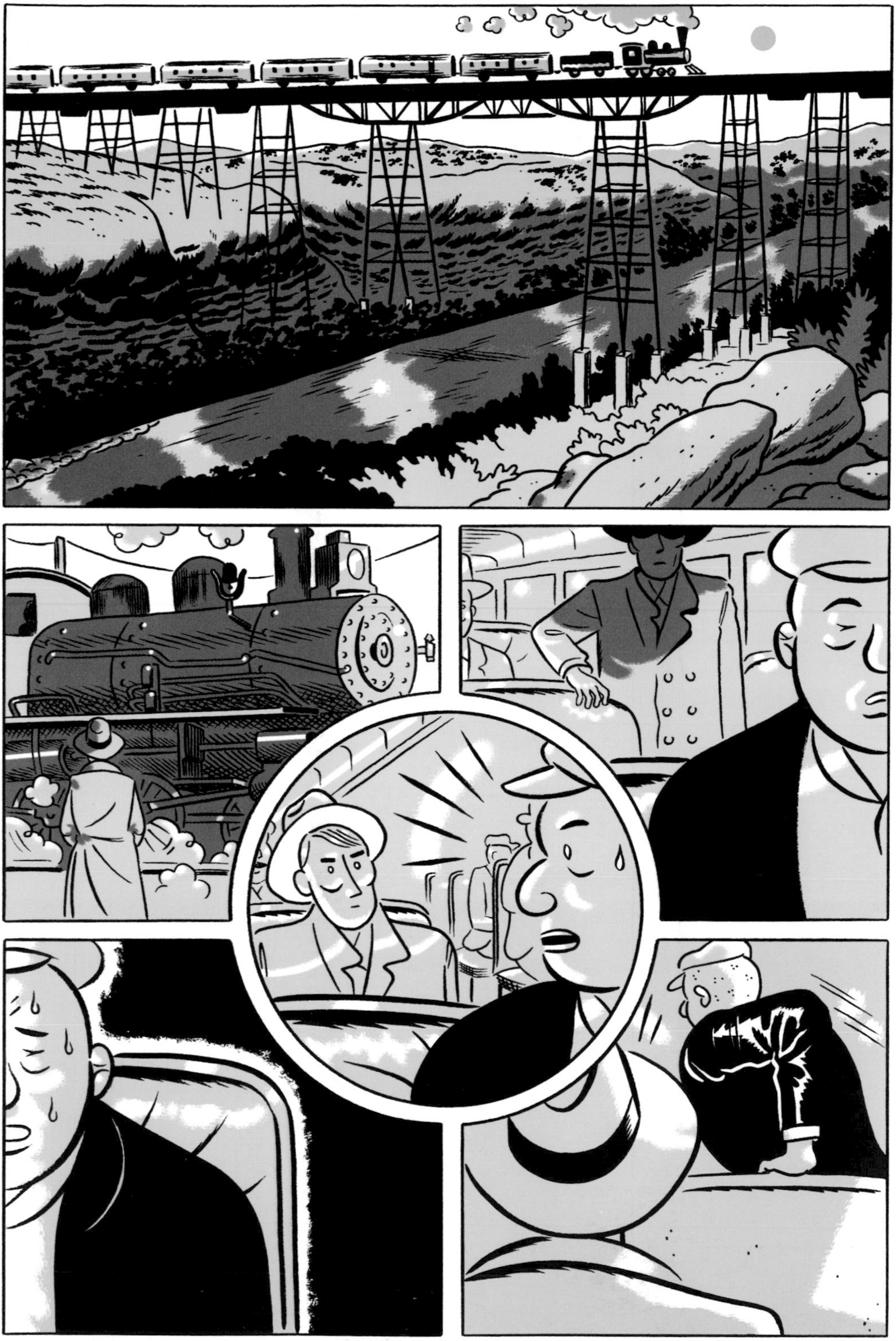

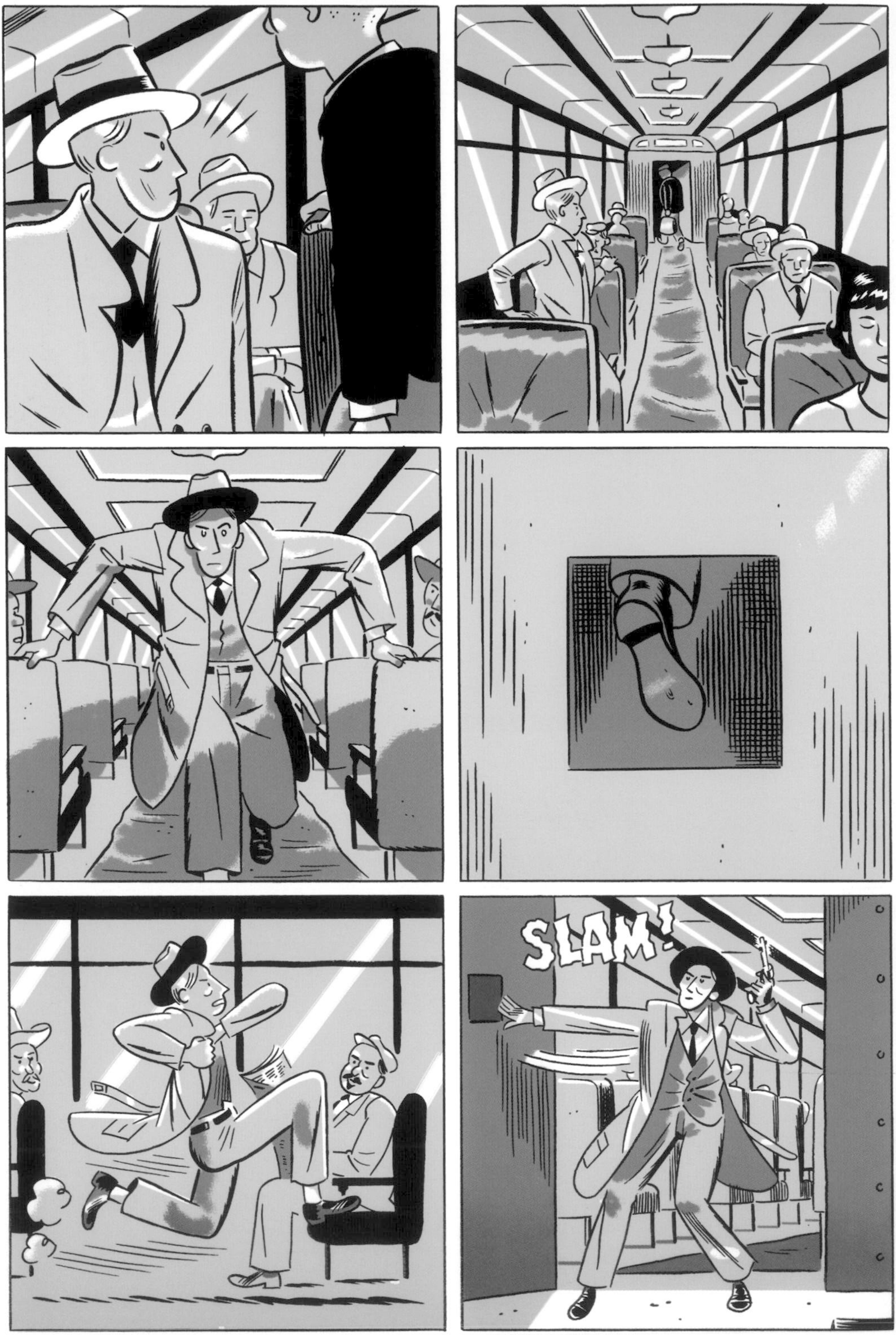
SLAM!

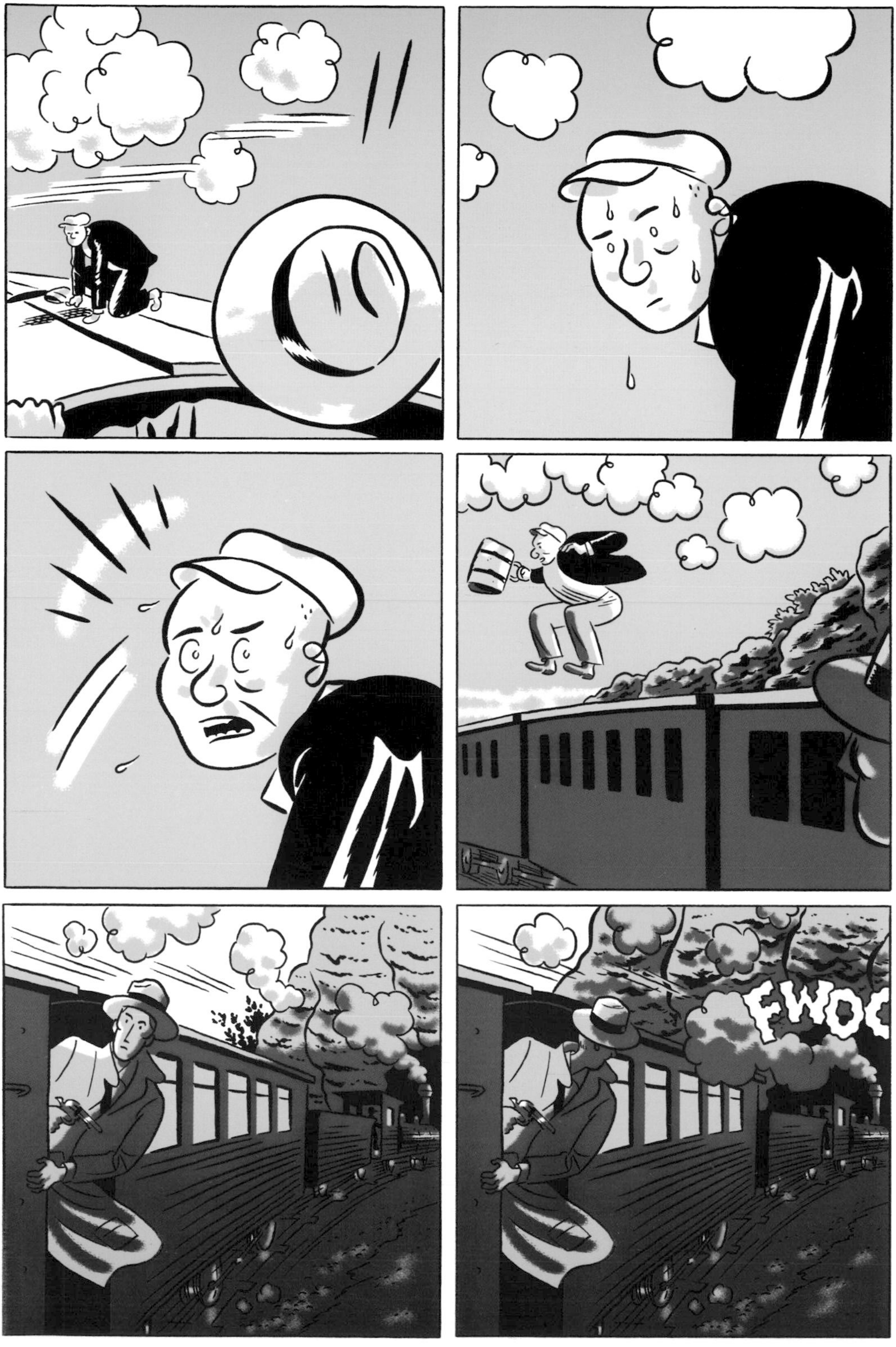
FWOO

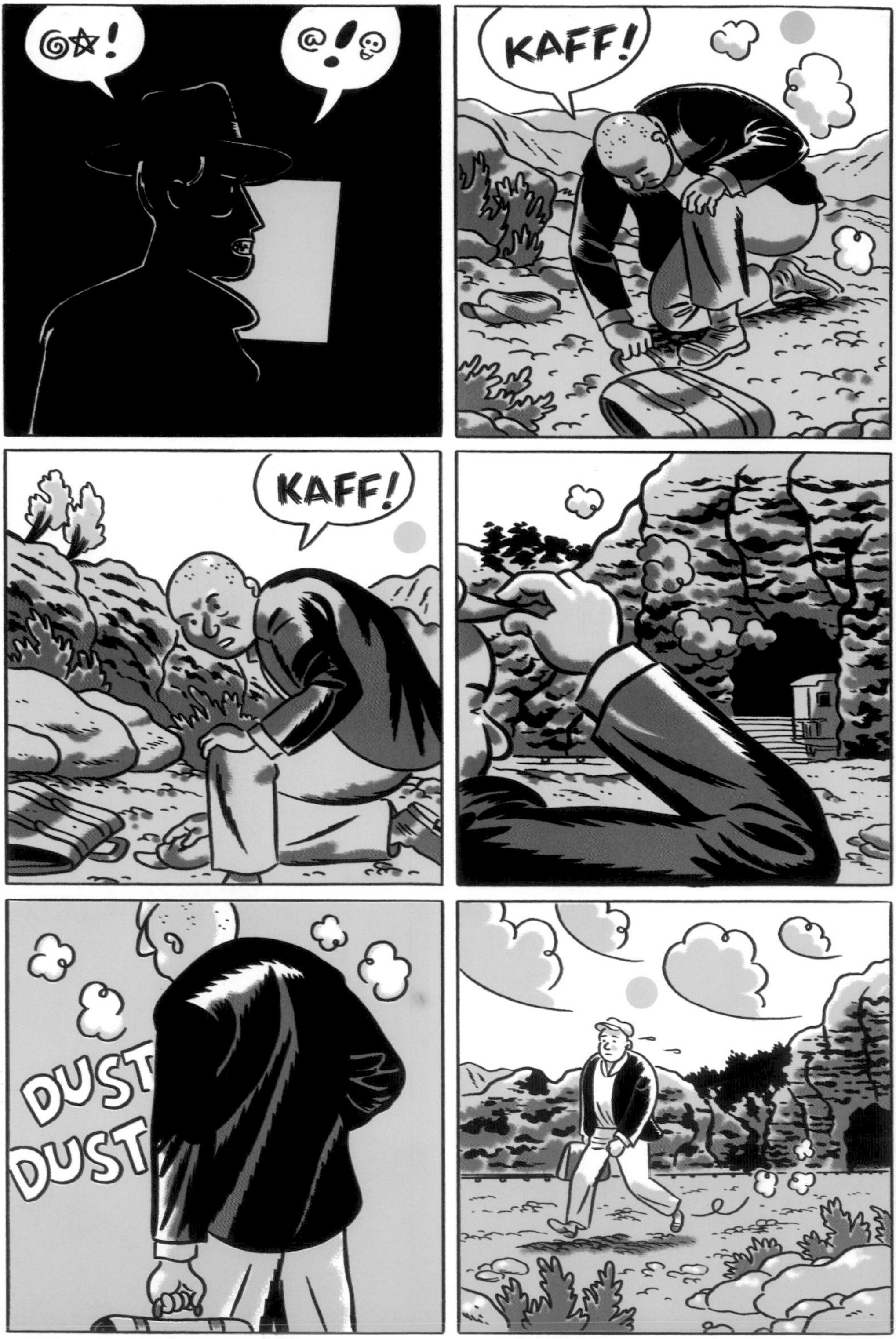

KAFF!
KAFF!
DUST
DUST

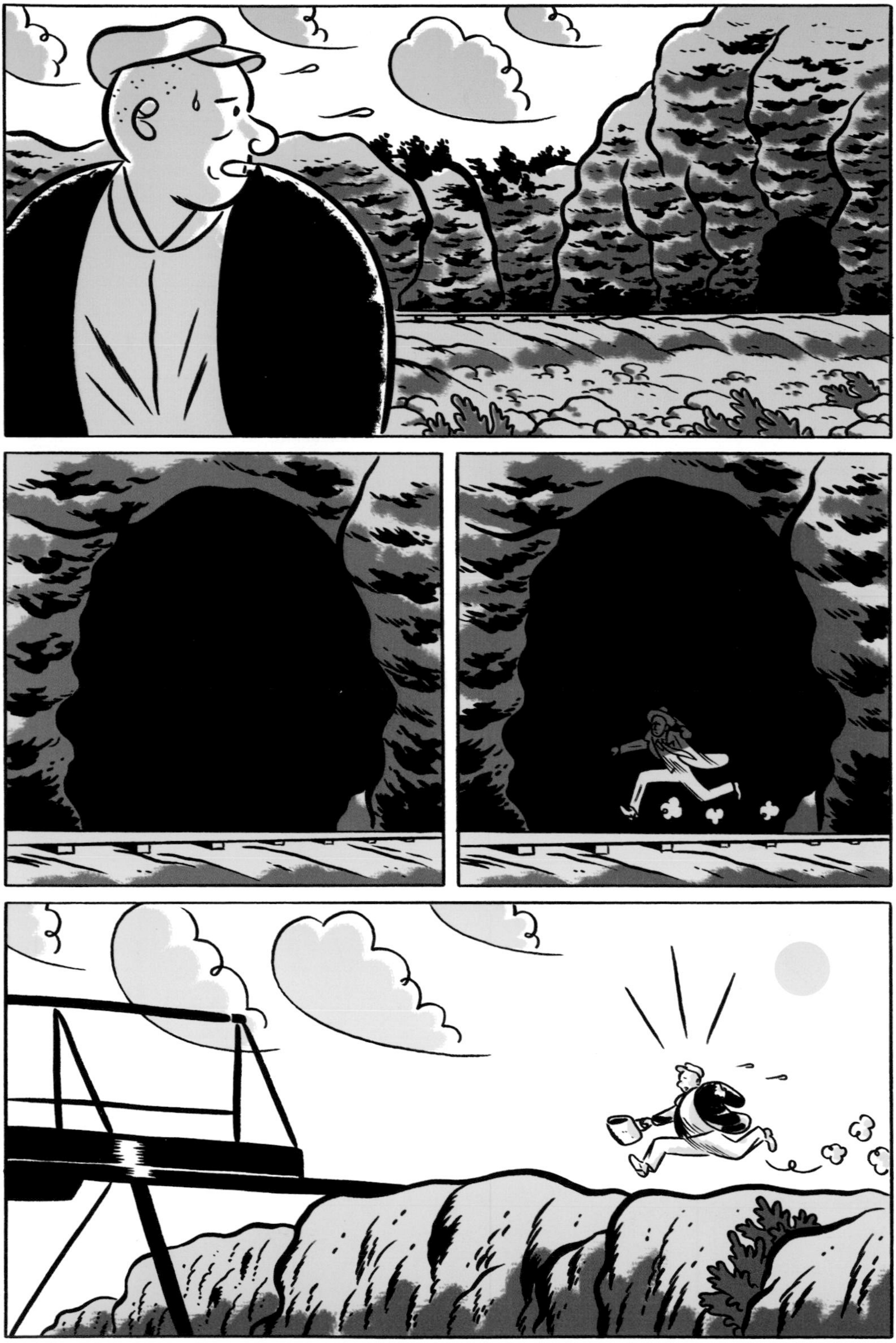

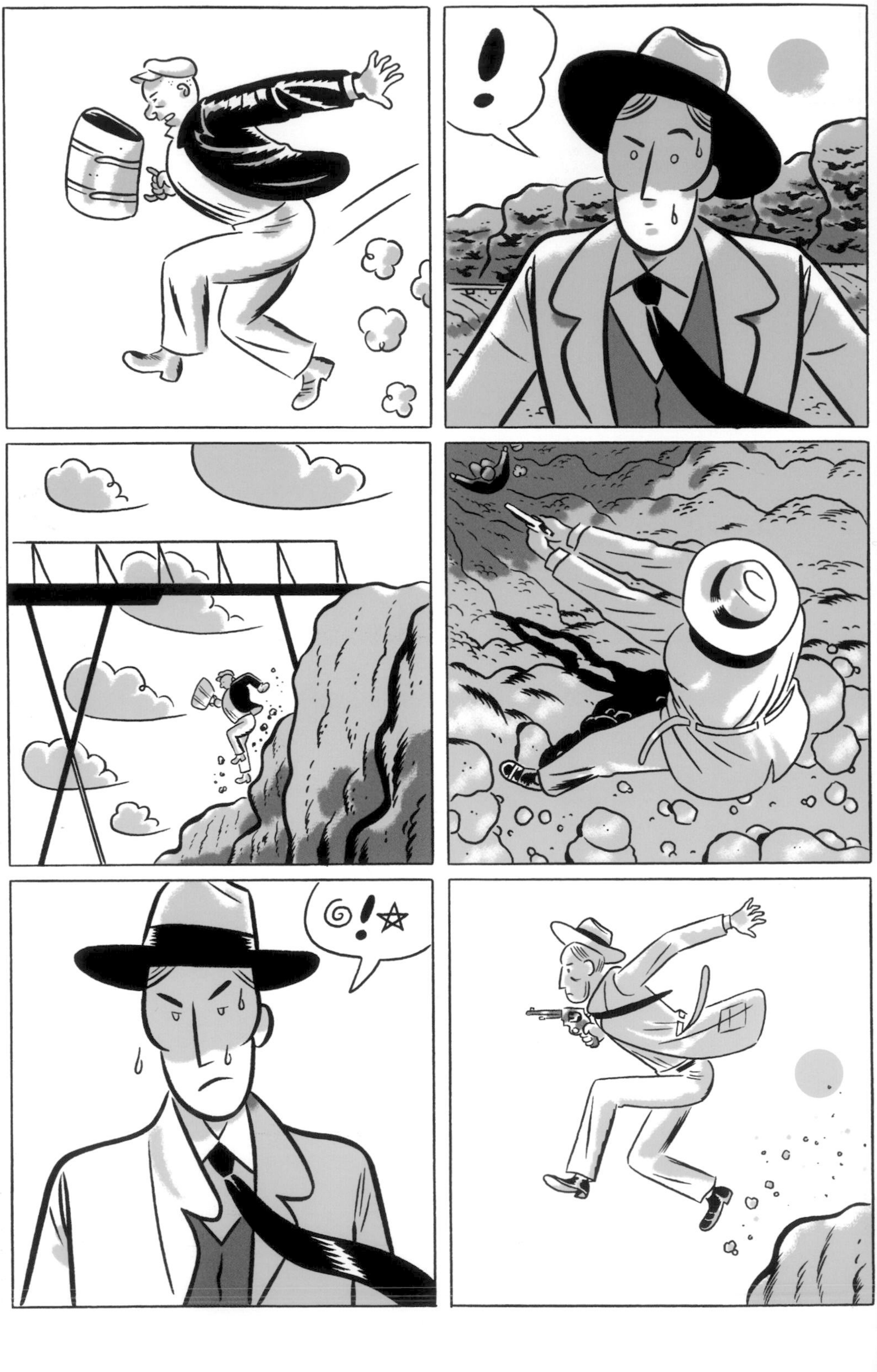
!
@!☆

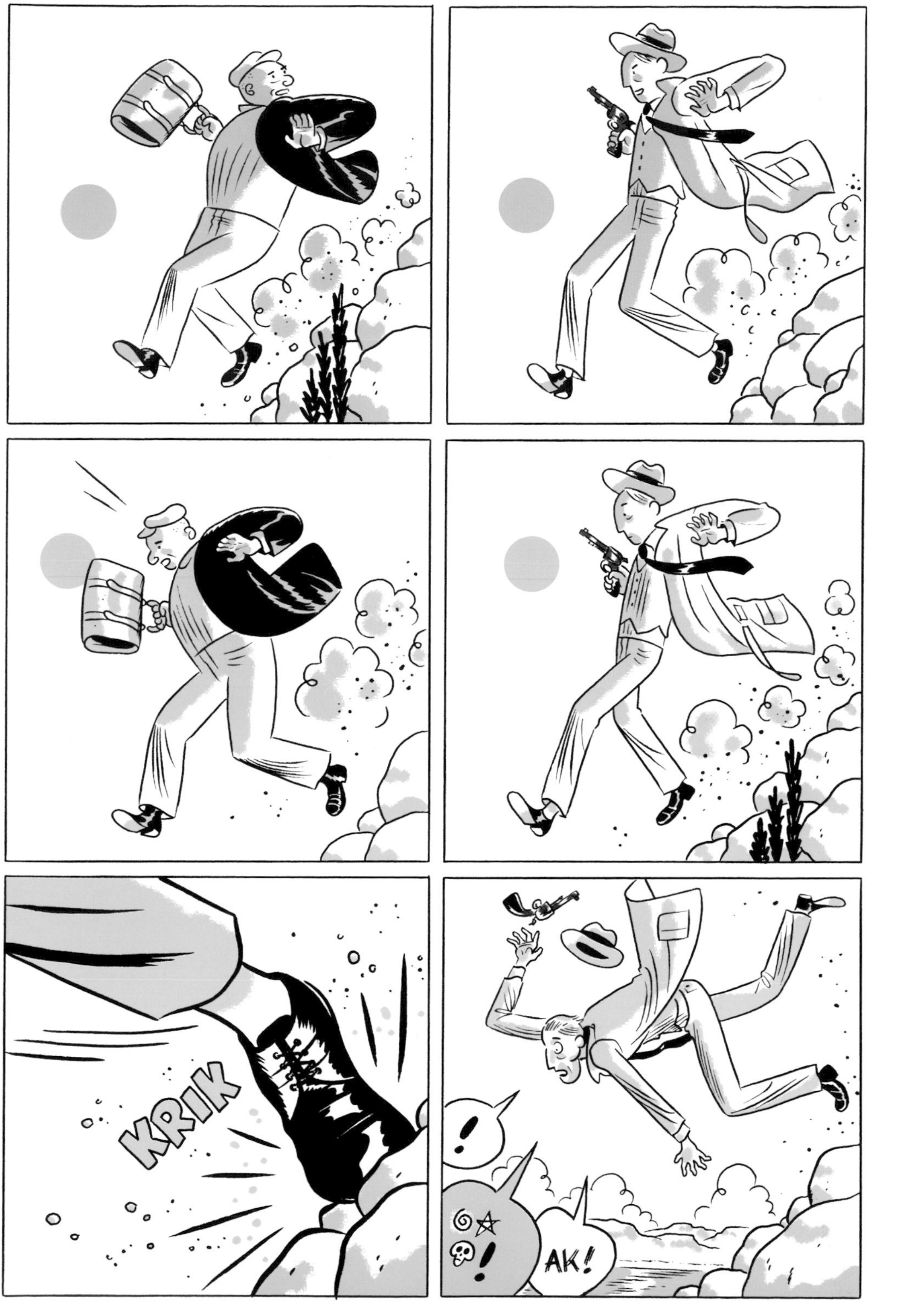
KRIK
!
AK!

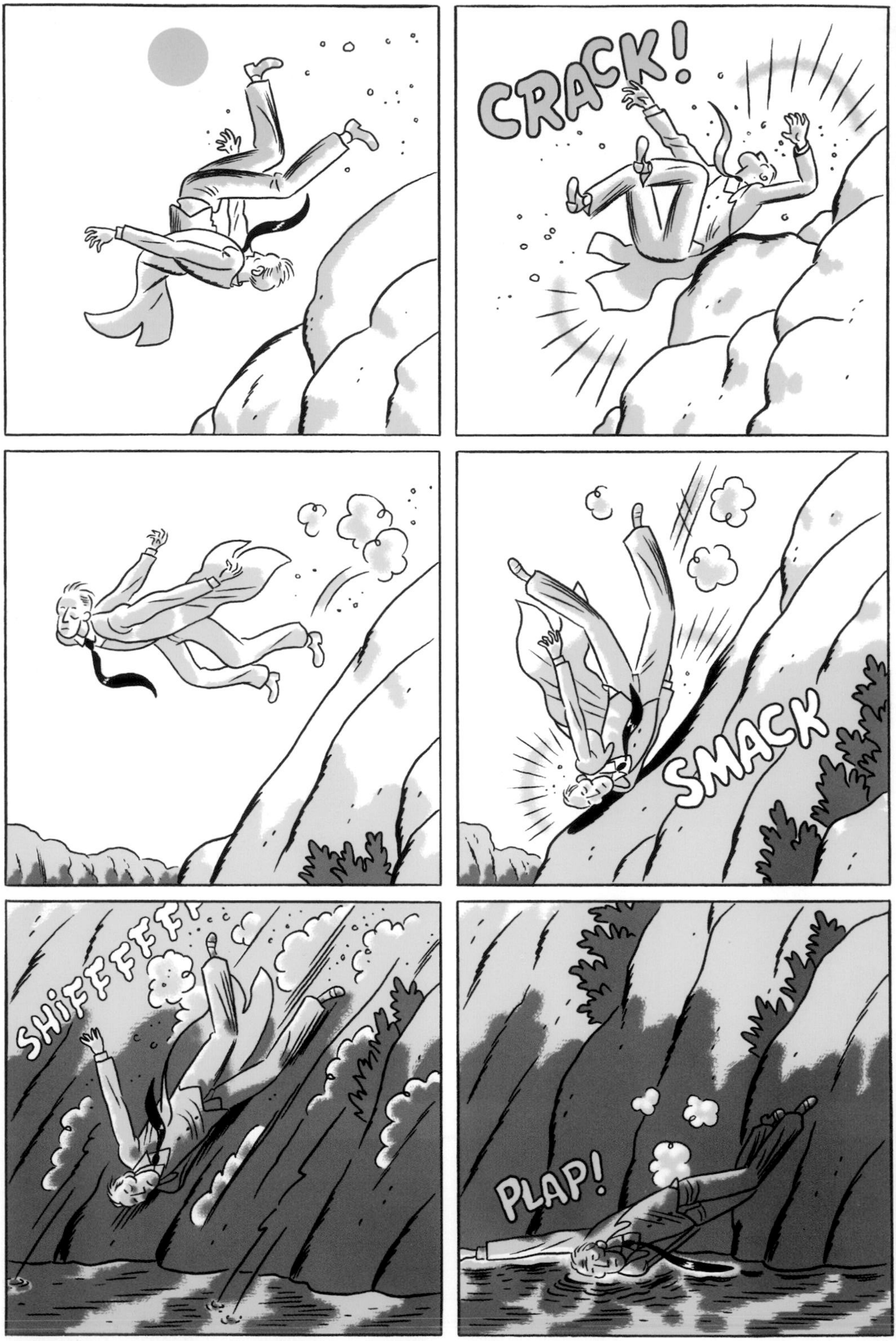
CRACK!
SMACK
SHIFFFFF
PLAP!

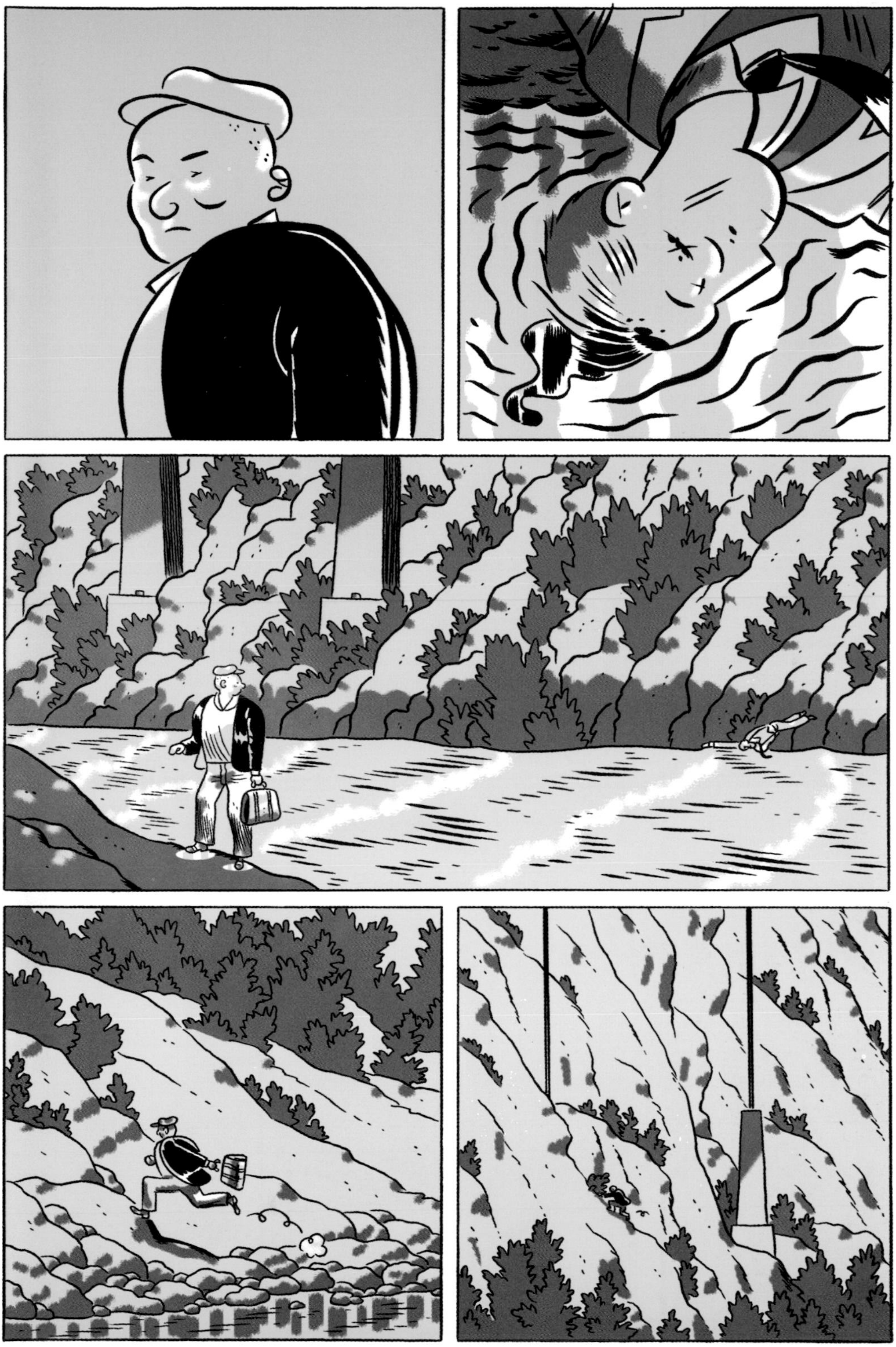

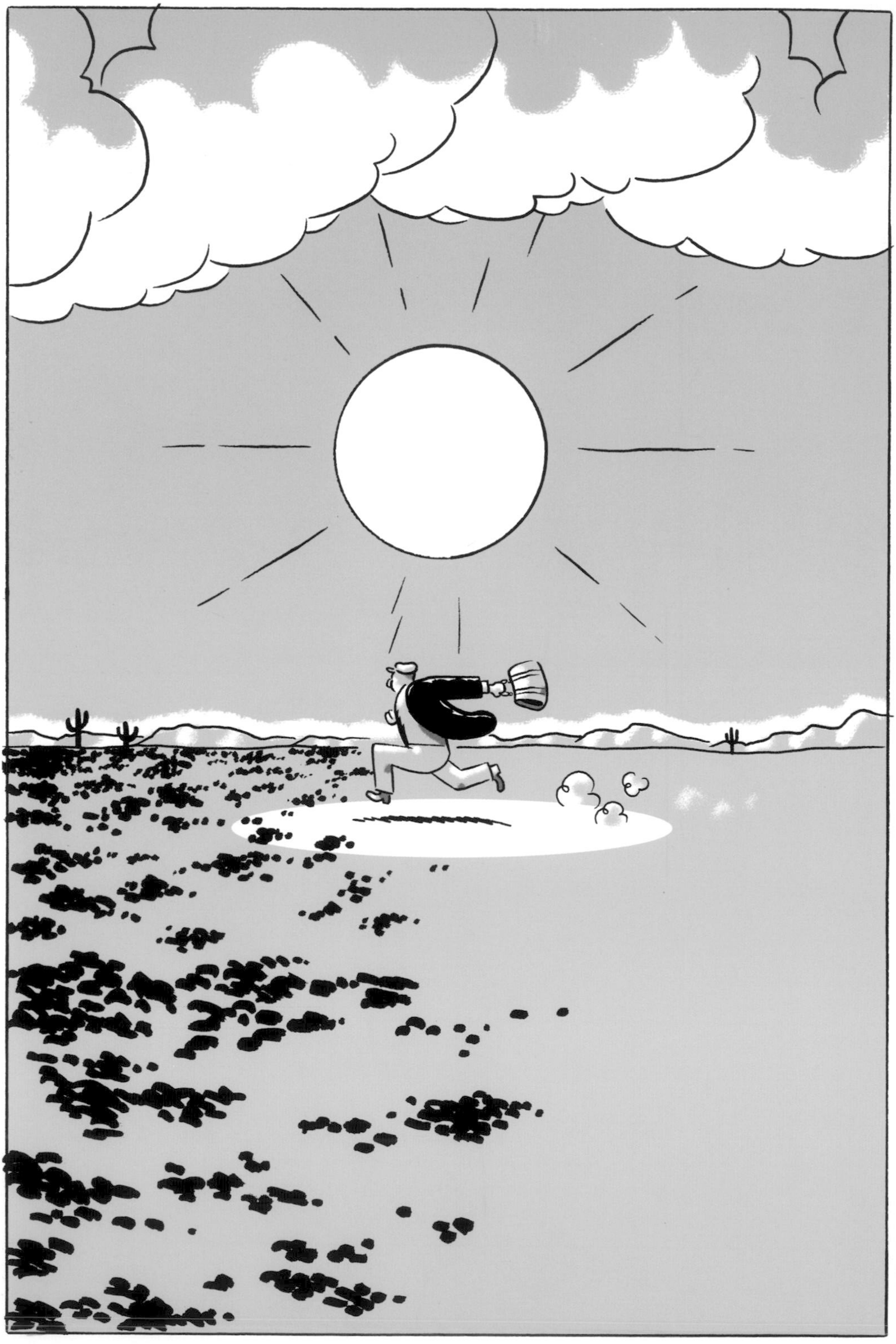

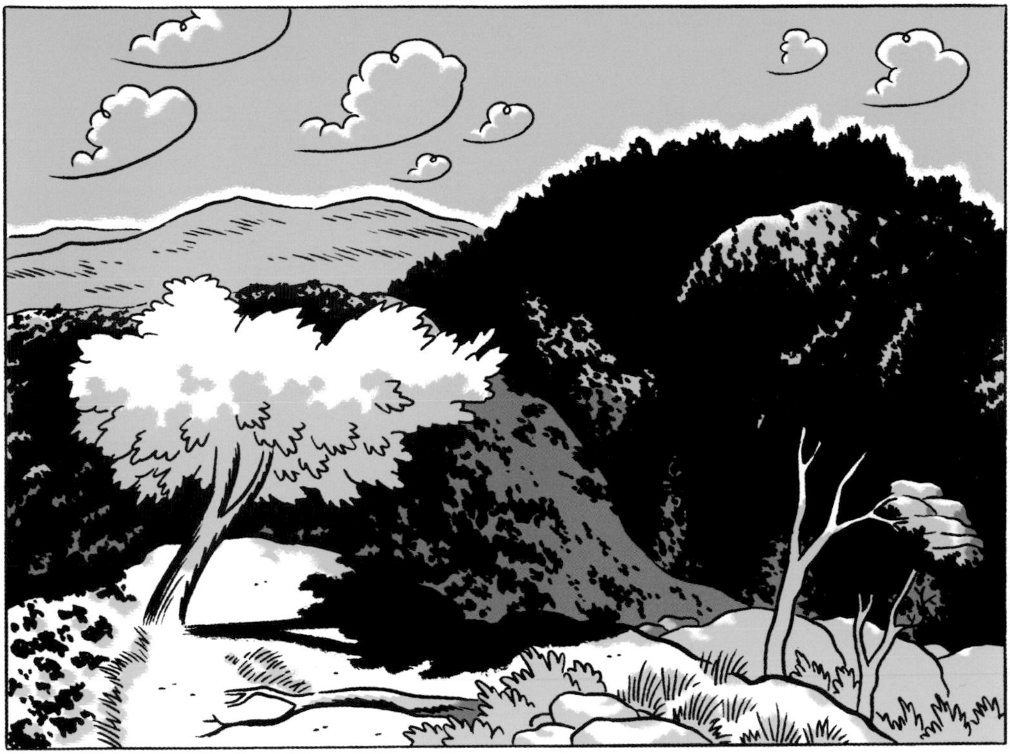

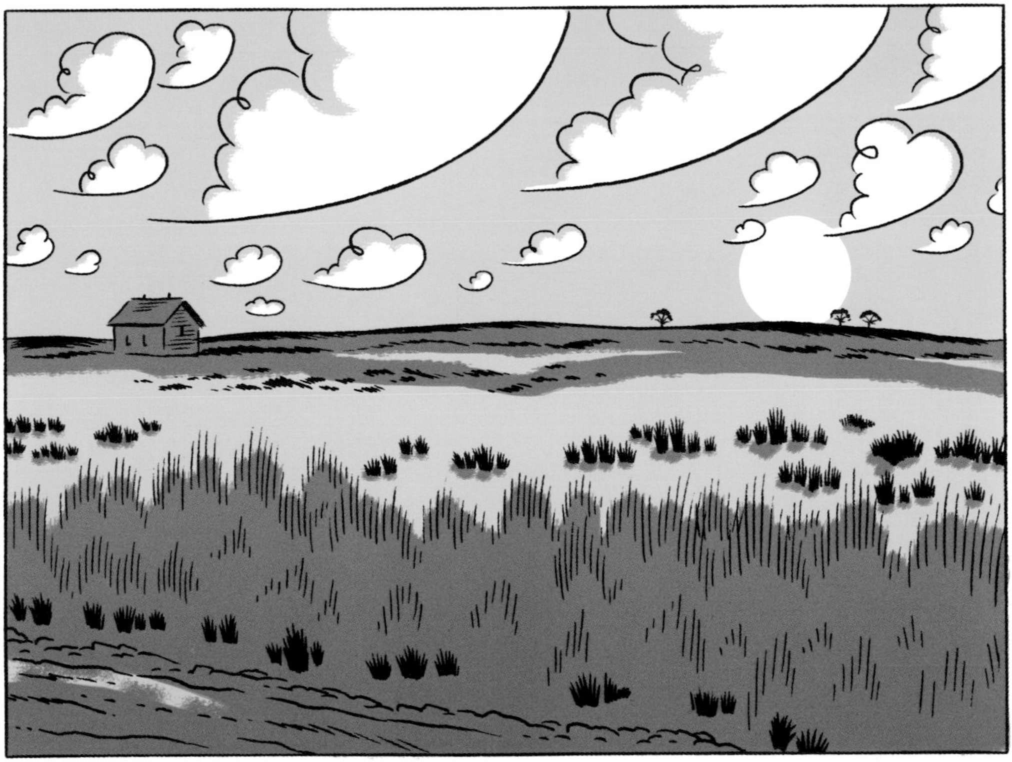

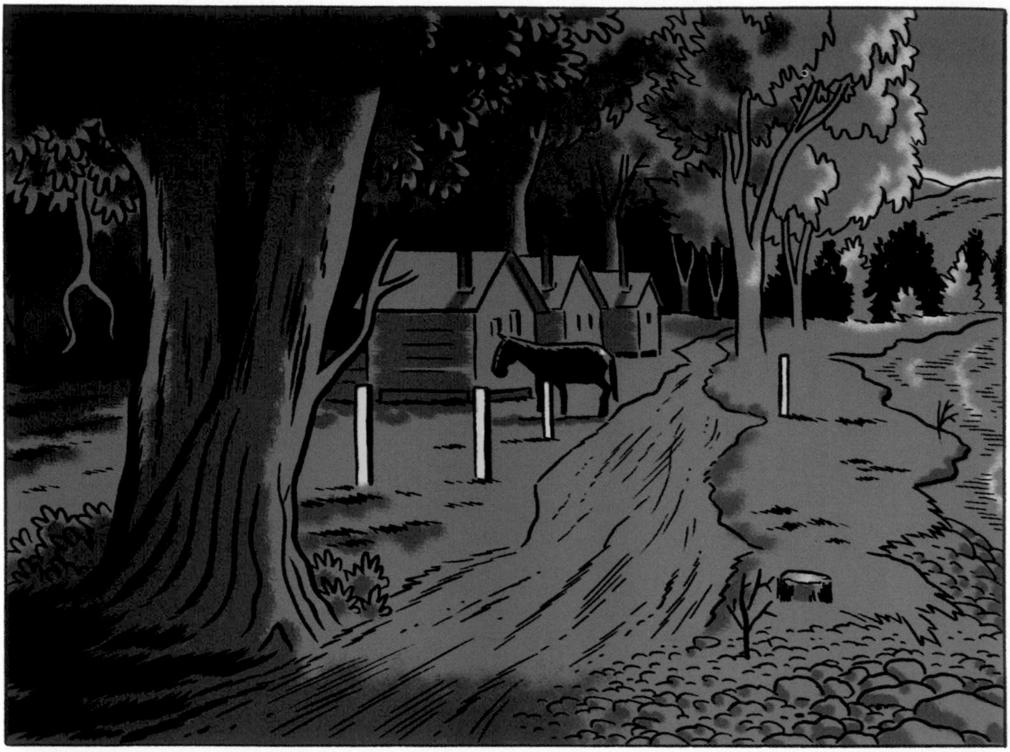
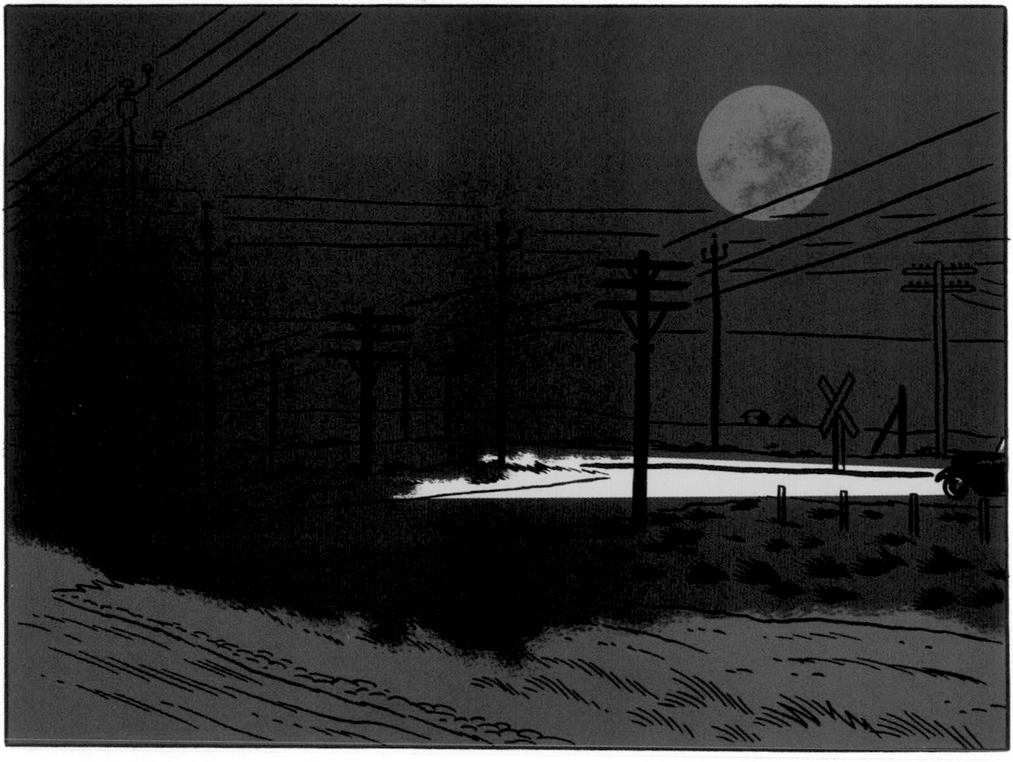

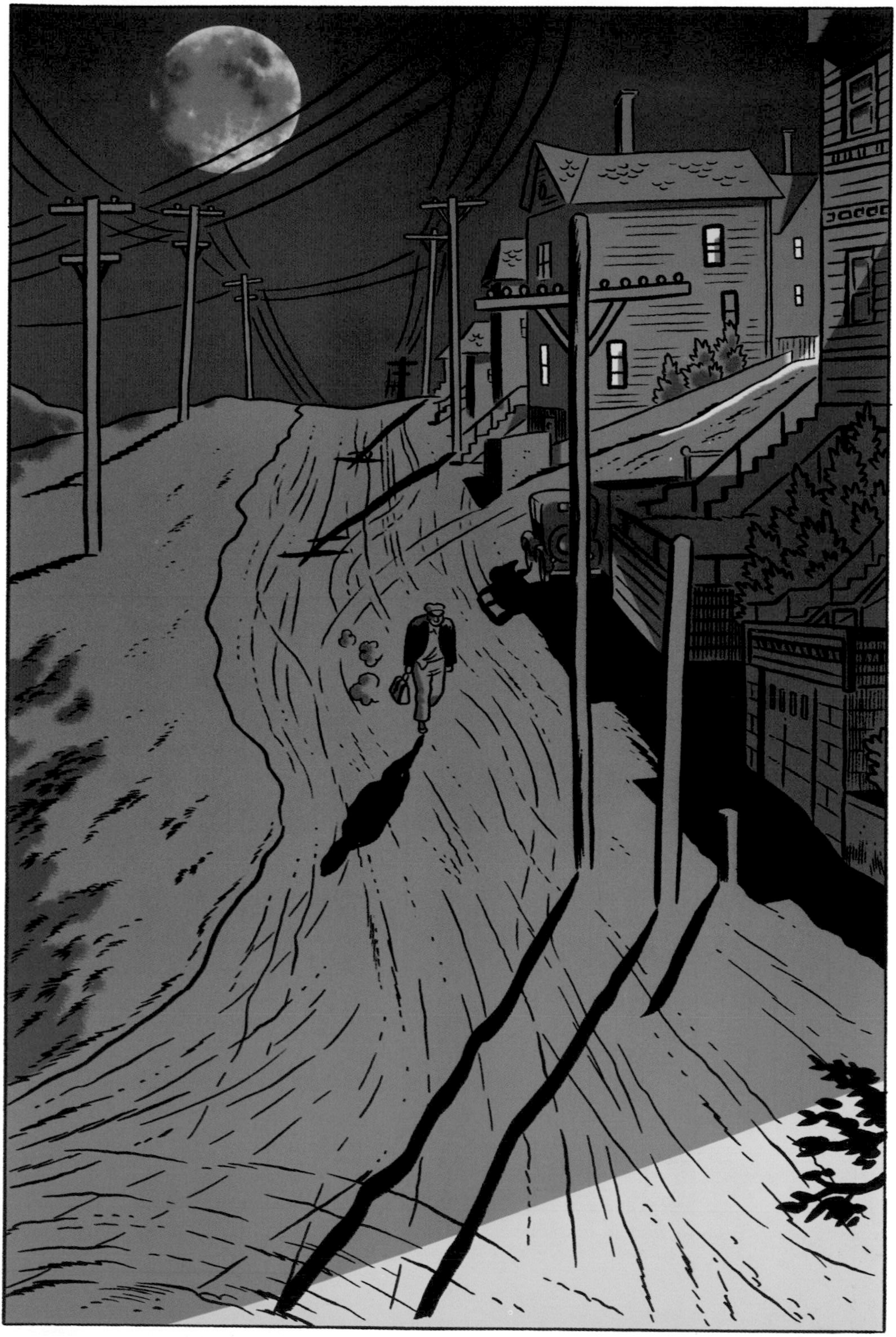

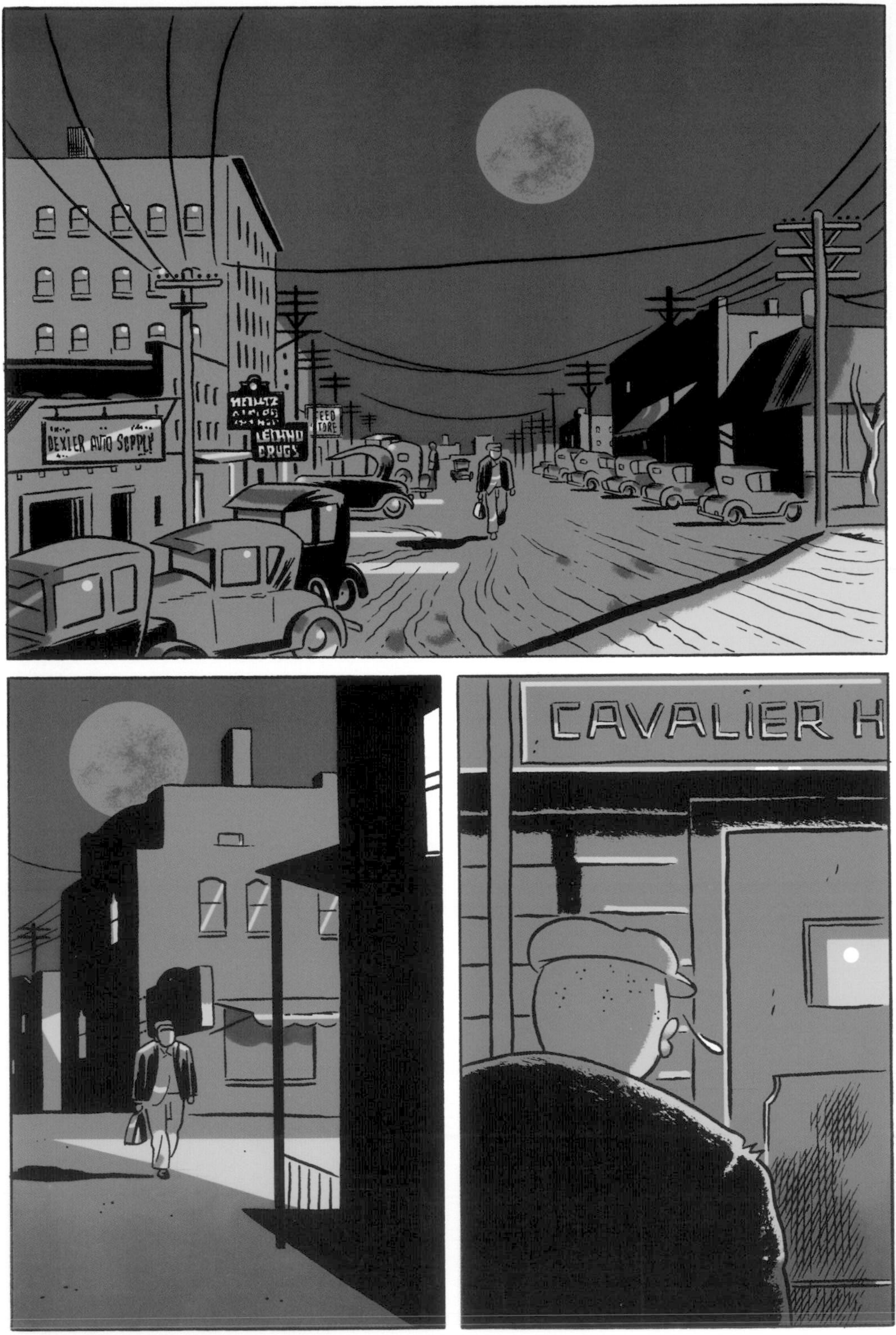
DEXLER AUTO SUPPLY
DRUGS
FEED STORE
CAVALIER H

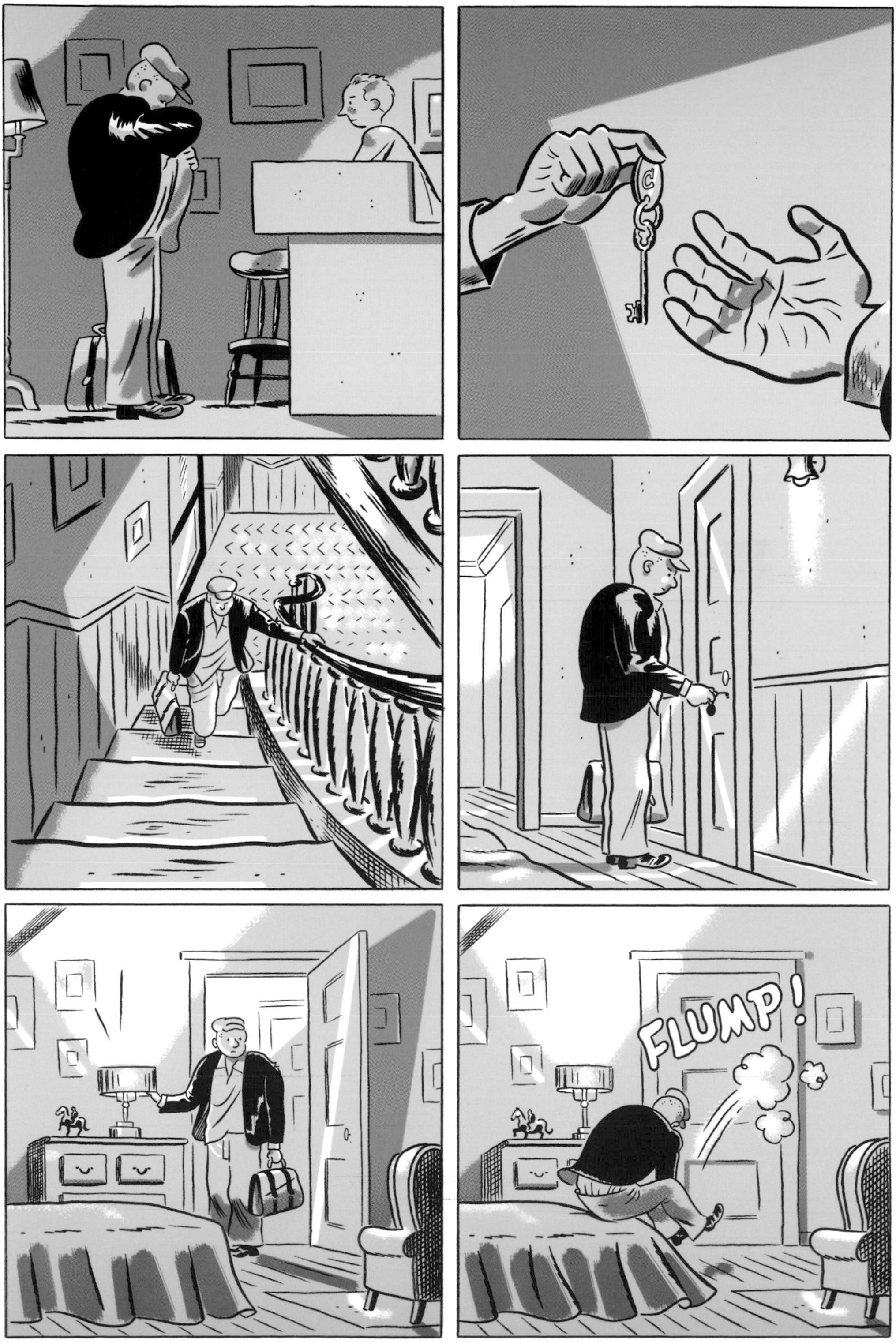
FLUMP!

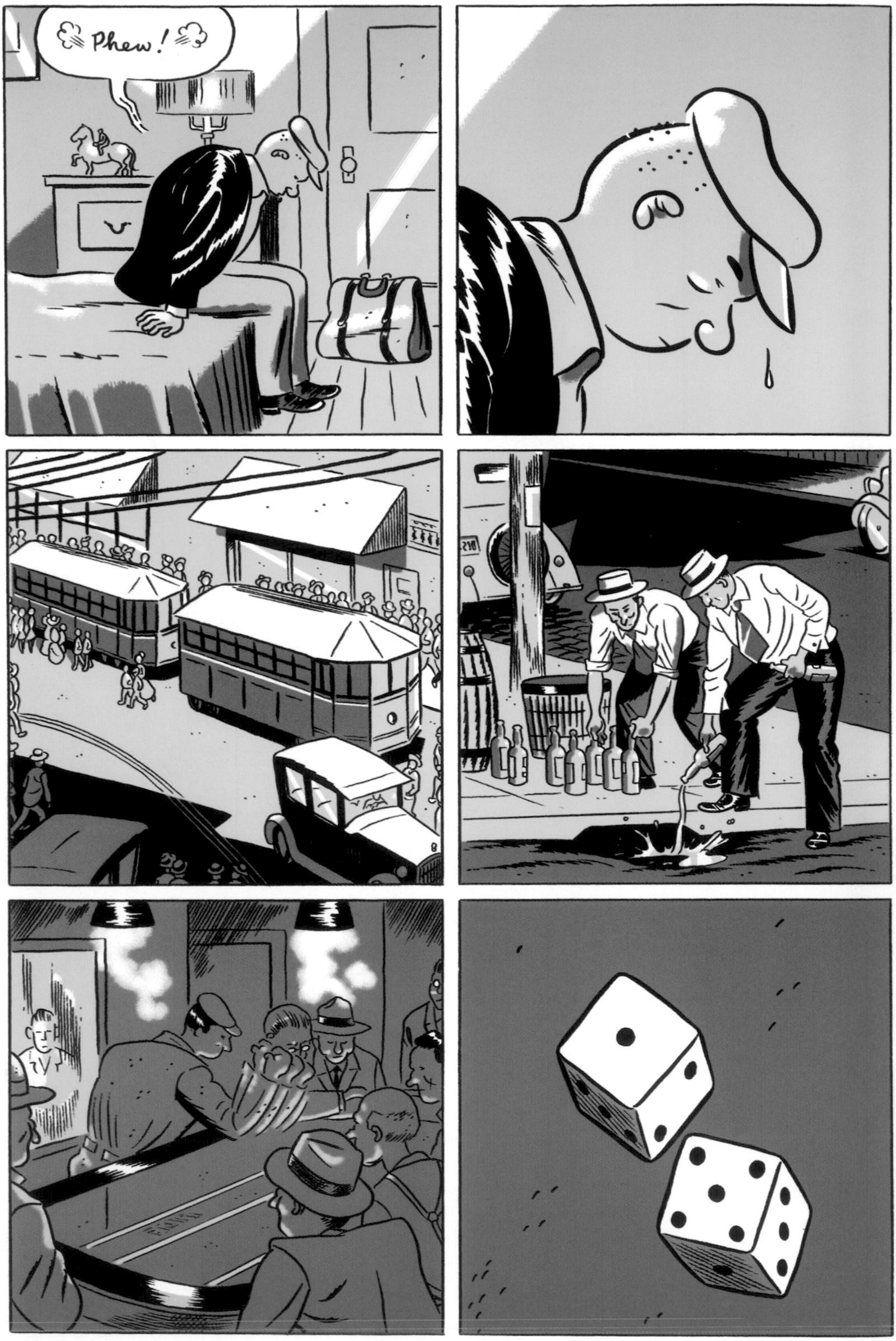
Phew!

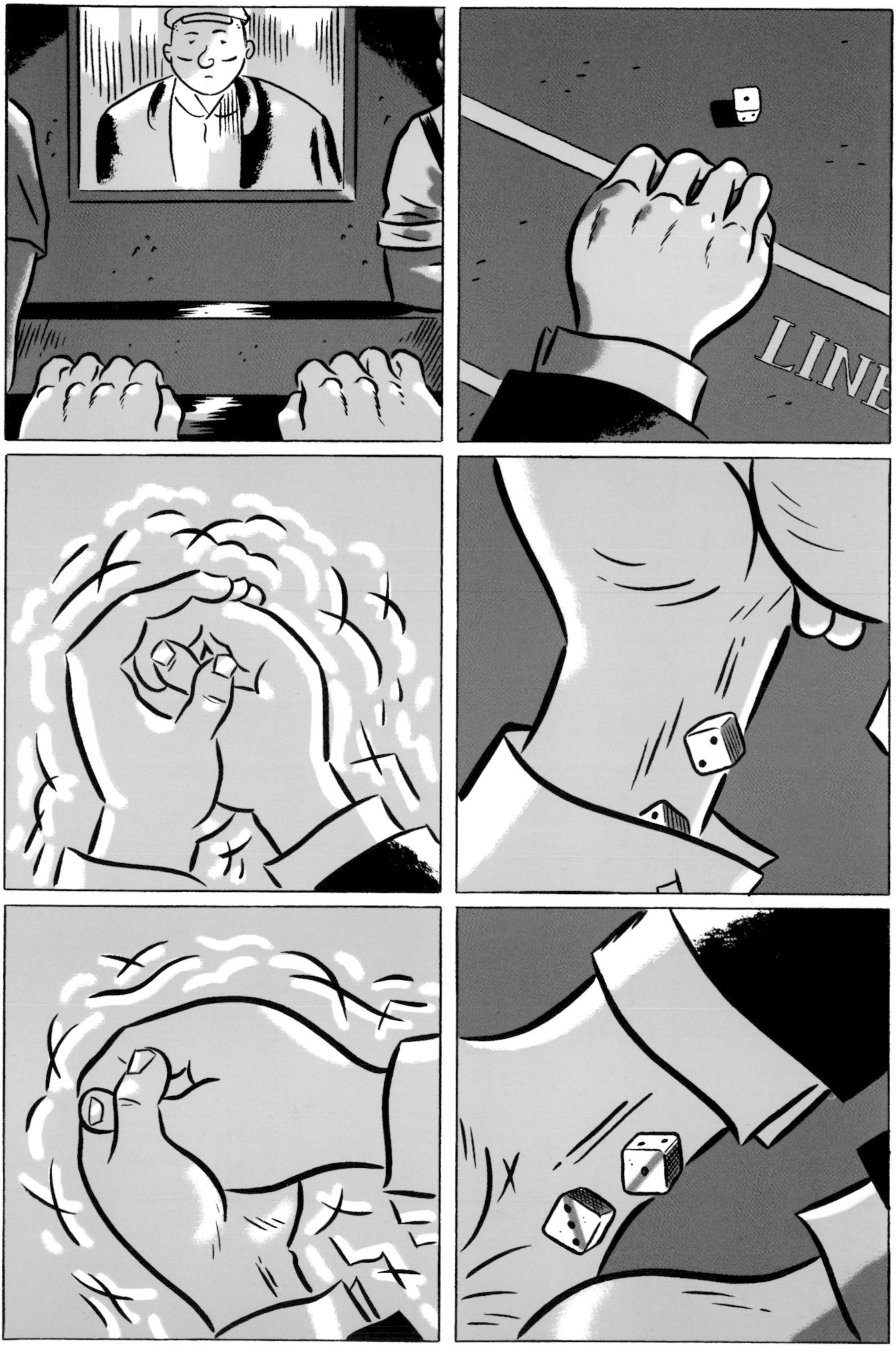
LINE

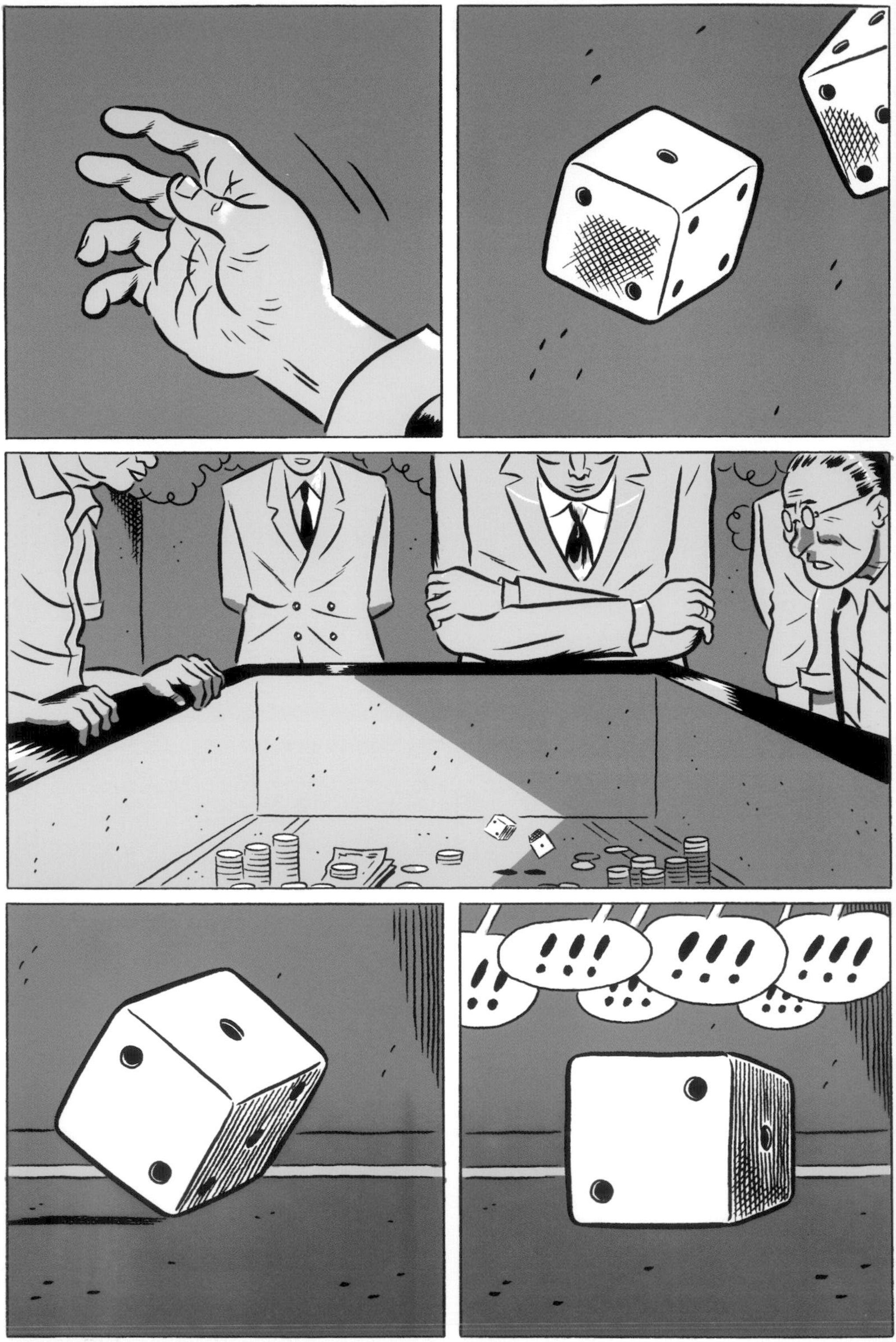
!!!
!!!
!!!
!!!

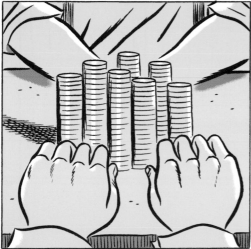

--YOU STUPID ~ YOU EVER HEAR OF THE SYNDICATE, YOU BIG OAF?...

THE TENANTS

THERE WERE MANY LONG-TERM RESIDENTS STAYING AT THE CAVALIER THAT SAM FELT NICK SHOULD BECOME "ACQUAINTED" WITH. SAM RAN DOWN THE LIST OF THESE COLORFUL CHARACTERS, BEGINNING WITH THE OCCUPANT OF ROOM SEVEN ~ MR. MCKENNA...

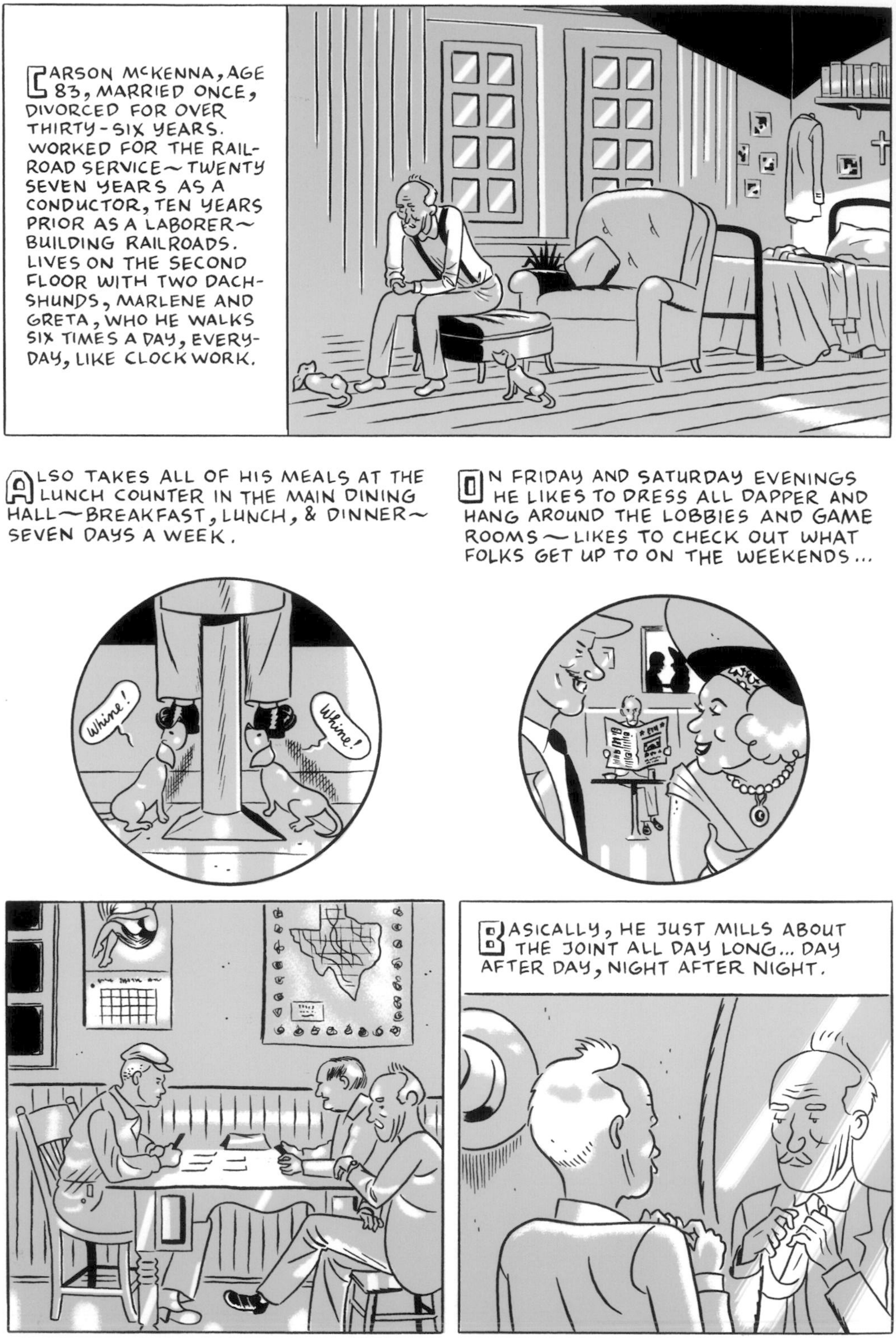
CARSON McKENNA, AGE 83, MARRIED ONCE, DIVORCED FOR OVER THIRTY-SIX YEARS. WORKED FOR THE RAILROAD SERVICE~ TWENTY SEVEN YEARS AS A CONDUCTOR, TEN YEARS PRIOR AS A LABORER~ BUILDING RAILROADS. LIVES ON THE SECOND FLOOR WITH TWO DACHSHUNDS, MARLENE AND GRETA, WHO HE WALKS SIX TIMES A DAY, EVERYDAY, LIKE CLOCK WORK.
ALSO TAKES ALL OF HIS MEALS AT THE LUNCH COUNTER IN THE MAIN DINING HALL~ BREAKFAST, LUNCH, & DINNER~ SEVEN DAYS A WEEK.
Whine!
Whine!
ON FRIDAY AND SATURDAY EVENINGS HE LIKES TO DRESS ALL DAPPER AND HANG AROUND THE LOBBIES AND GAME ROOMS ~ LIKES TO CHECK OUT WHAT FOLKS GET UP TO ON THE WEEKENDS...
BASICALLY, HE JUST MILLS ABOUT THE JOINT ALL DAY LONG... DAY AFTER DAY, NIGHT AFTER NIGHT.

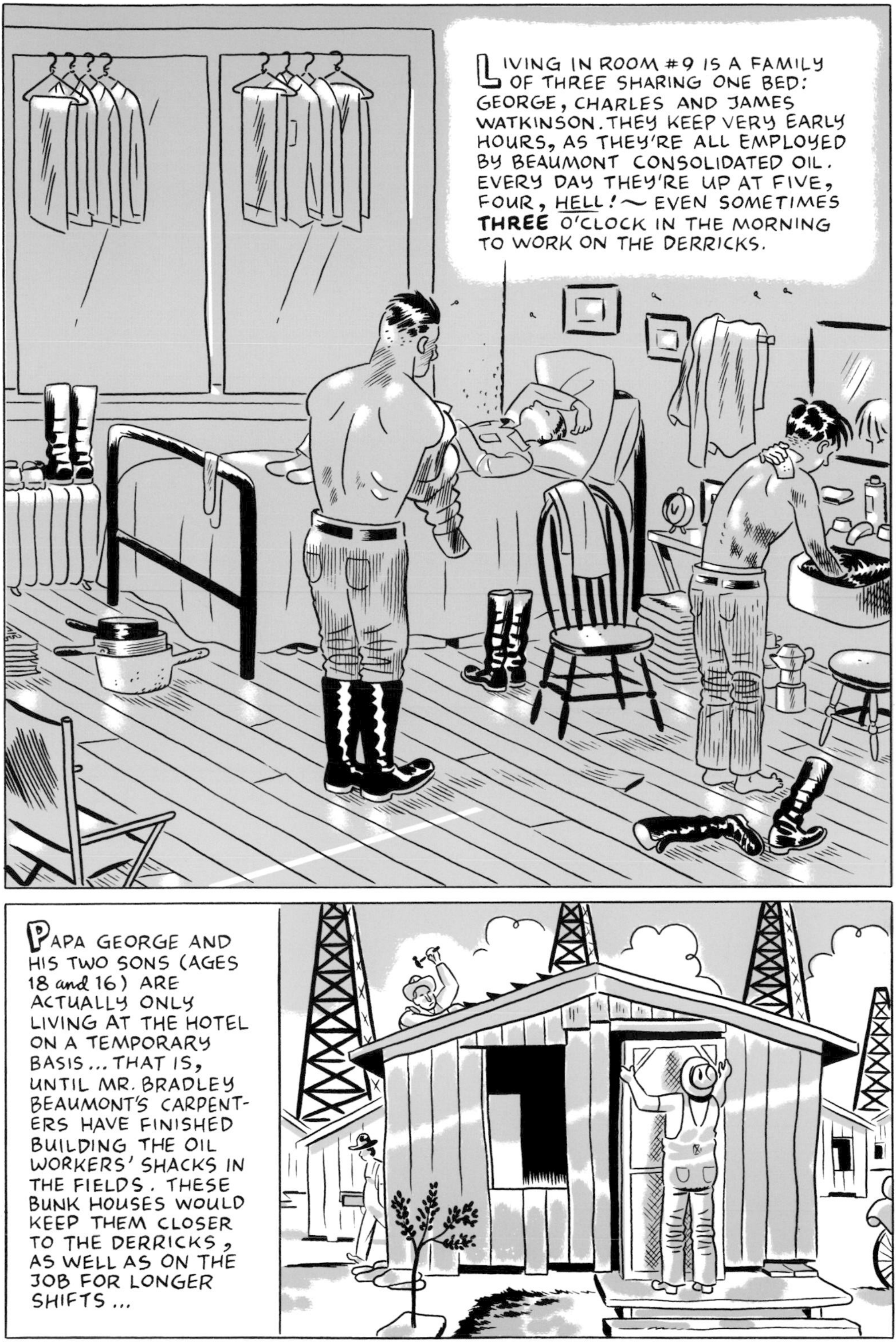
LIVING IN ROOM #9 IS A FAMILY OF THREE SHARING ONE BED: GEORGE, CHARLES AND JAMES WATKINSON. THEY KEEP VERY EARLY HOURS, AS THEY'RE ALL EMPLOYED BY BEAUMONT CONSOLIDATED OIL. EVERY DAY THEY'RE UP AT FIVE, FOUR, HELL! ~ EVEN SOMETIMES THREE O'CLOCK IN THE MORNING TO WORK ON THE DERRICKS.
PAPA GEORGE AND HIS TWO SONS (AGES 18 and 16) ARE ACTUALLY ONLY LIVING AT THE HOTEL ON A TEMPORARY BASIS... THAT IS, UNTIL MR. BRADLEY BEAUMONT'S CARPENTERS HAVE FINISHED BUILDING THE OIL WORKERS' SHACKS IN THE FIELDS. THESE BUNK HOUSES WOULD KEEP THEM CLOSER TO THE DERRICKS, AS WELL AS ON THE JOB FOR LONGER SHIFTS...

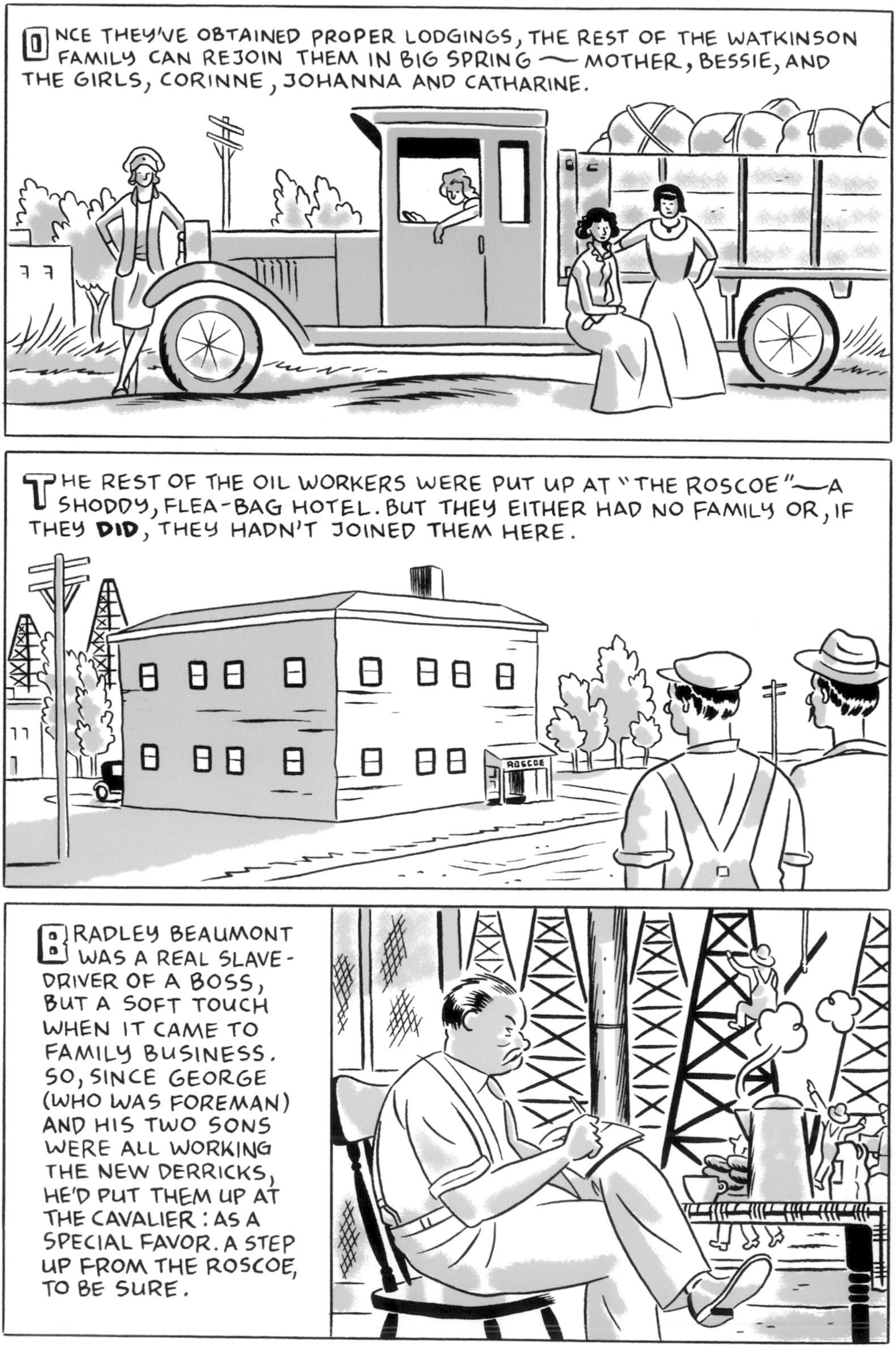
ONCE THEY'VE OBTAINED PROPER LODGINGS, THE REST OF THE WATKINSON FAMILY CAN REJOIN THEM IN BIG SPRING — MOTHER, BESSIE, AND THE GIRLS, CORINNE, JOHANNA AND CATHARINE.
THE REST OF THE OIL WORKERS WERE PUT UP AT "THE ROSCOE" — A SHODDY, FLEA-BAG HOTEL. BUT THEY EITHER HAD NO FAMILY OR, IF THEY **DID**, THEY HADN'T JOINED THEM HERE.
ROSCOE
BRADLEY BEAUMONT WAS A REAL SLAVE-DRIVER OF A BOSS, BUT A SOFT TOUCH WHEN IT CAME TO FAMILY BUSINESS. SO, SINCE GEORGE (WHO WAS FOREMAN) AND HIS TWO SONS WERE ALL WORKING THE NEW DERRICKS, HE'D PUT THEM UP AT THE CAVALIER: AS A SPECIAL FAVOR. A STEP UP FROM THE ROSCOE, TO BE SURE.

ON THE FIRST FLOOR, IN ROOM # 3, LIVES MITCH McCOY; A TALL, HANDSOME, WELL-GROOMED MAN, THIRTYISH, VERY POLITE TO THE STAFF, VERY SOCIABLE--ALWAYS SEEMS TO BE ON-THE-GO.

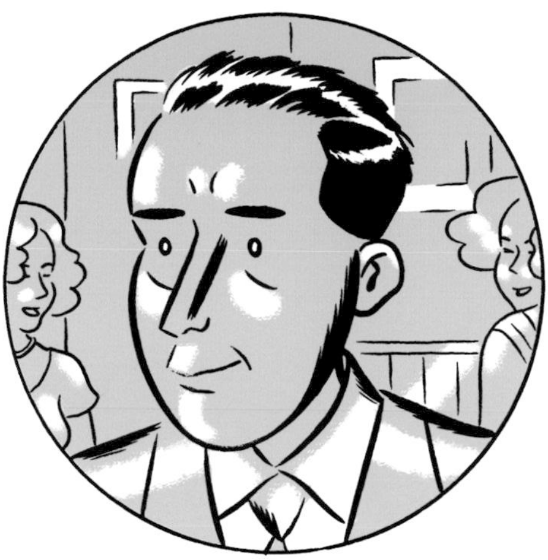

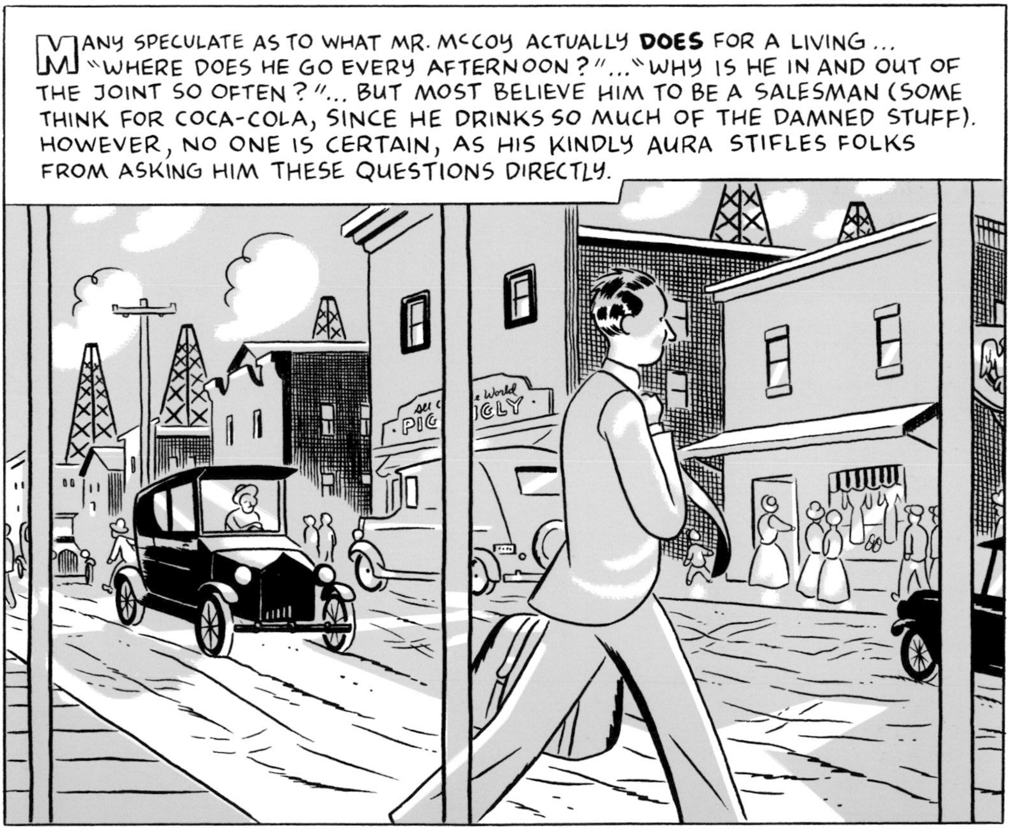
MANY SPECULATE AS TO WHAT MR. McCOY ACTUALLY **DOES** FOR A LIVING ... "WHERE DOES HE GO EVERY AFTERNOON?" ... "WHY IS HE IN AND OUT OF THE JOINT SO OFTEN?" ... BUT MOST BELIEVE HIM TO BE A SALESMAN (SOME THINK FOR COCA-COLA, SINCE HE DRINKS SO MUCH OF THE DAMNED STUFF). HOWEVER, NO ONE IS CERTAIN, AS HIS KINDLY AURA STIFLES FOLKS FROM ASKING HIM THESE QUESTIONS DIRECTLY.

SINGLE MOTHER, GERALDINE NORMAND, AND CHILD, HENRY, LIVE UPSTAIRS IN ROOM # 11. GERALDINE WORKS AS A TEACHER AT THE ELEMENTARY SCHOOL IN BIG SPRING. HENRY IS WITH HER ALL DAY LONG, THROUGH EVERY SESSION UP UNTIL HER END-OF-THE-DAY DUTIES.

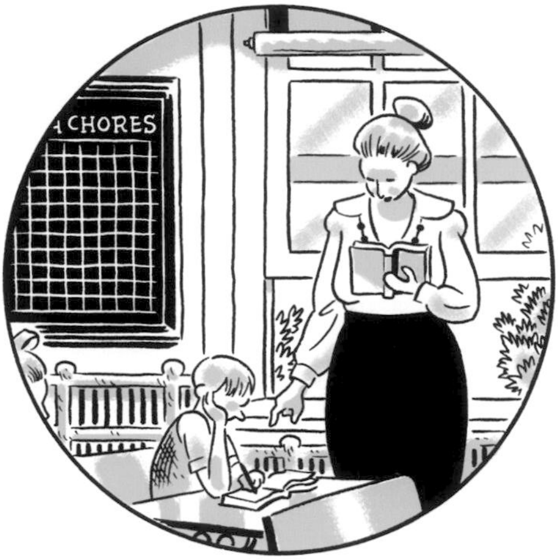
CHORES

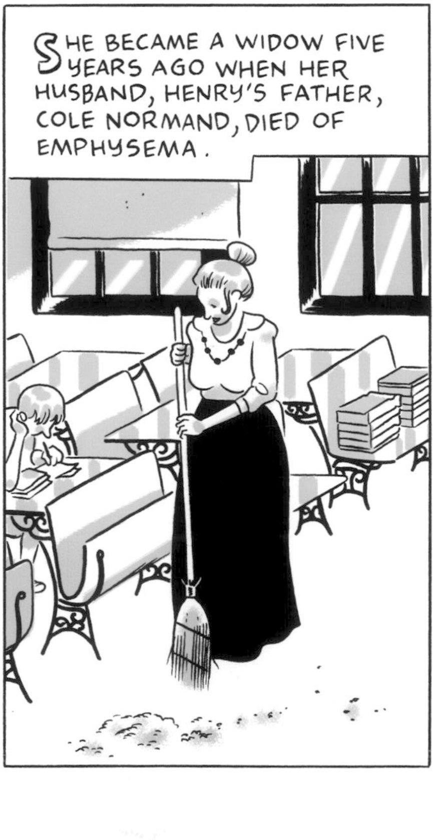
SHE BECAME A WIDOW FIVE YEARS AGO WHEN HER HUSBAND, HENRY'S FATHER, COLE NORMAND, DIED OF EMPHYSEMA.

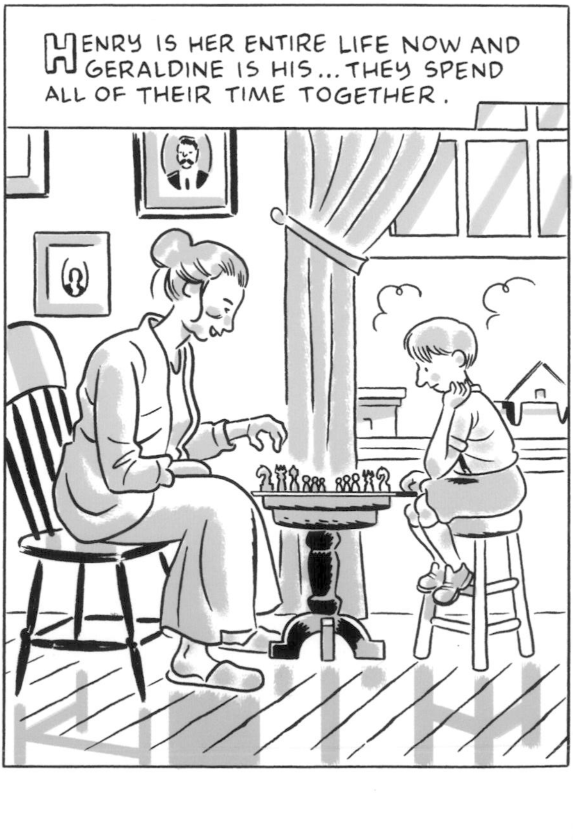
HENRY IS HER ENTIRE LIFE NOW AND GERALDINE IS HIS... THEY SPEND ALL OF THEIR TIME TOGETHER.

DEWEY OLIVER, WHO WORKS AS MAINTENANCE MAN, JANITOR, AND WAITER, LIVES IN A TINY ROOM IN THE BASEMENT THAT USED TO BE A STORAGE ROOM. HE'S THE ONLY STAFF MEMBER RESIDING AT THE HOTEL...

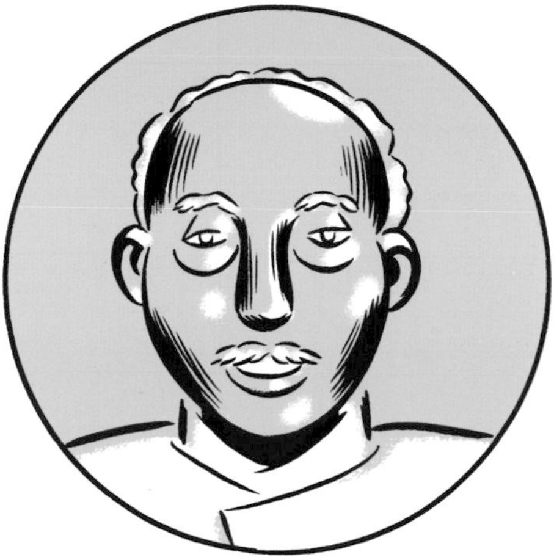

THAT IS, BESIDES NEWCOMERS NICK AND WILLA FORD... WHO LIVE UP IN ROOM #16. WILLA SOMETIMES HELPS OUT AT THE CAVALIER DOING HOUSEKEEPING ON BUSY WEEKENDS AND HOLIDAYS AND SUCH.

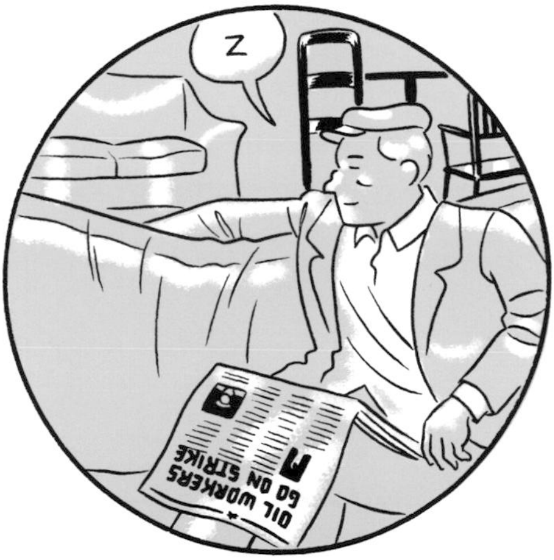
Z
OIL WORKERS GO ON STRIKE

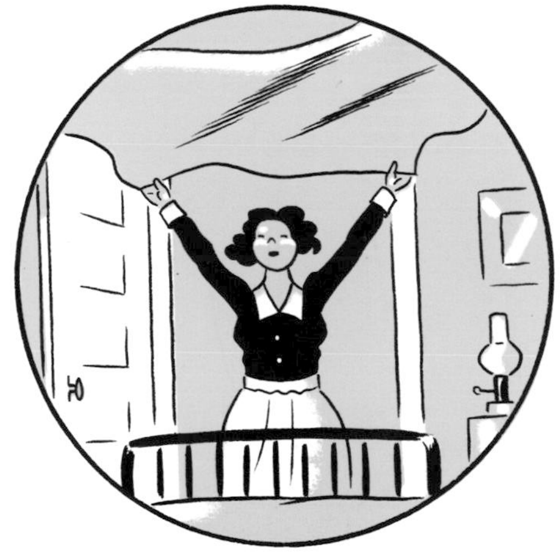

OCCASSIONALLY THE HILLS SLEEP THERE AS WELL, BUT NORMALLY THEY PREFER SLEEPING IN THEIR BEDS AT HOME—AWAY FROM DOWNTOWN... A BIG OL' HOUSE OUT ON THE HIGH PLAINS...

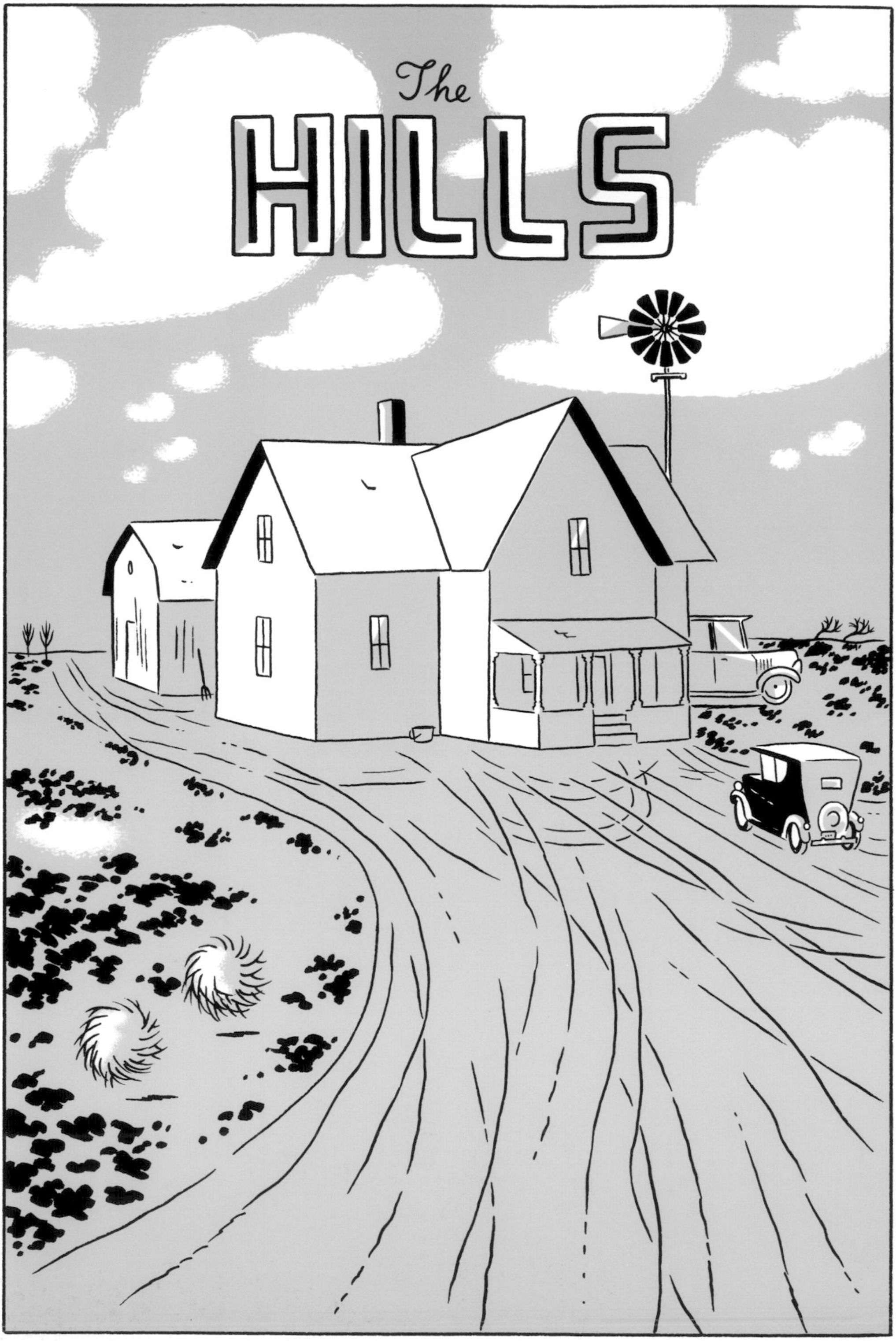
The
HILLS

THIS IS THE HOME THAT FRANK HILL PURCHASED FOR HIS **ENTIRE** FAMILY BACK IN 1923... ACQUIRED WITH A SMALL FORTUNE ACCRUED DURING HIS STINT AS AN INDEPENDENT OIL MAN.

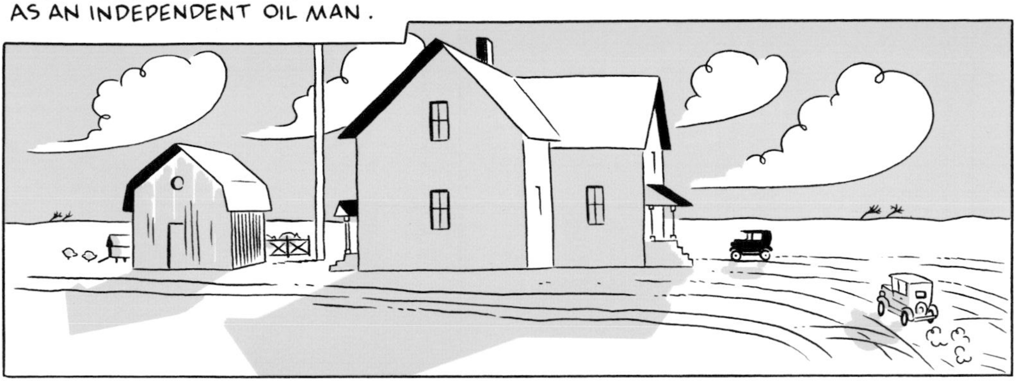

NOT KNOWING A THING ABOUT THE OIL TRADE (BEYOND THAT OF A WILDCATTER), HE QUICKLY SOLD THE LOT OF LAND HE SO LUCKILY STRUCK OIL BENEATH TO FAIRFAX & WEBB CONSOLIDATED. HE SOLD OUT FOR A VERY REASONABLE SUM, UNDER THE CONDITION THAT THEY SHOW HIM A THING OR TWO ABOUT THE DRILLING BUSINESS — TO WHICH THEY GRACIOUSLY AGREED.

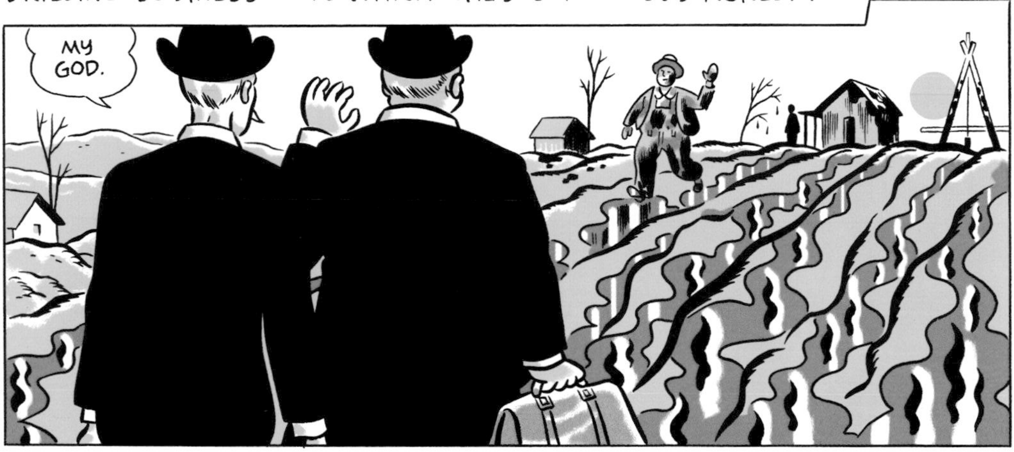
MY GOD.

FRANK AND THE OTHER NEIGHBORING LAND OWNERS MADE QUITE A BIT OF MONEY ON THEIR FIND, BUT THEY COULD'VE BEEN MILLIONAIRES FIVE TIMES OVER, HAD THEY HELD OUT A LITTLE LONGER FOR A MORE **SCRUPULOUS** PARTNER TO DO BUSINESS WITH. FRANK DIDN'T SUFFER **SO** MUCH, AS IT WAS **HIS** DISCOVERY, THUS AWARDING HIM THE LION'S SHARE OF PROFITS...

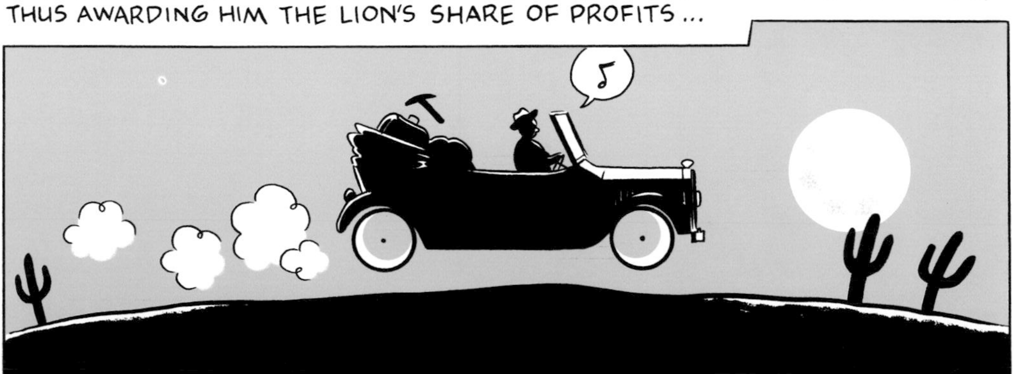

BUT THIS WAS IN 1918 ... AND AFTER ONLY A SHORT VISIT WITH HIS WIFE AND CHILDREN, FRANK LEFT HOME AGAIN — TO START HIS OWN OIL DRILLING COMPANY.

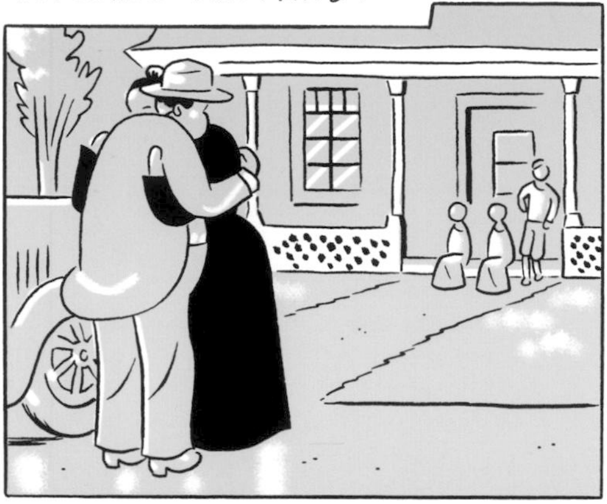

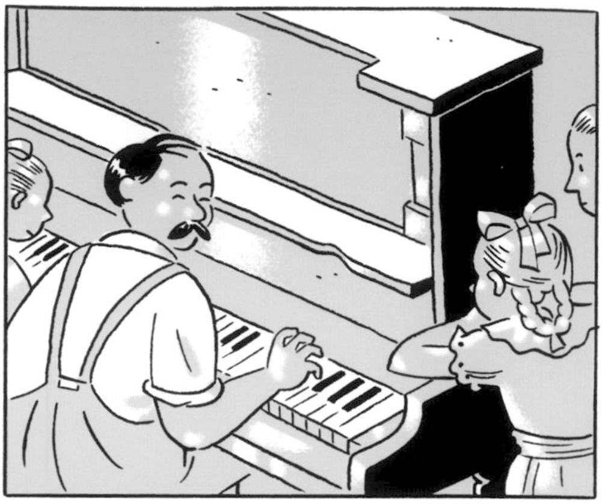

NOW THAT HE HAD A BETTER UNDERSTANDING OF THE TRADE, HE SET OUT TO SEEK HIS BIG FORTUNE! HE FELT THAT HE COULD FIND LAND THAT WOULD PRODUCE EVEN MORE BLACK GOLD THAN THAT OLD LOT HE'D GIVEN TO FAIRFAX & WEBB (*pictured below*).

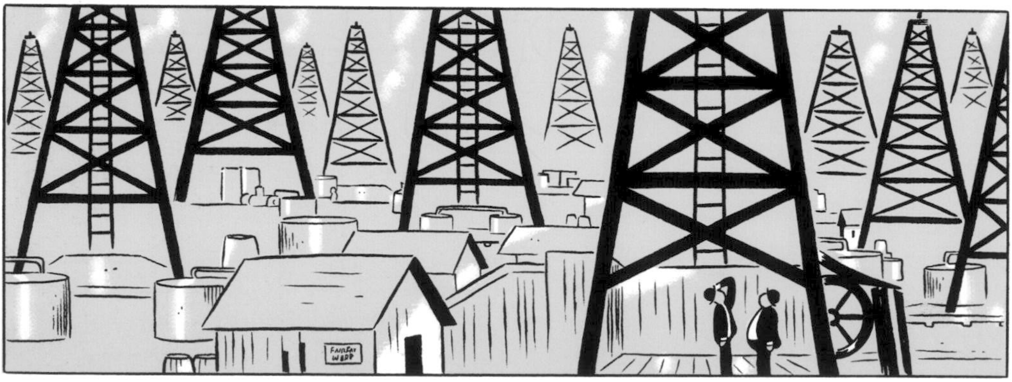

—FAIRFAX & WEBB OIL FIELD IN 1919, TWENTY PUMPS PRODUCING.

SO FRANK STARTED ANEW, IN A NEW SPOT WITH PROPER EQUIPMENT. HE HIRED SOME OLD **CLOSE** FRIENDS TO HELP HIM OUT AS WELL.

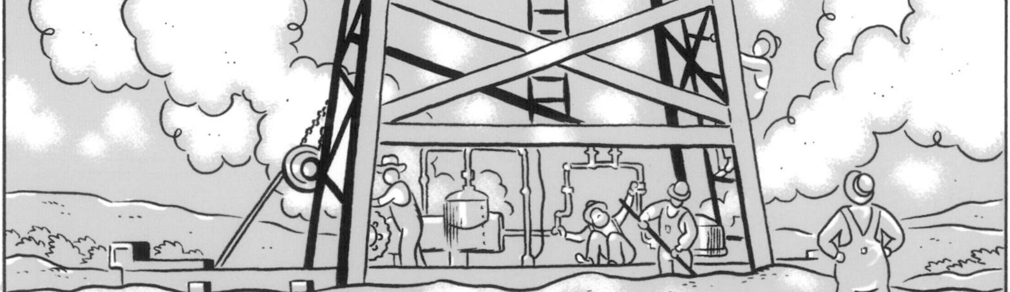

FRANK NEEDED PEOPLE HE COULD TRUST AROUND HIM. GUYS LIKE NICK FORD, WHO CAME OUT EARLY INTO FRANK'S ENDEAVOR. OF COURSE NOT EVERYONE WAS A FRIEND — HE NEEDED KNOWLEDGE-ABLE FOLKS ON THE SITE AS WELL — GEOLOGISTS AND WHAT NOT.

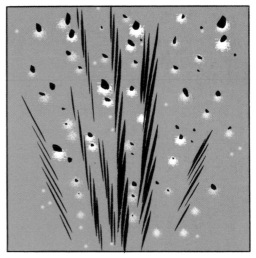

FOR A BUNCH OF RANK AMATEURS, FRANK AND COMPANY MADE OUT PRETTY DAMN WELL... THEY HAD SIX RIGS PUMPING THE FIRST YEAR, AND NINE BY YEAR TWO... NOT A HUGE OUTFIT, BUT **PROFITABLE** NONETHELESS!...OF COURSE AFTER TWO YEARS OF THIS, FRANK BECAME BORED WITH OIL AND BEGAN LEAP-FROGGING FROM ONE BUSINESS TO ANOTHER...AND ANOTHER...

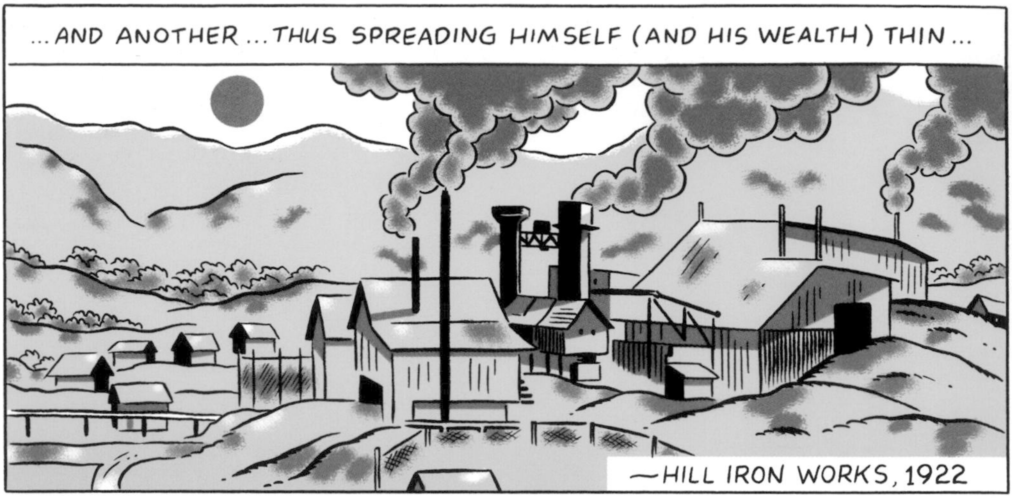
...AND ANOTHER...THUS SPREADING HIMSELF (AND HIS WEALTH) THIN...
—HILL IRON WORKS, 1922

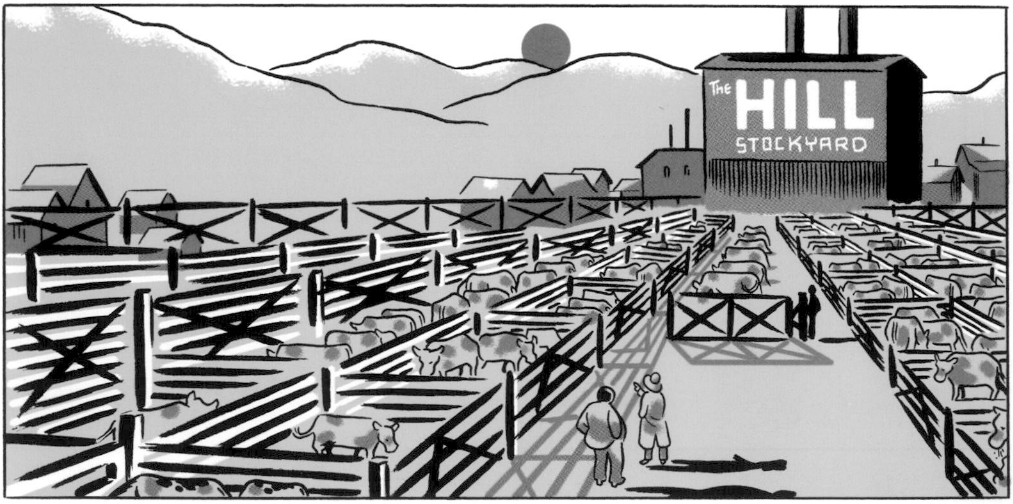
THE HILL STOCKYARD

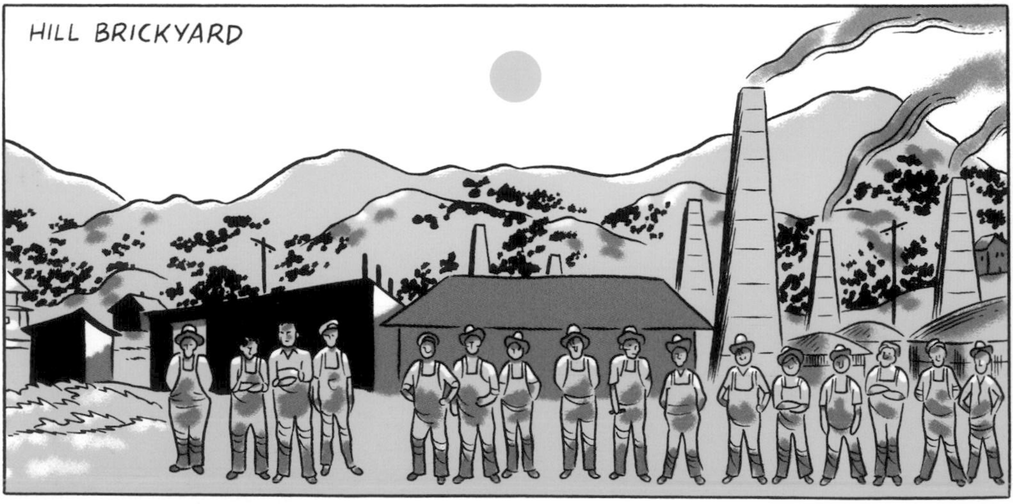
HILL BRICKYARD

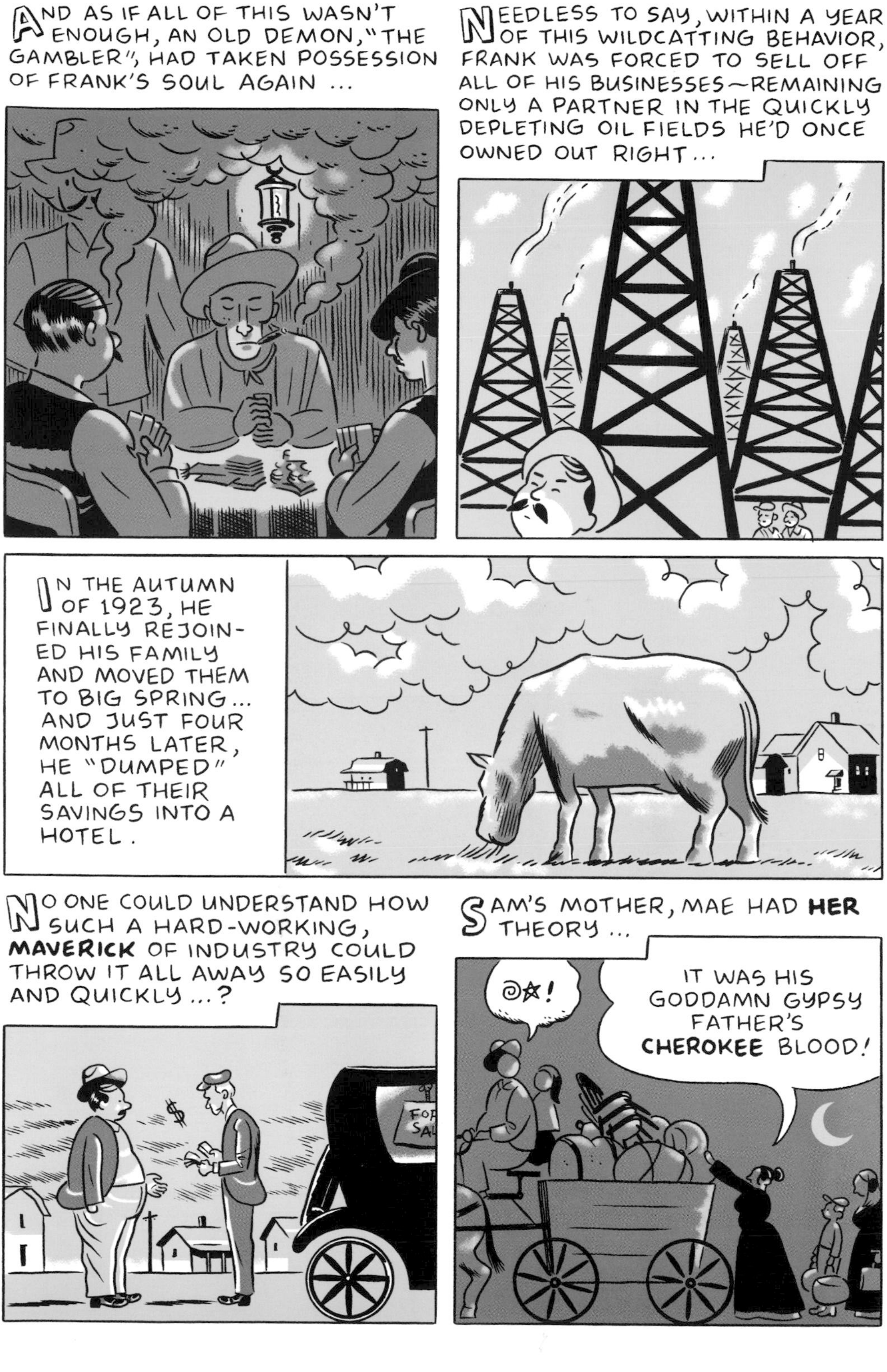
AND AS IF ALL OF THIS WASN'T ENOUGH, AN OLD DEMON, "THE GAMBLER", HAD TAKEN POSSESSION OF FRANK'S SOUL AGAIN ...
NEEDLESS TO SAY, WITHIN A YEAR OF THIS WILDCATTING BEHAVIOR, FRANK WAS FORCED TO SELL OFF ALL OF HIS BUSINESSES—REMAINING ONLY A PARTNER IN THE QUICKLY DEPLETING OIL FIELDS HE'D ONCE OWNED OUT RIGHT...
IN THE AUTUMN OF 1923, HE FINALLY REJOINED HIS FAMILY AND MOVED THEM TO BIG SPRING... AND JUST FOUR MONTHS LATER, HE "DUMPED" ALL OF THEIR SAVINGS INTO A HOTEL.
NO ONE COULD UNDERSTAND HOW SUCH A HARD-WORKING, **MAVERICK** OF INDUSTRY COULD THROW IT ALL AWAY SO EASILY AND QUICKLY ...?
$
SAM'S MOTHER, MAE HAD **HER** THEORY ...
@☆!
IT WAS HIS GODDAMN GYPSY FATHER'S **CHEROKEE** BLOOD!

WILLA

BACK AT THE CAVALIER **HOTEL**, WE FIND SAM AND WILLA KEEPING THEIR "DATE" WITH THAT CHOCOLATE MALT SHE'D PROMISED HIM WEEKS AGO...

AS THEY SIPPED THEIR DRINKS, WILLA GOT SAM CAUGHT UP ON HER FAMILY HISTORY—

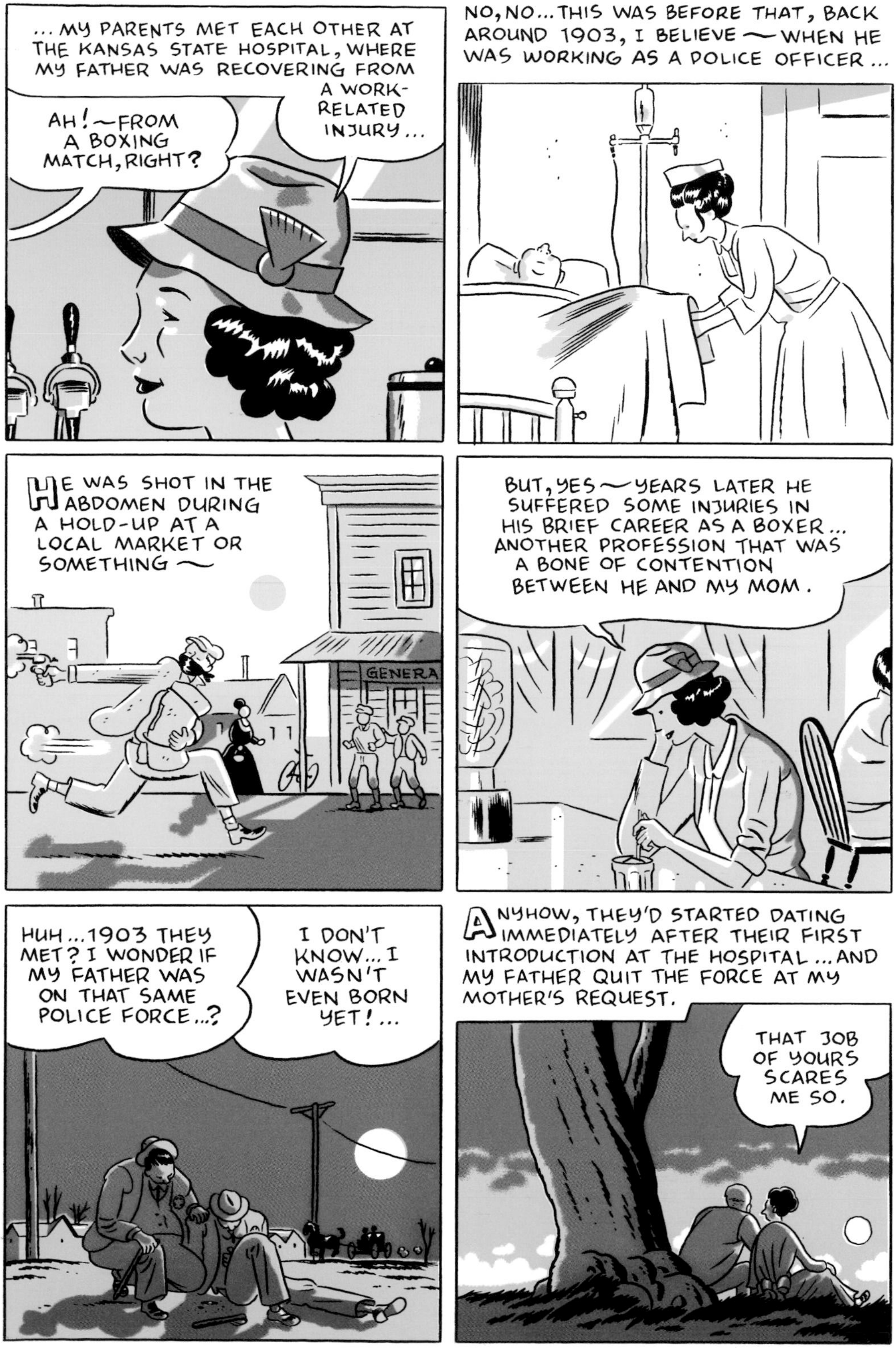
... MY PARENTS MET EACH OTHER AT THE KANSAS STATE HOSPITAL, WHERE MY FATHER WAS RECOVERING FROM A WORK-RELATED INJURY...
AH!~FROM A BOXING MATCH, RIGHT?
NO, NO... THIS WAS BEFORE THAT, BACK AROUND 1903, I BELIEVE ~ WHEN HE WAS WORKING AS A POLICE OFFICER...
HE WAS SHOT IN THE ABDOMEN DURING A HOLD-UP AT A LOCAL MARKET OR SOMETHING ~
GENERA
BUT, YES ~ YEARS LATER HE SUFFERED SOME INJURIES IN HIS BRIEF CAREER AS A BOXER... ANOTHER PROFESSION THAT WAS A BONE OF CONTENTION BETWEEN HE AND MY MOM.
HUH...1903 THEY MET? I WONDER IF MY FATHER WAS ON THAT SAME POLICE FORCE...?
I DON'T KNOW... I WASN'T EVEN BORN YET!...
ANYHOW, THEY'D STARTED DATING IMMEDIATELY AFTER THEIR FIRST INTRODUCTION AT THE HOSPITAL... AND MY FATHER QUIT THE FORCE AT MY MOTHER'S REQUEST.
THAT JOB OF YOURS SCARES ME SO.

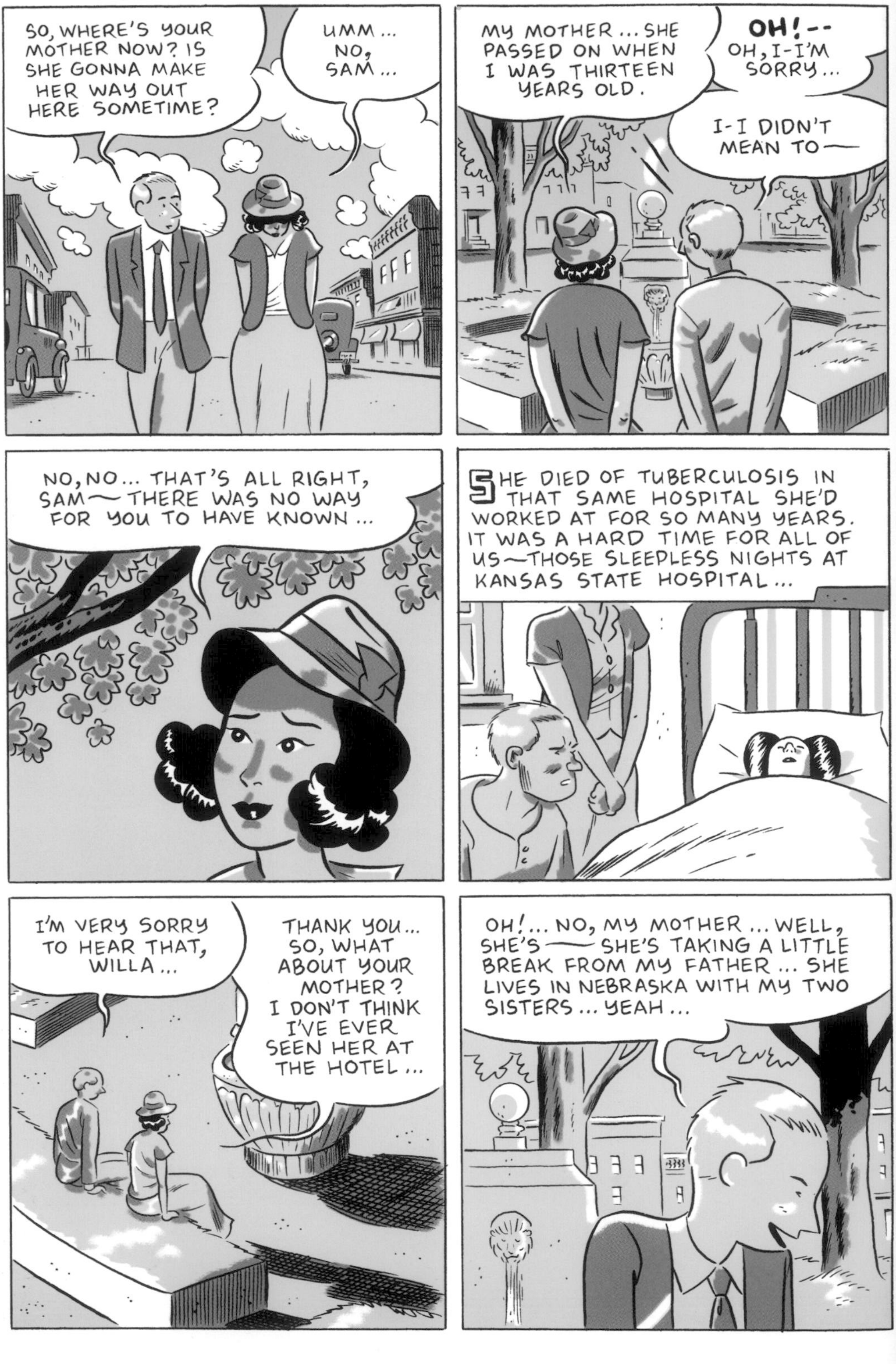
SO, WHERE'S YOUR MOTHER NOW? IS SHE GONNA MAKE HER WAY OUT HERE SOMETIME?
UMM... NO, SAM...
MY MOTHER... SHE PASSED ON WHEN I WAS THIRTEEN YEARS OLD.
OH!-- OH, I-I'M SORRY...
I-I DIDN'T MEAN TO—
NO, NO... THAT'S ALL RIGHT, SAM— THERE WAS NO WAY FOR YOU TO HAVE KNOWN...
SHE DIED OF TUBERCULOSIS IN THAT SAME HOSPITAL SHE'D WORKED AT FOR SO MANY YEARS. IT WAS A HARD TIME FOR ALL OF US—THOSE SLEEPLESS NIGHTS AT KANSAS STATE HOSPITAL...
I'M VERY SORRY TO HEAR THAT, WILLA...
THANK YOU... SO, WHAT ABOUT YOUR MOTHER? I DON'T THINK I'VE EVER SEEN HER AT THE HOTEL...
OH!... NO, MY MOTHER... WELL, SHE'S — SHE'S TAKING A LITTLE BREAK FROM MY FATHER... SHE LIVES IN NEBRASKA WITH MY TWO SISTERS... YEAH...

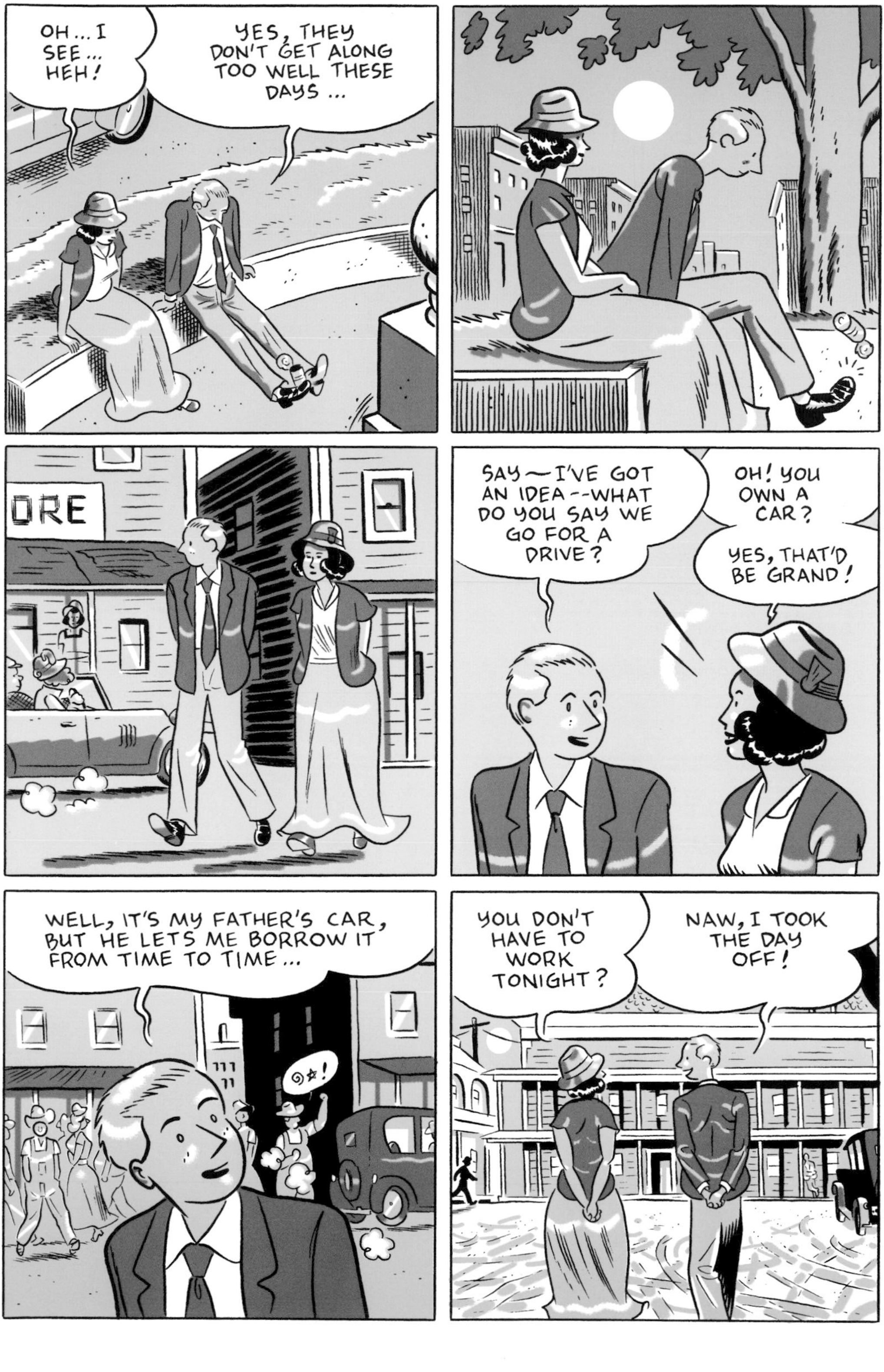
OH... I SEE... HEH!
YES, THEY DON'T GET ALONG TOO WELL THESE DAYS...
ORE
SAY—I'VE GOT AN IDEA--WHAT DO YOU SAY WE GO FOR A DRIVE?
OH! YOU OWN A CAR?
YES, THAT'D BE GRAND!
WELL, IT'S MY FATHER'S CAR, BUT HE LETS ME BORROW IT FROM TIME TO TIME...
YOU DON'T HAVE TO WORK TONIGHT?
NAW, I TOOK THE DAY OFF!

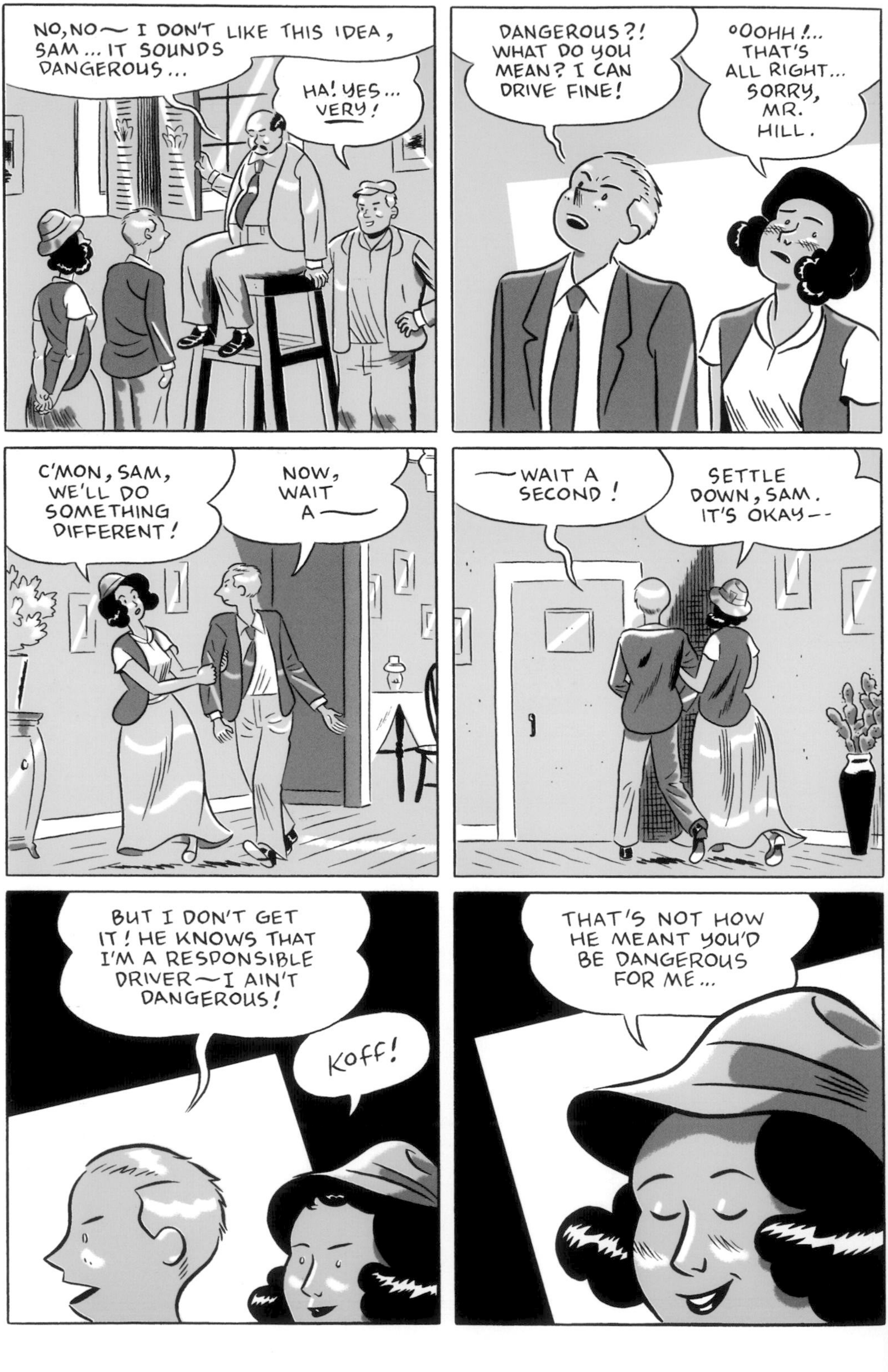
NO, NO— I DON'T LIKE THIS IDEA, SAM... IT SOUNDS DANGEROUS...
HA! YES... VERY!
DANGEROUS?! WHAT DO YOU MEAN? I CAN DRIVE FINE!
OOOHH!... THAT'S ALL RIGHT... SORRY, MR. HILL.
C'MON, SAM, WE'LL DO SOMETHING DIFFERENT!
NOW, WAIT A—
—WAIT A SECOND!
SETTLE DOWN, SAM. IT'S OKAY--
BUT I DON'T GET IT! HE KNOWS THAT I'M A RESPONSIBLE DRIVER—I AIN'T DANGEROUS!
KOFF!
THAT'S NOT HOW HE MEANT YOU'D BE DANGEROUS FOR ME...

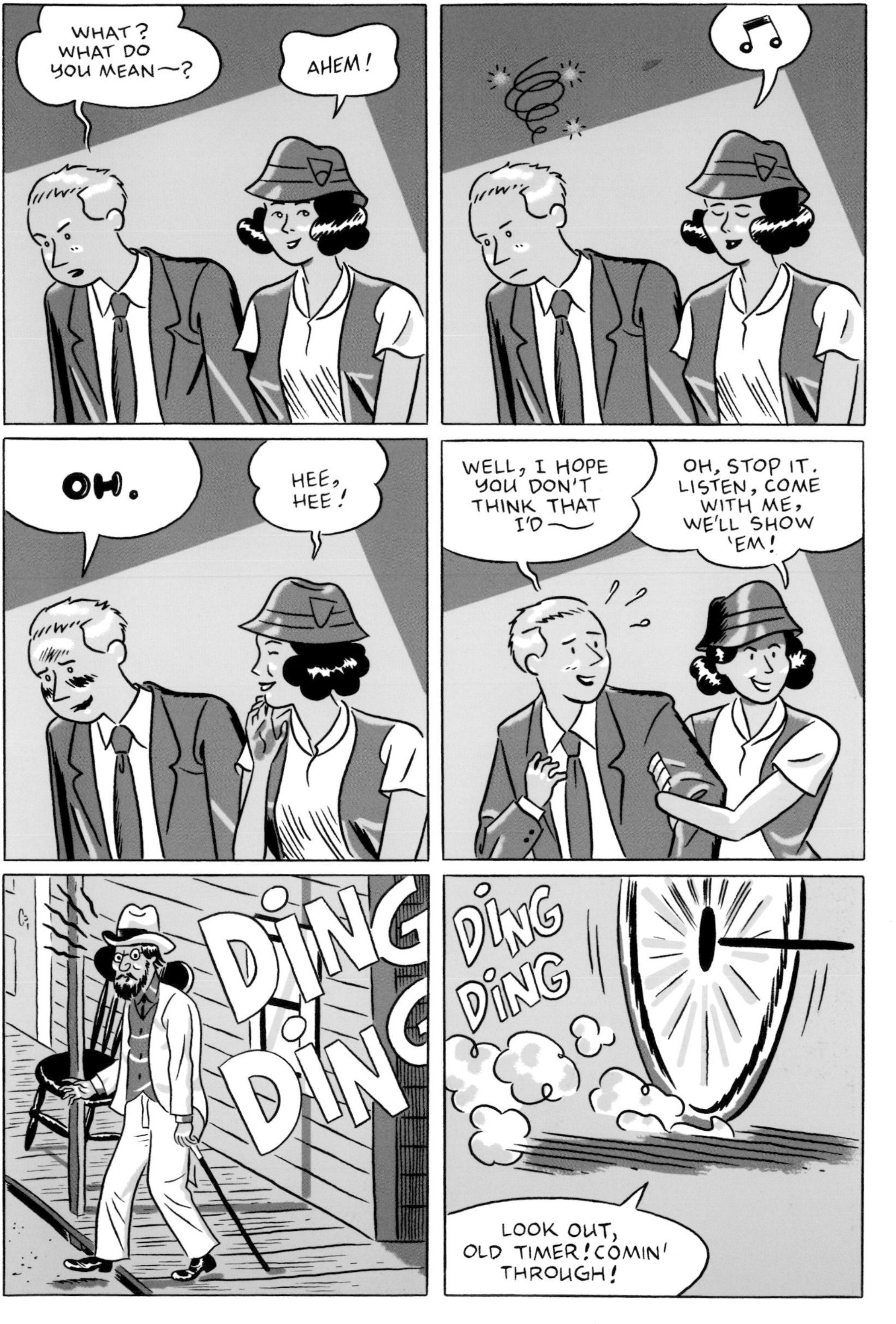
WHAT? WHAT DO YOU MEAN~?
AHEM!
♫
OH.
HEE, HEE!
WELL, I HOPE YOU DON'T THINK THAT I'D~
OH, STOP IT. LISTEN, COME WITH ME, WE'LL SHOW 'EM!
DING DING
DING DING
LOOK OUT, OLD TIMER! COMIN' THROUGH!

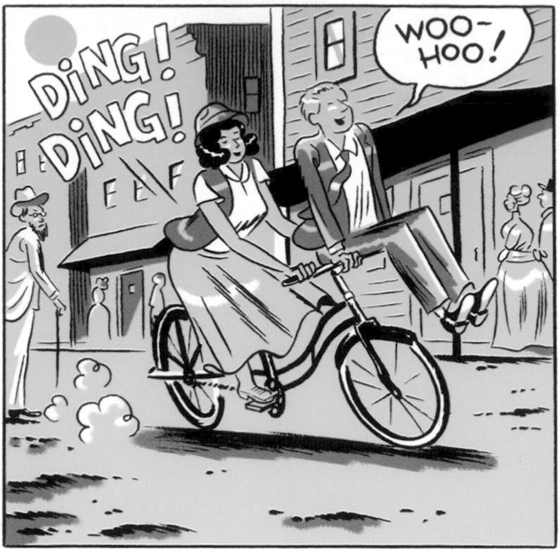
DING! DING!
WOO-HOO!

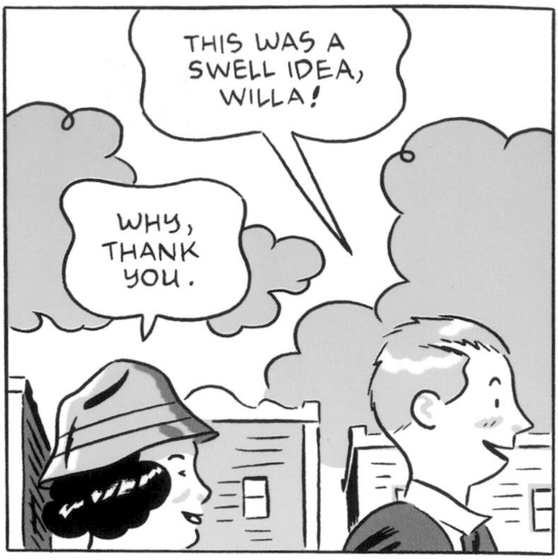
THIS WAS A SWELL IDEA, WILLA!
WHY, THANK YOU.

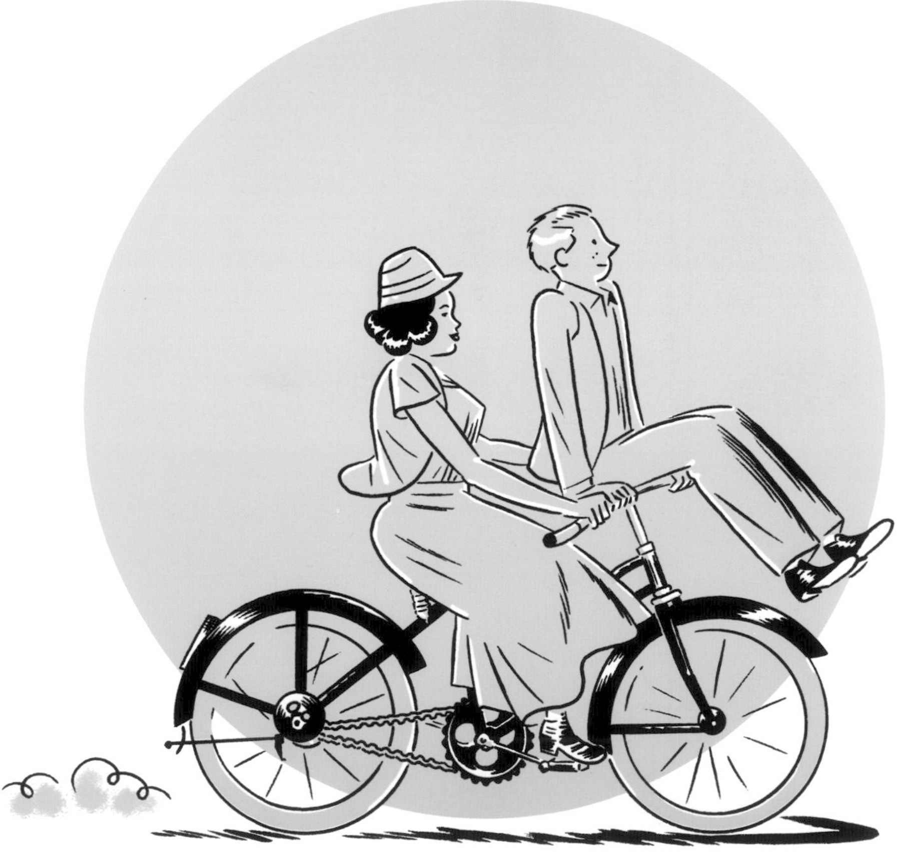

MADE

L ET'S CHECK BACK IN WITH OL' ROSS THOMPSON NOW.
FOR THE PAST FEW DAYS HE'D SEEN VERY LITTLE
OUTSIDE OF THE FOUR WALLS OF HIS HOTEL ROOM...
BUT TODAY HE'S DECIDED TO SEE THE TOWN A BIT MORE
THAN USUAL.

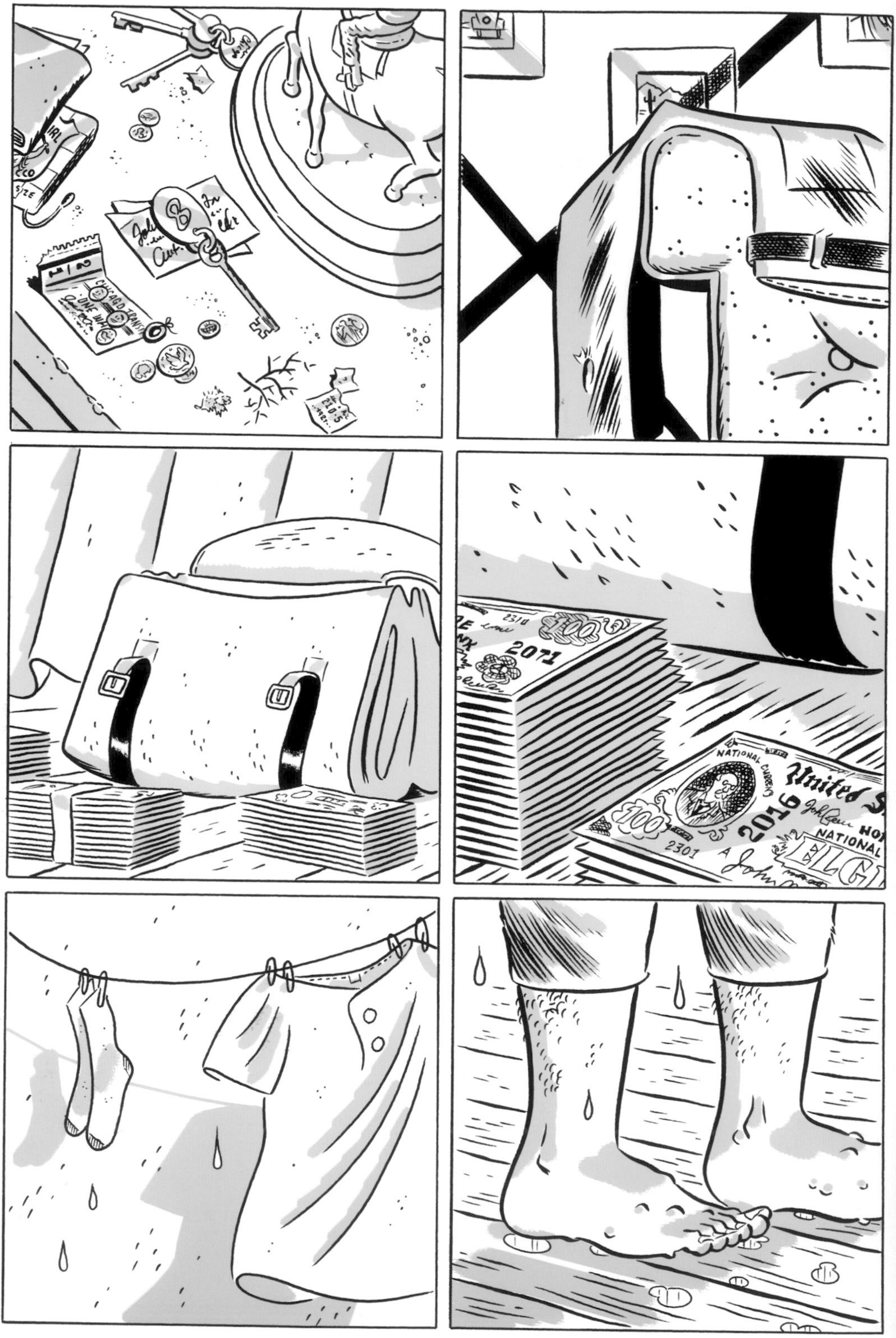
CHICAGO TRANSIT
2071
NATIONAL CURRENCY
2016
NATIONAL
2301

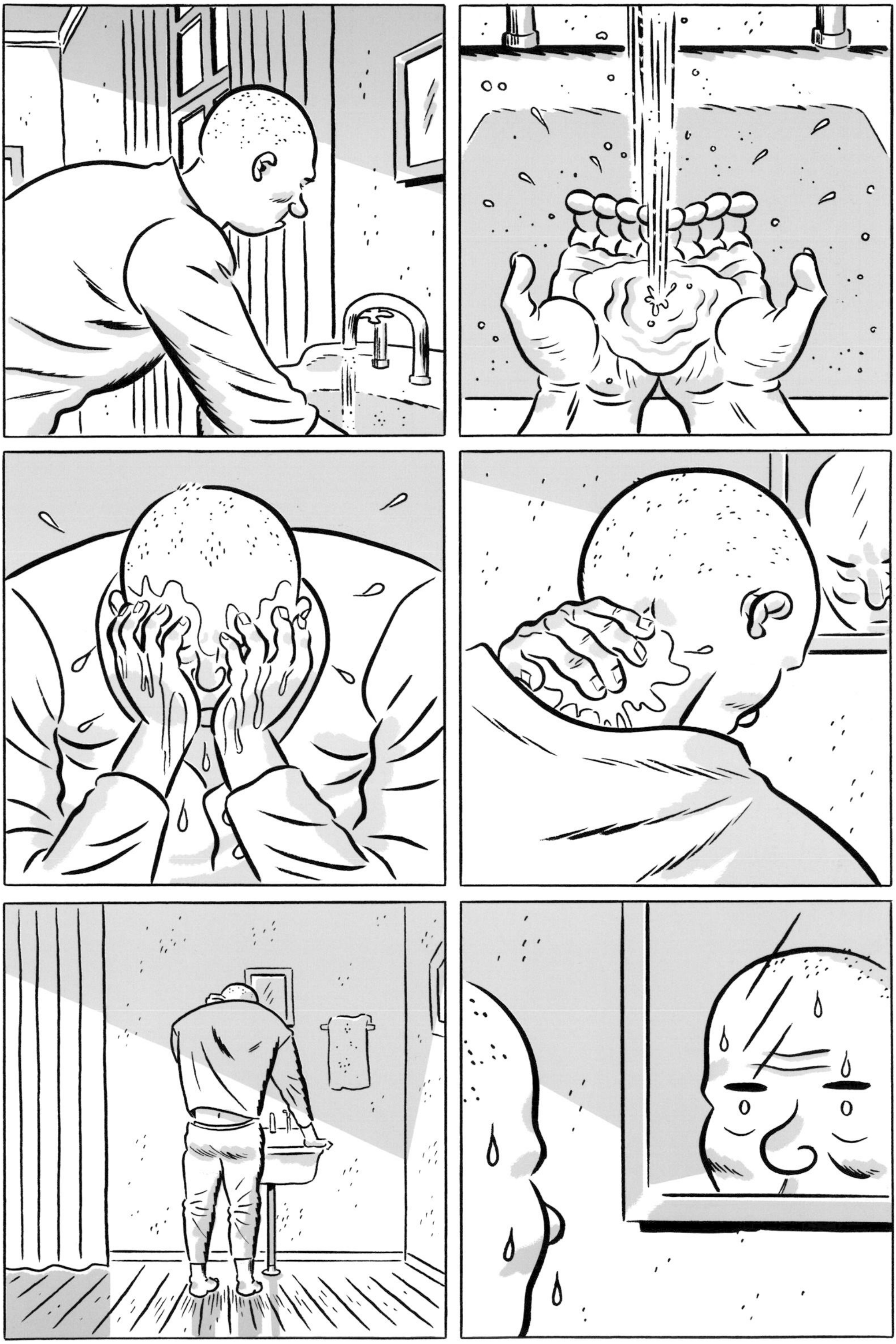

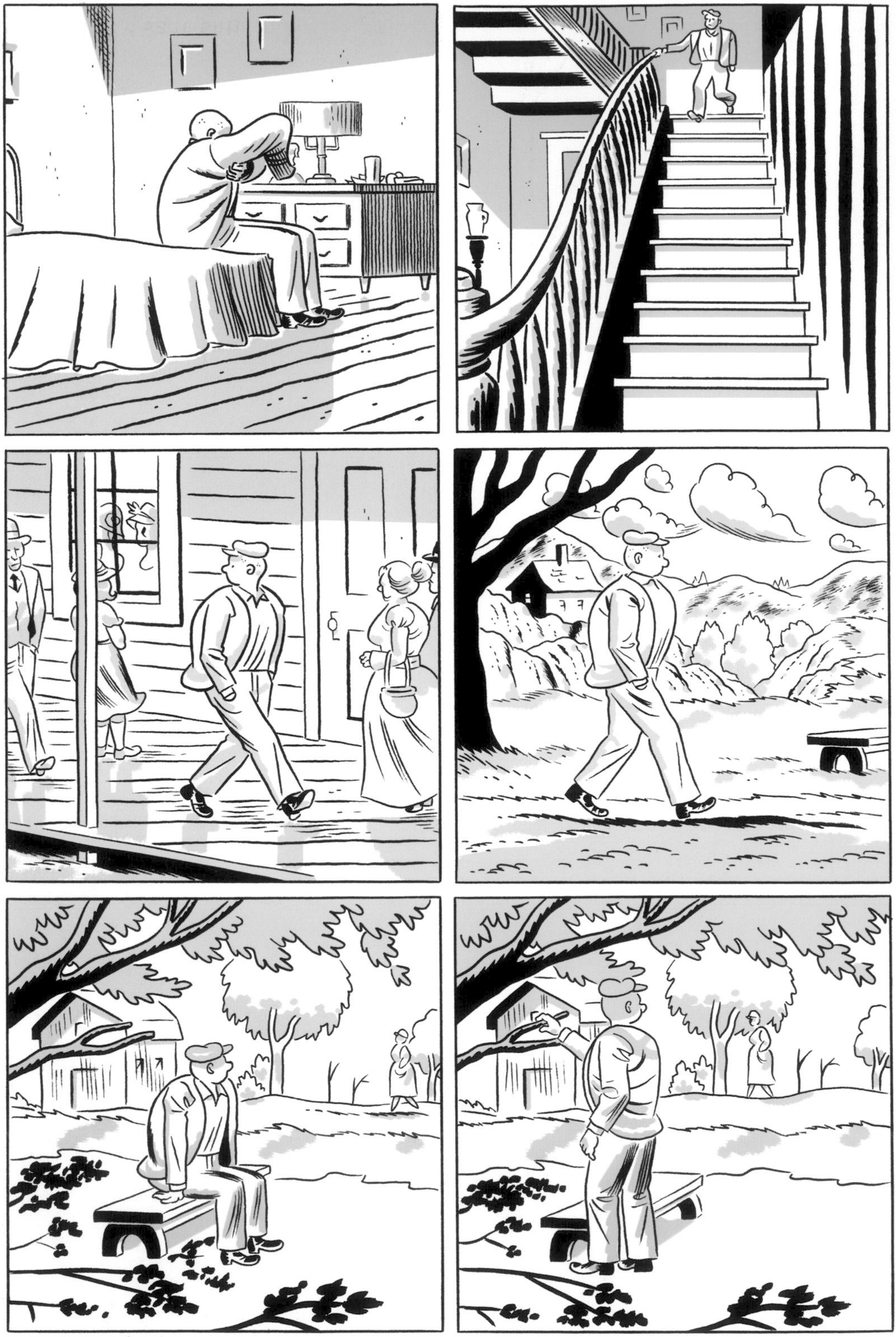

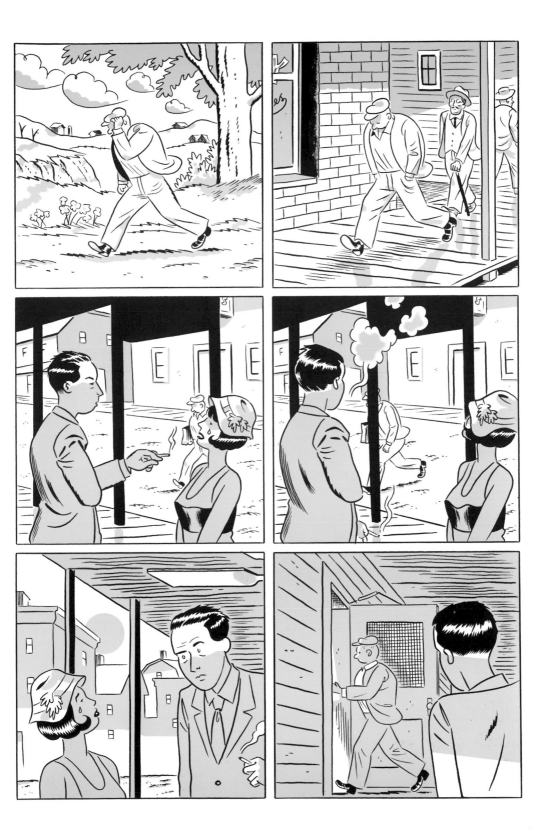

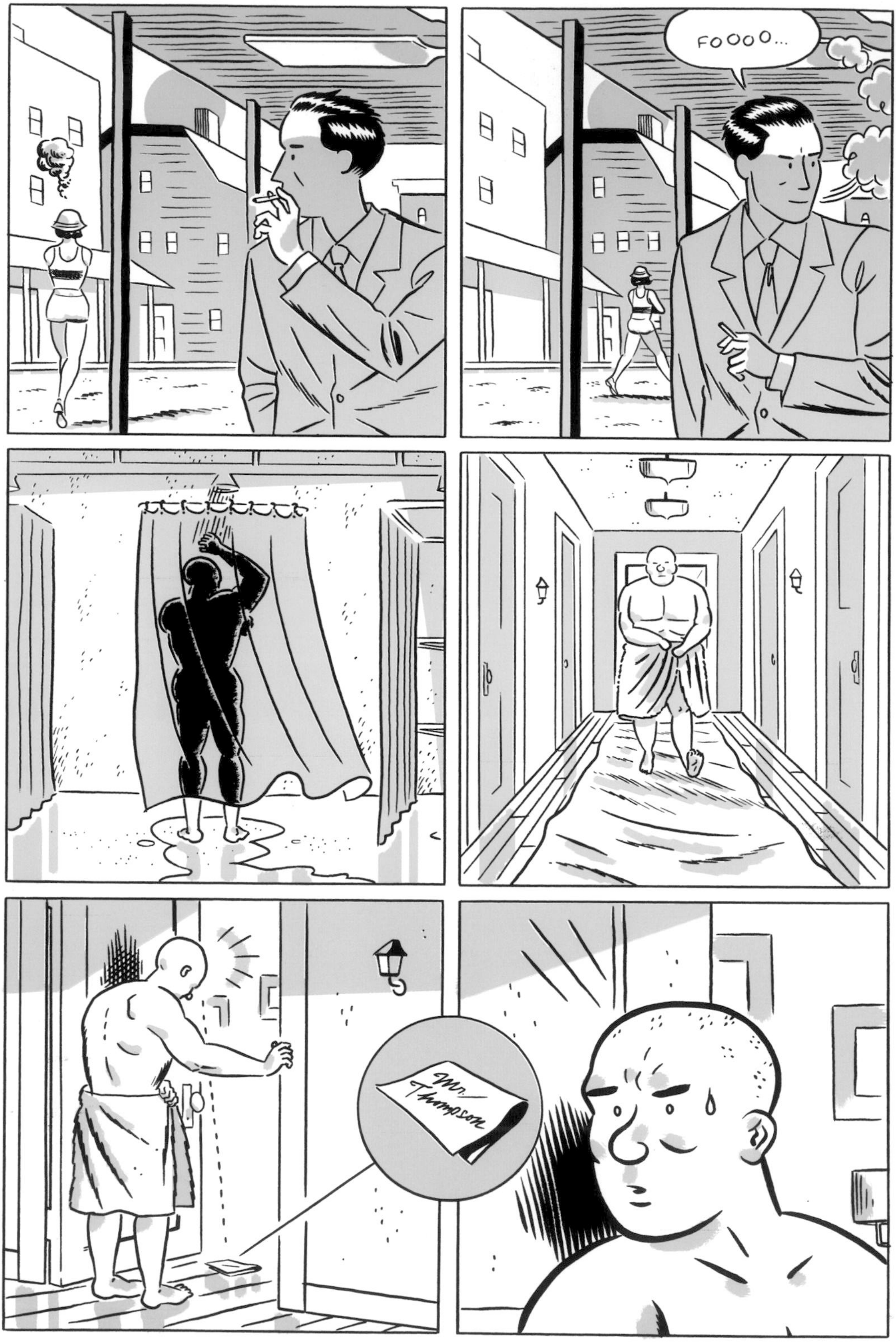
FOOOO...
Mr. Thompson

WORKING MAN'S BLUES

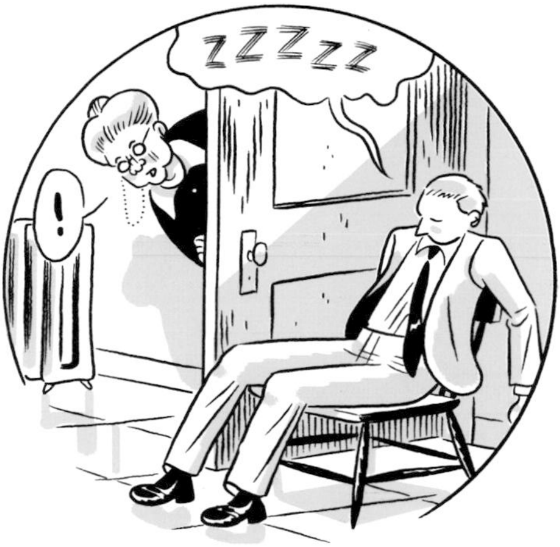
ZZZZZ
!

LIFE AS A WORKING STUDENT WAS WEARING OUR SAM DOWN— ESPECIALLY WITH HIS FATHER'S CONTINUED ABSENCE FROM THE HOTEL. OUTSIDE OF SCHOOL, MOST PEOPLE WOULD GUESS THAT SAM WAS WELL INTO HIS TWENTIES...

OR, POSSIBLY EVEN **THIRTY**...

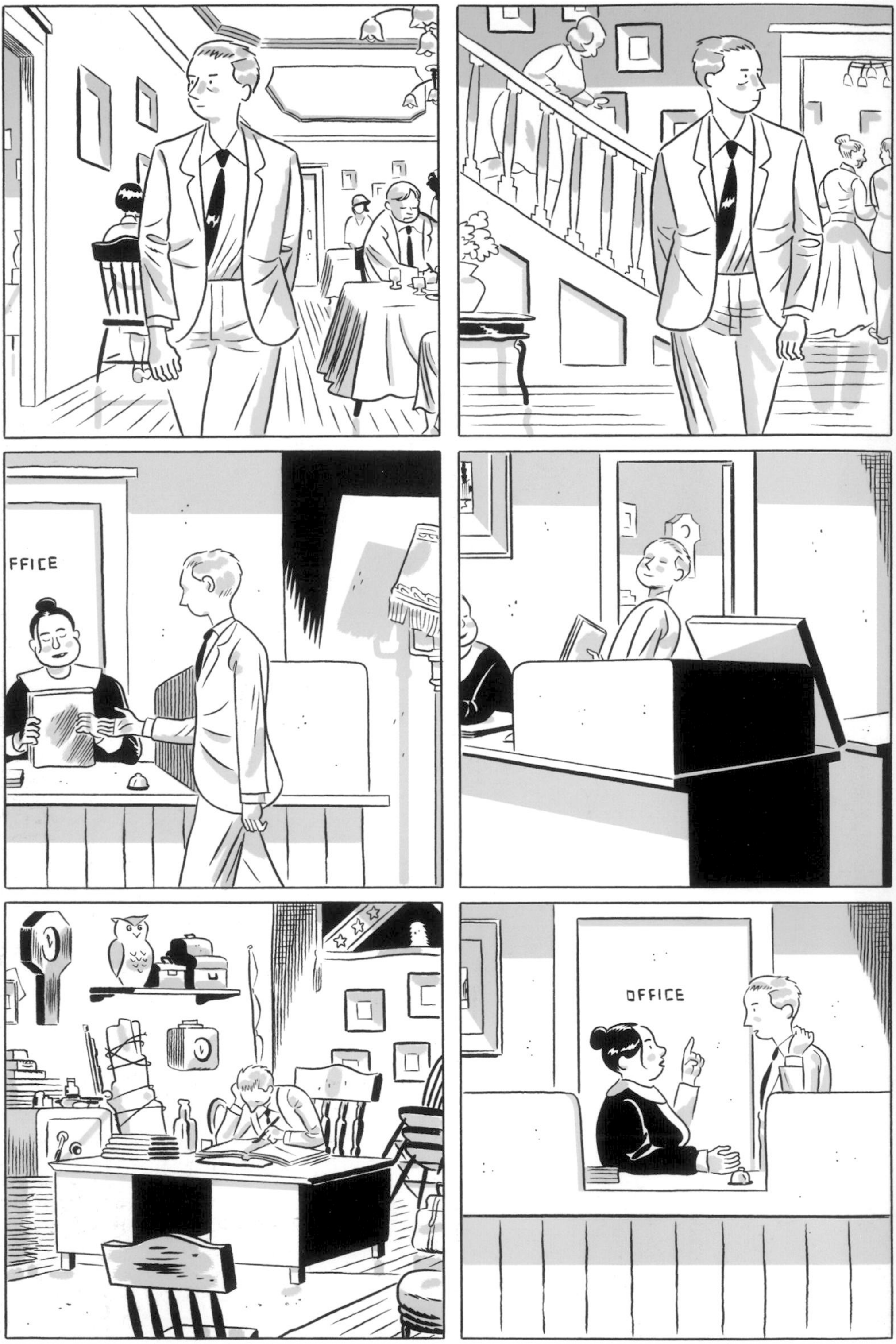
FFICE
OFFICE

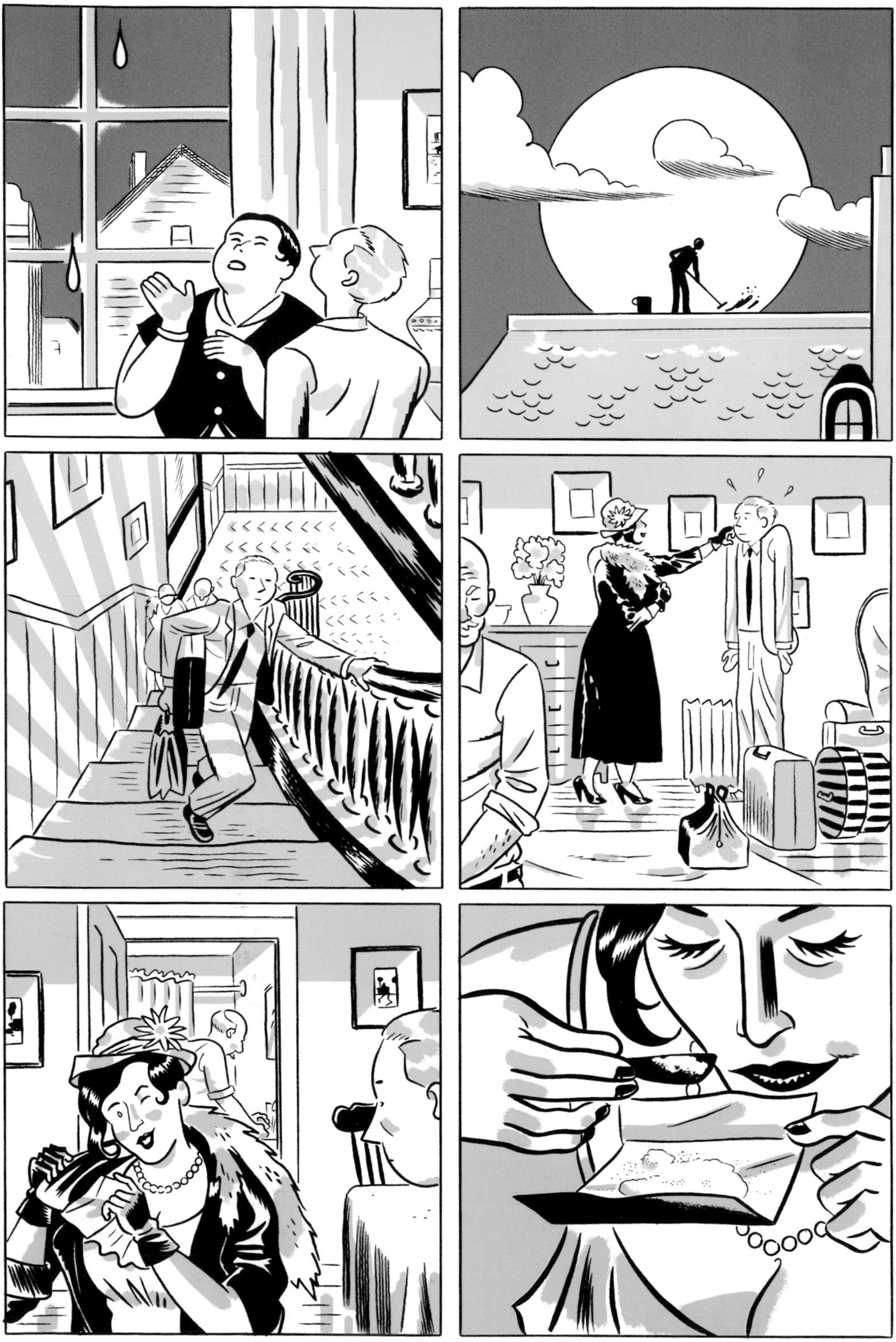

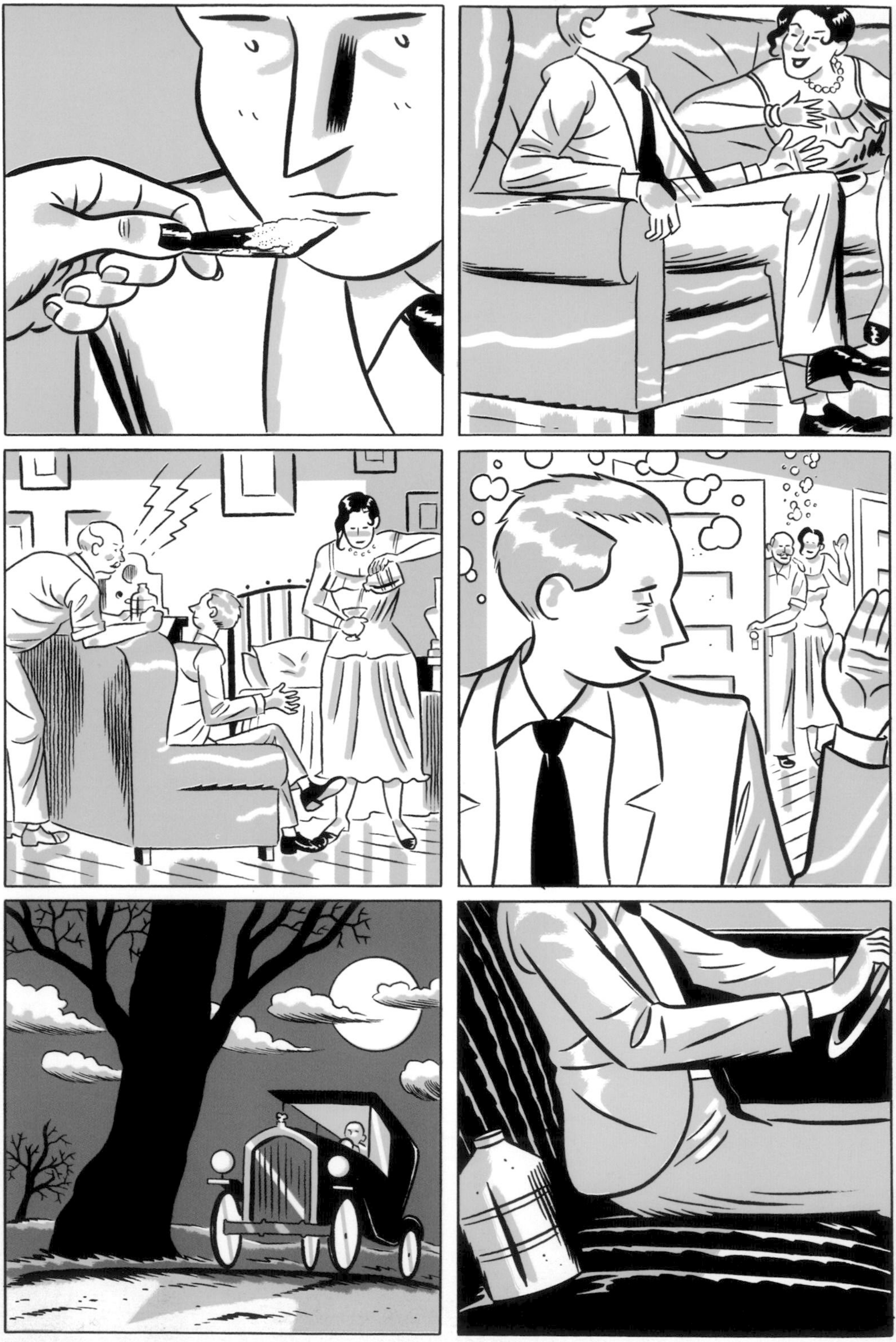

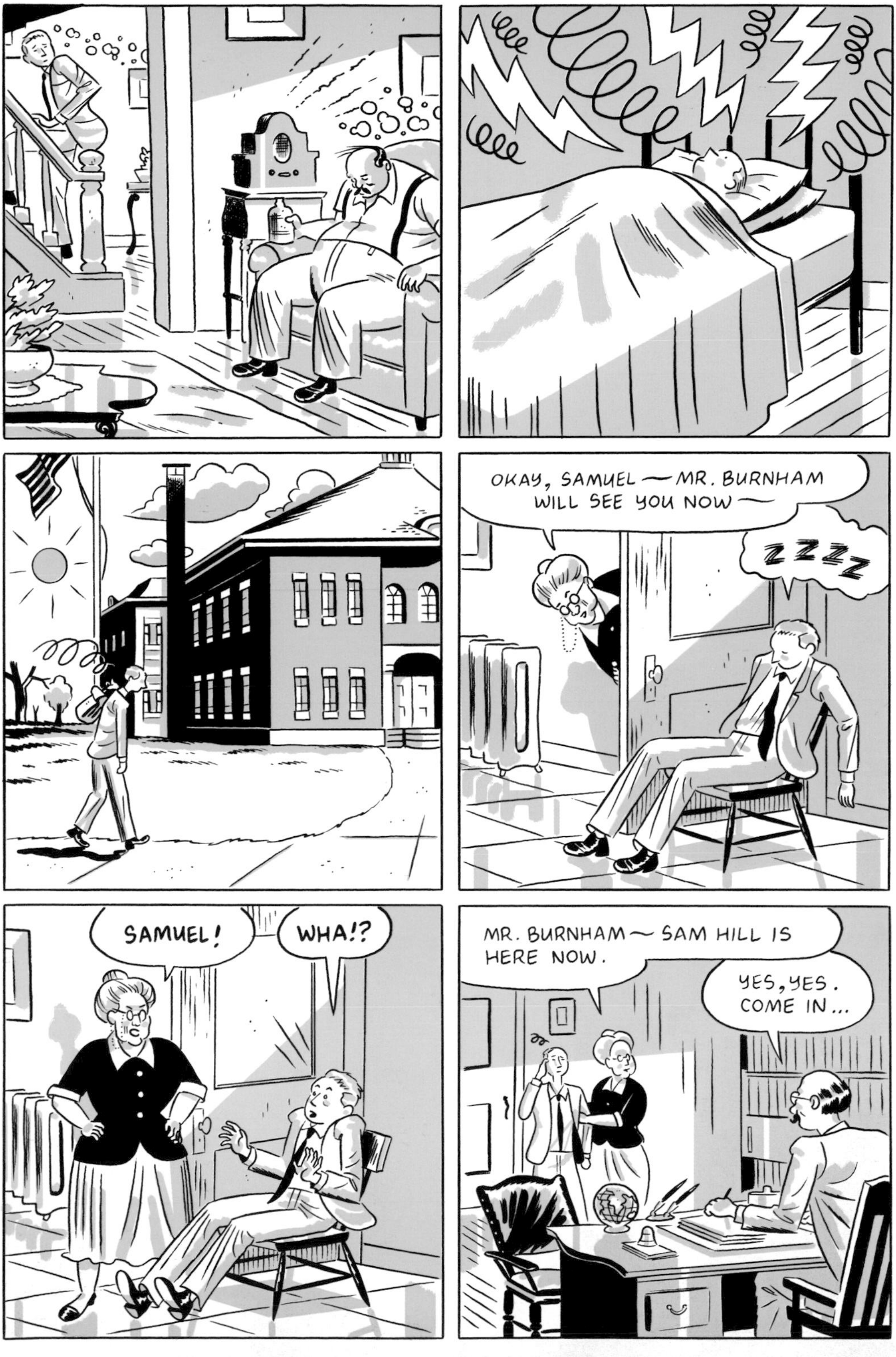
OKAY, SAMUEL — MR. BURNHAM WILL SEE YOU NOW —
ZZZZ
SAMUEL!
WHA!?
MR. BURNHAM — SAM HILL IS HERE NOW.
YES, YES. COME IN...

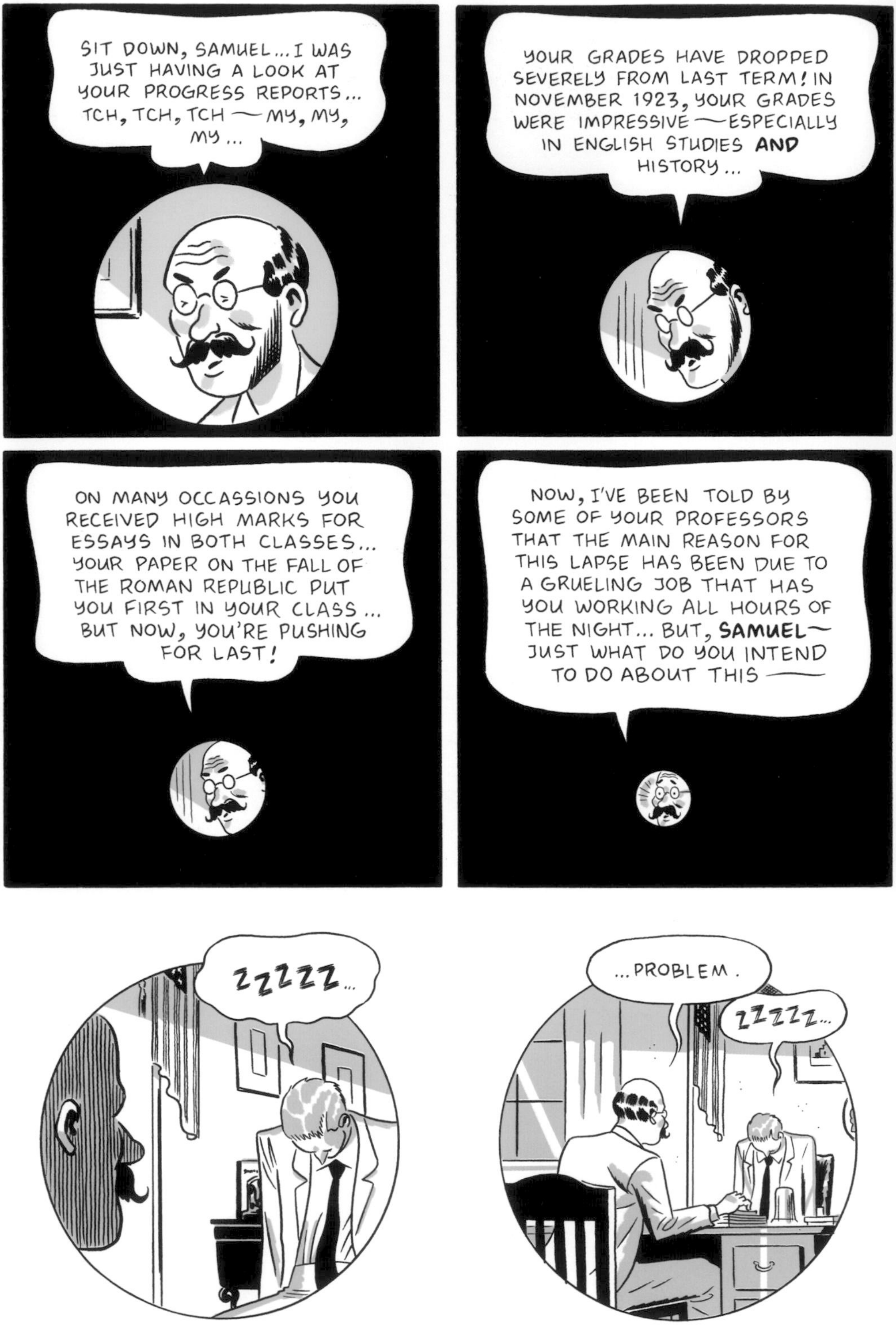
SIT DOWN, SAMUEL... I WAS JUST HAVING A LOOK AT YOUR PROGRESS REPORTS... TCH, TCH, TCH — MY, MY, MY...
YOUR GRADES HAVE DROPPED SEVERELY FROM LAST TERM! IN NOVEMBER 1923, YOUR GRADES WERE IMPRESSIVE — ESPECIALLY IN ENGLISH STUDIES **AND** HISTORY...
ON MANY OCCASSIONS YOU RECEIVED HIGH MARKS FOR ESSAYS IN BOTH CLASSES... YOUR PAPER ON THE FALL OF THE ROMAN REPUBLIC PUT YOU FIRST IN YOUR CLASS... BUT NOW, YOU'RE PUSHING FOR LAST!
NOW, I'VE BEEN TOLD BY SOME OF YOUR PROFESSORS THAT THE MAIN REASON FOR THIS LAPSE HAS BEEN DUE TO A GRUELING JOB THAT HAS YOU WORKING ALL HOURS OF THE NIGHT... BUT, **SAMUEL** — JUST WHAT DO YOU INTEND TO DO ABOUT THIS —
ZZZZZ...
...PROBLEM.
ZZZZZ...

CON MEN

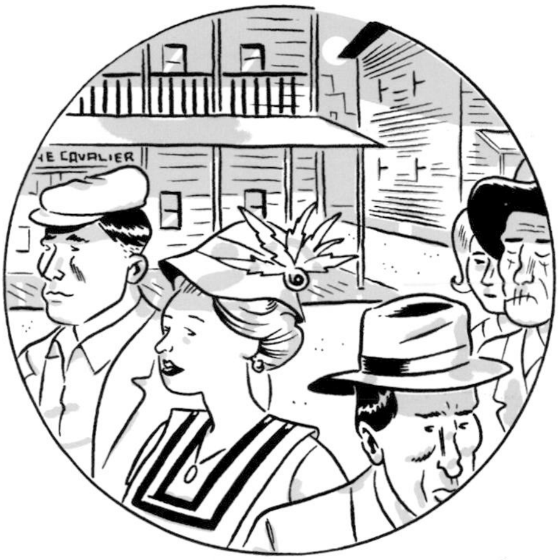
HE CAVALIER

THOMPSON HAD BEEN AWAKE THE ENTIRE NIGHT— HIS MIND REELING WITH THOUGHTS OF HIS SECRET "PEN PAL".

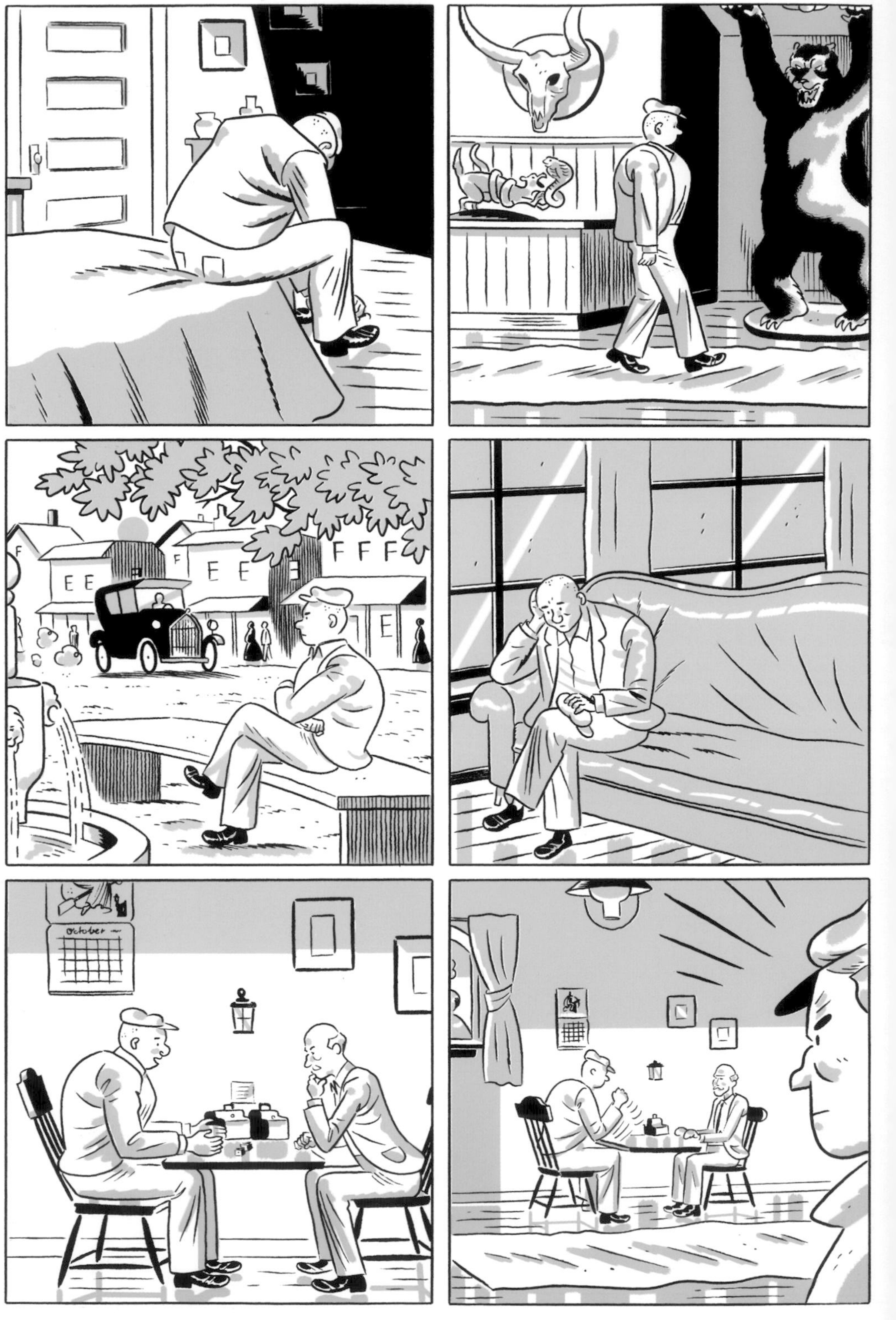
October

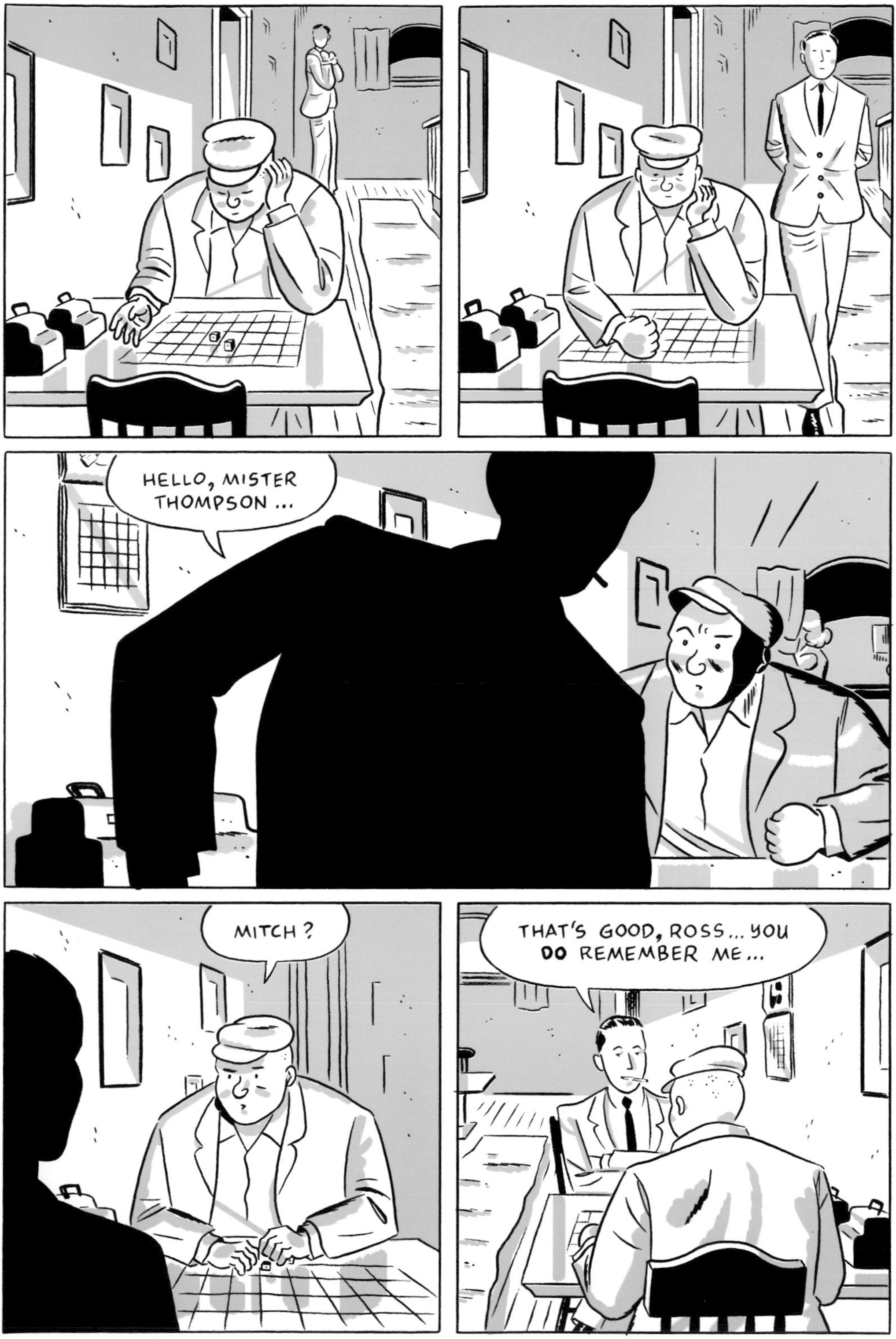
HELLO, MISTER THOMPSON ...
MITCH?
THAT'S GOOD, ROSS... YOU **DO** REMEMBER ME...

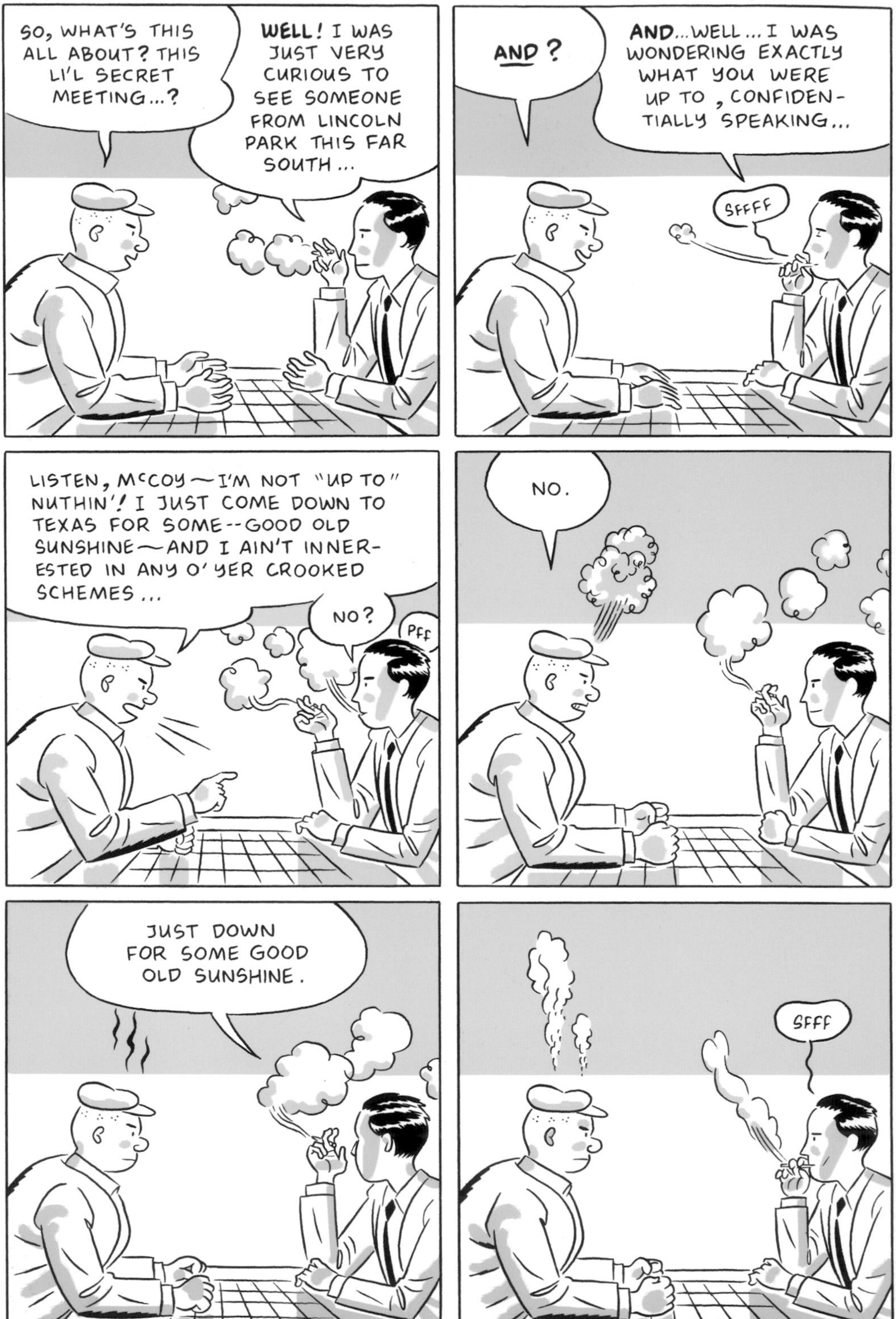
SO, WHAT'S THIS ALL ABOUT? THIS LI'L SECRET MEETING...?
WELL! I WAS JUST VERY CURIOUS TO SEE SOMEONE FROM LINCOLN PARK THIS FAR SOUTH...
AND?
AND... WELL... I WAS WONDERING EXACTLY WHAT YOU WERE UP TO, CONFIDENTIALLY SPEAKING...
SFFFF
LISTEN, McCOY— I'M NOT "UP TO" NUTHIN'! I JUST COME DOWN TO TEXAS FOR SOME--GOOD OLD SUNSHINE— AND I AIN'T INNERESTED IN ANY O' YER CROOKED SCHEMES...
NO?
PFF
NO.
JUST DOWN FOR SOME GOOD OLD SUNSHINE.
SFFF

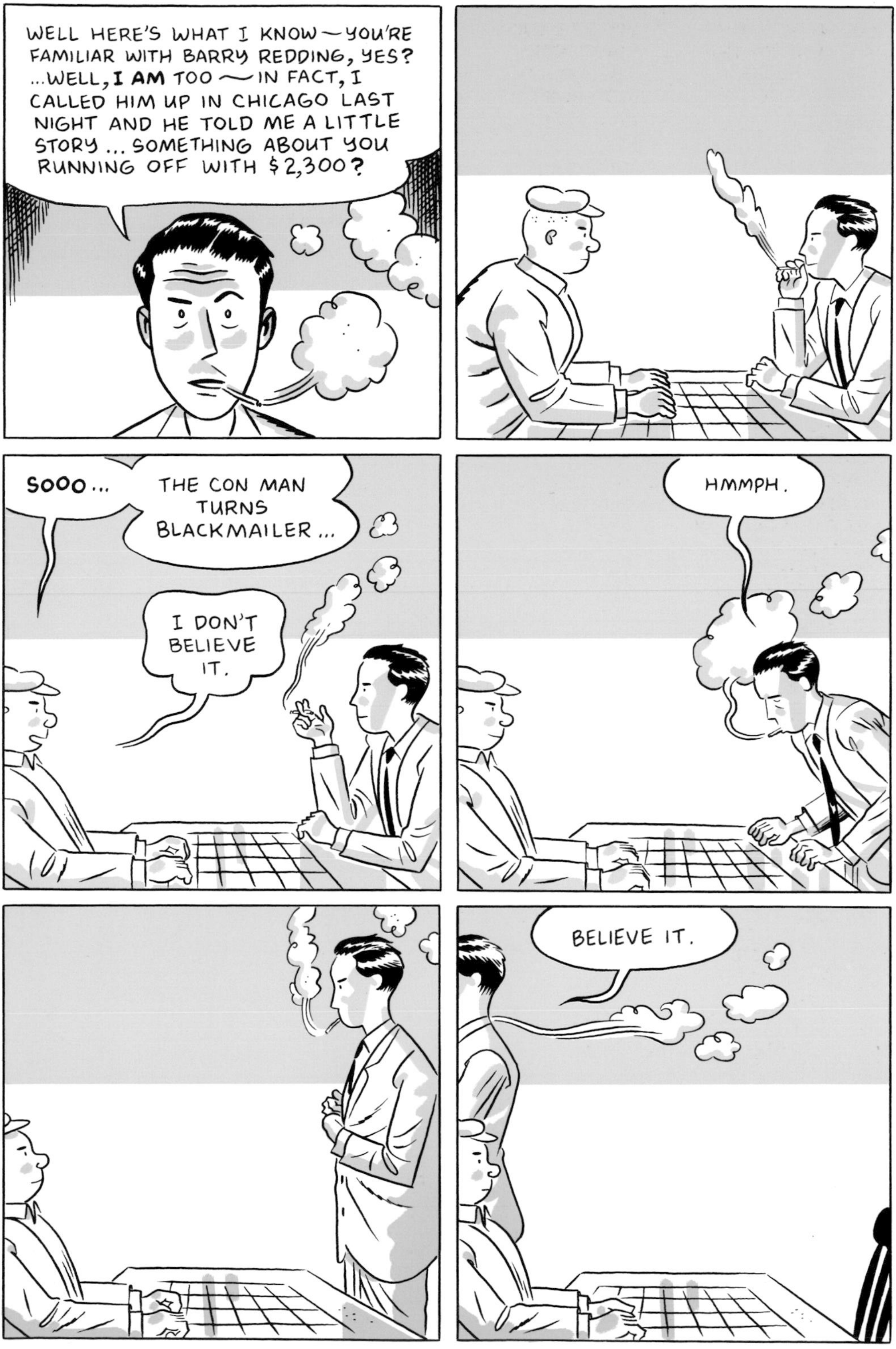
WELL HERE'S WHAT I KNOW — YOU'RE FAMILIAR WITH BARRY REDDING, YES? ...WELL, **I AM** TOO — IN FACT, I CALLED HIM UP IN CHICAGO LAST NIGHT AND HE TOLD ME A LITTLE STORY ... SOMETHING ABOUT YOU RUNNING OFF WITH $2,300?
SOOO...
THE CON MAN TURNS BLACKMAILER...
I DON'T BELIEVE IT.
HMMPH.
BELIEVE IT.

FRANK'S BLUES

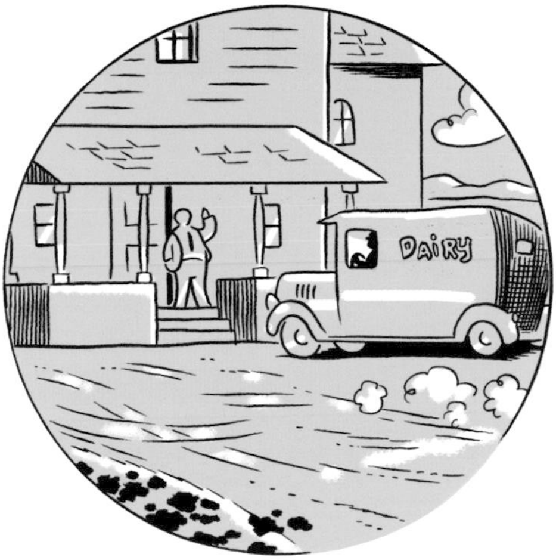
DAIRY

STORMY WEATHER IS ON EVERYONE'S MIND AS SEPTEMBER COMES TO A CLOSE IN BIG SPRING... AND AFTER SUCH A BOILING HOT SUMMER, IT IS HEARTILY WELCOMED...

EVEN HURRICANES ARE PRACTICALLY PRAYED FOR IN ORDER FOR TEXANS TO GET A BREAK FROM THE INFERNAL HEAT.

MR. FRANK HILL HAS HIS OWN REMEDY FOR THE HEAT—HIS VERY OWN, HAND-DELIVERED WHITE LIGHTNING... IN A BOTTLE!

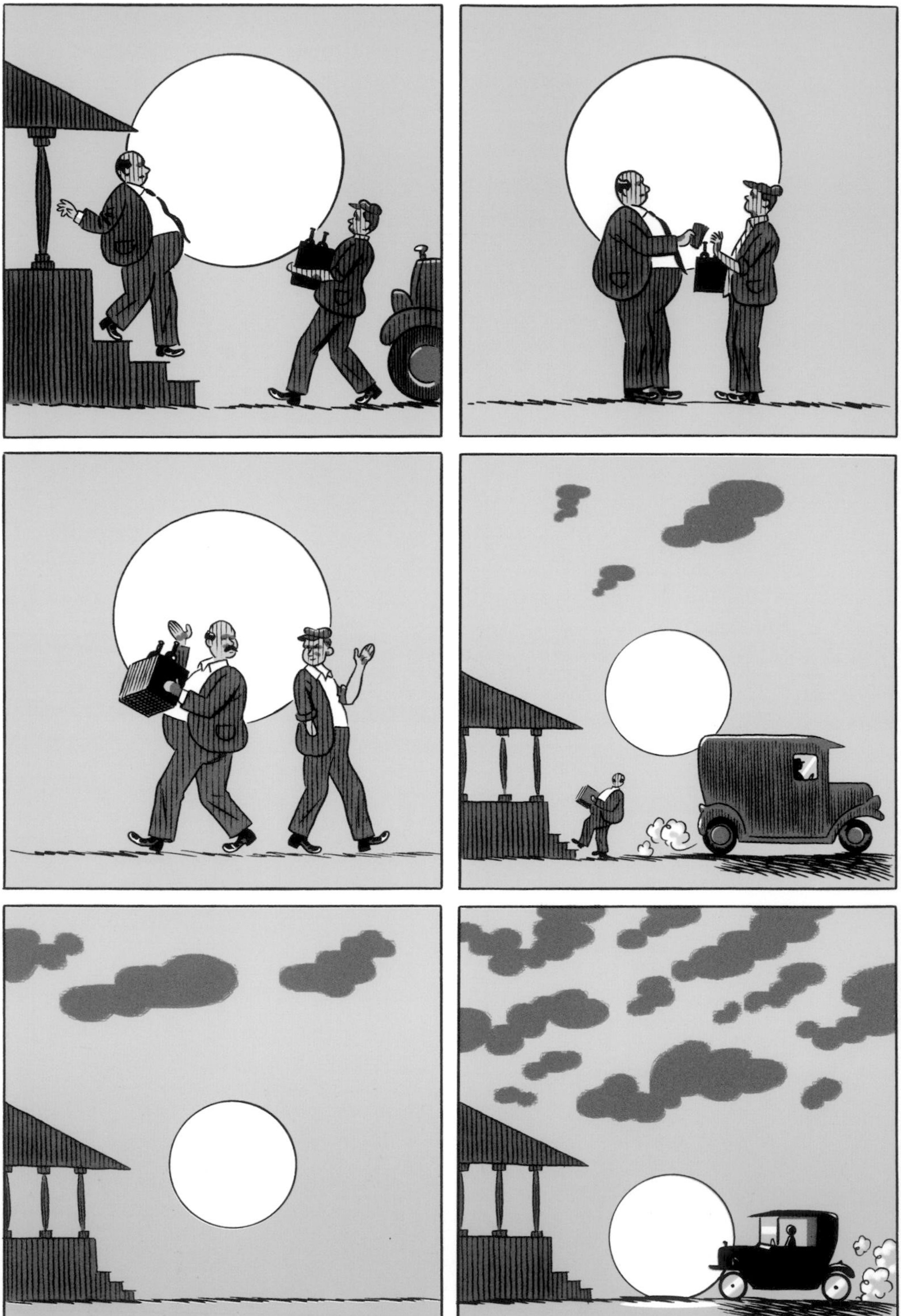

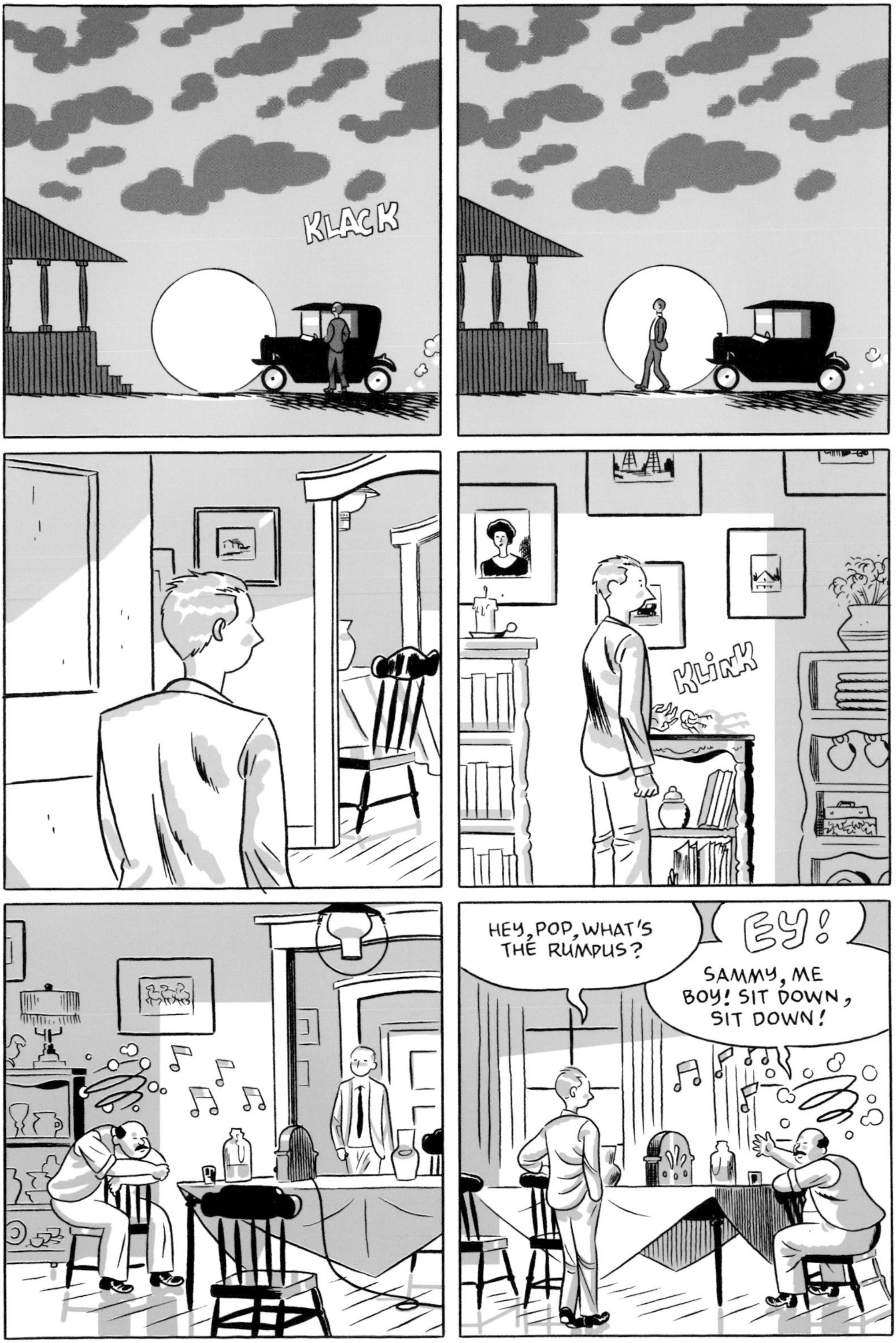
KLACK
KLINK
HEY, POP, WHAT'S THE RUMPUS?
EY!
SAMMY, ME BOY! SIT DOWN, SIT DOWN!

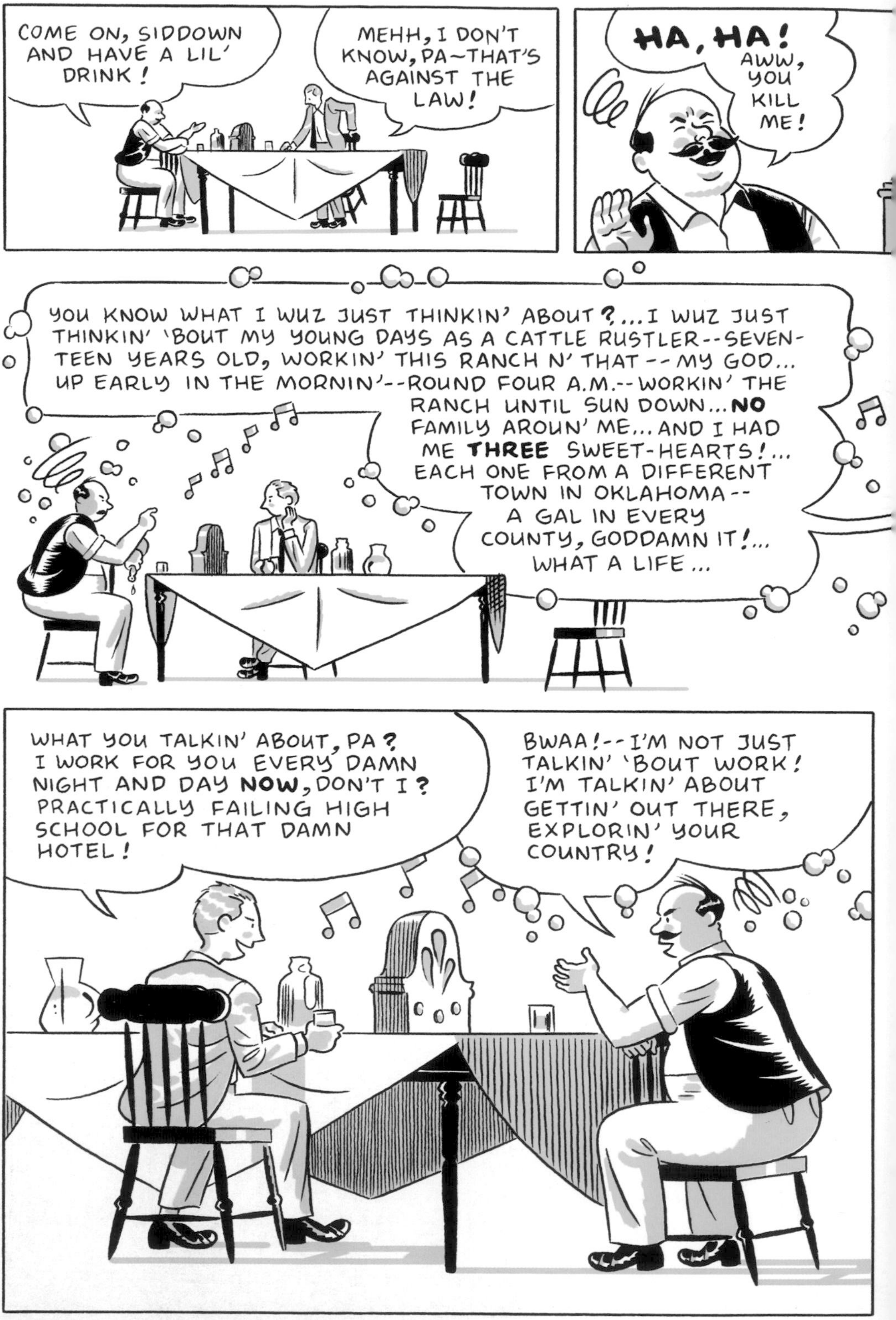

COME ON, SIDDOWN AND HAVE A LIL' DRINK!
MEHH, I DON'T KNOW, PA~THAT'S AGAINST THE LAW!
HA, HA! AWW, YOU KILL ME!
YOU KNOW WHAT I WUZ JUST THINKIN' ABOUT?... I WUZ JUST THINKIN' 'BOUT MY YOUNG DAYS AS A CATTLE RUSTLER--SEVENTEEN YEARS OLD, WORKIN' THIS RANCH N' THAT--MY GOD... UP EARLY IN THE MORNIN'--ROUND FOUR A.M.--WORKIN' THE RANCH UNTIL SUN DOWN... NO FAMILY AROUN' ME... AND I HAD ME THREE SWEET-HEARTS!... EACH ONE FROM A DIFFERENT TOWN IN OKLAHOMA--A GAL IN EVERY COUNTY, GODDAMN IT!... WHAT A LIFE...
WHAT YOU TALKIN' ABOUT, PA? I WORK FOR YOU EVERY DAMN NIGHT AND DAY NOW, DON'T I? PRACTICALLY FAILING HIGH SCHOOL FOR THAT DAMN HOTEL!
BWAA!--I'M NOT JUST TALKIN' 'BOUT WORK! I'M TALKIN' ABOUT GETTIN' OUT THERE, EXPLORIN' YOUR COUNTRY!

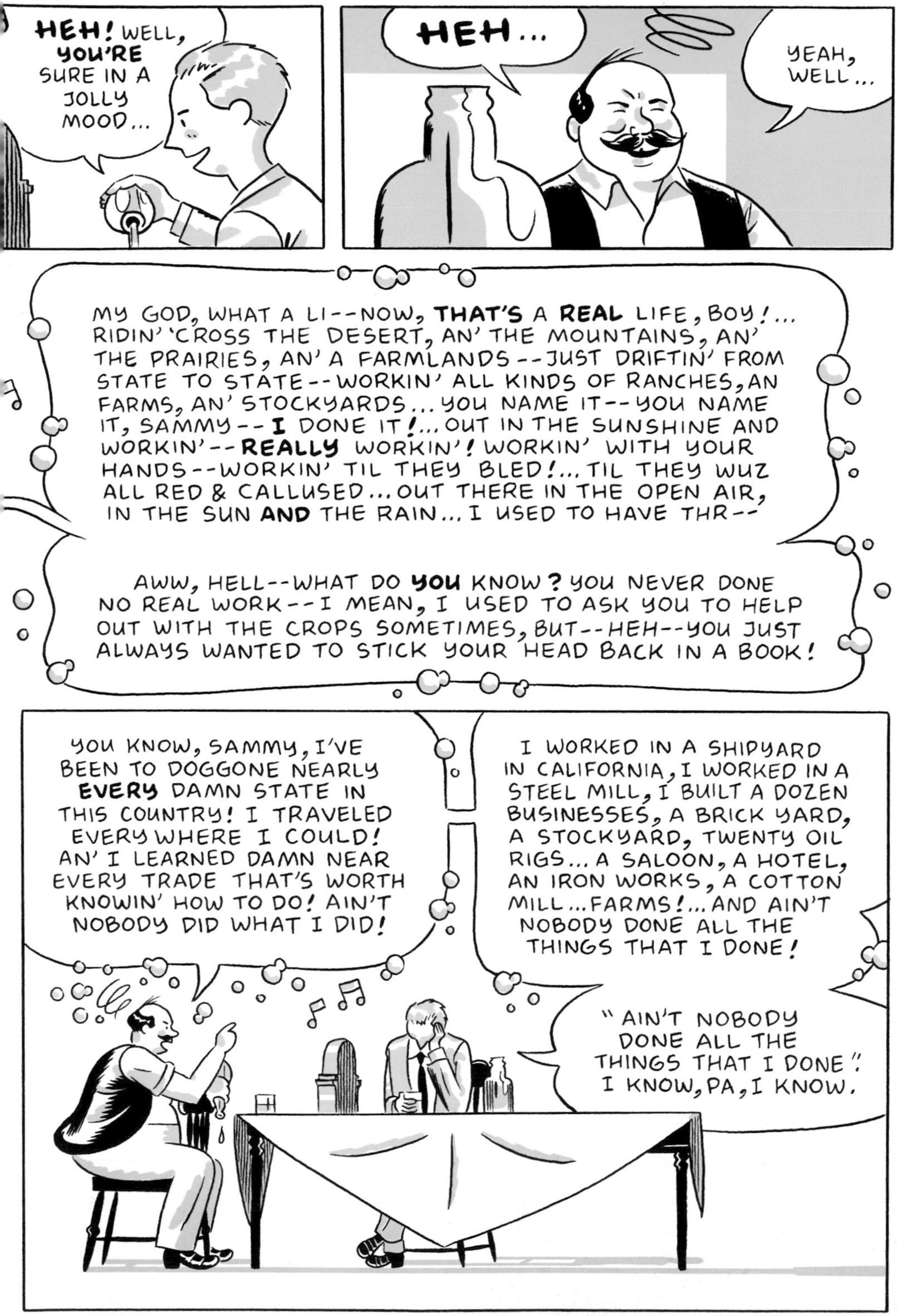
HEH! WELL, YOU'RE SURE IN A JOLLY MOOD...
HEH...
YEAH, WELL...
MY GOD, WHAT A LI--NOW, THAT'S A REAL LIFE, BOY!... RIDIN' 'CROSS THE DESERT, AN' THE MOUNTAINS, AN' THE PRAIRIES, AN' A FARMLANDS--JUST DRIFTIN' FROM STATE TO STATE--WORKIN' ALL KINDS OF RANCHES, AN FARMS, AN' STOCKYARDS... YOU NAME IT--YOU NAME IT, SAMMY--I DONE IT!... OUT IN THE SUNSHINE AND WORKIN'--REALLY WORKIN'! WORKIN' WITH YOUR HANDS--WORKIN' TIL THEY BLED!... TIL THEY WUZ ALL RED & CALLUSED... OUT THERE IN THE OPEN AIR, IN THE SUN AND THE RAIN... I USED TO HAVE THR--
AWW, HELL--WHAT DO YOU KNOW? YOU NEVER DONE NO REAL WORK--I MEAN, I USED TO ASK YOU TO HELP OUT WITH THE CROPS SOMETIMES, BUT--HEH--YOU JUST ALWAYS WANTED TO STICK YOUR HEAD BACK IN A BOOK!
YOU KNOW, SAMMY, I'VE BEEN TO DOGGONE NEARLY EVERY DAMN STATE IN THIS COUNTRY! I TRAVELED EVERYWHERE I COULD! AN' I LEARNED DAMN NEAR EVERY TRADE THAT'S WORTH KNOWIN' HOW TO DO! AIN'T NOBODY DID WHAT I DID!
I WORKED IN A SHIPYARD IN CALIFORNIA, I WORKED IN A STEEL MILL, I BUILT A DOZEN BUSINESSES, A BRICK YARD, A STOCKYARD, TWENTY OIL RIGS... A SALOON, A HOTEL, AN IRON WORKS, A COTTON MILL... FARMS!... AND AIN'T NOBODY DONE ALL THE THINGS THAT I DONE!
"AIN'T NOBODY DONE ALL THE THINGS THAT I DONE". I KNOW, PA, I KNOW.

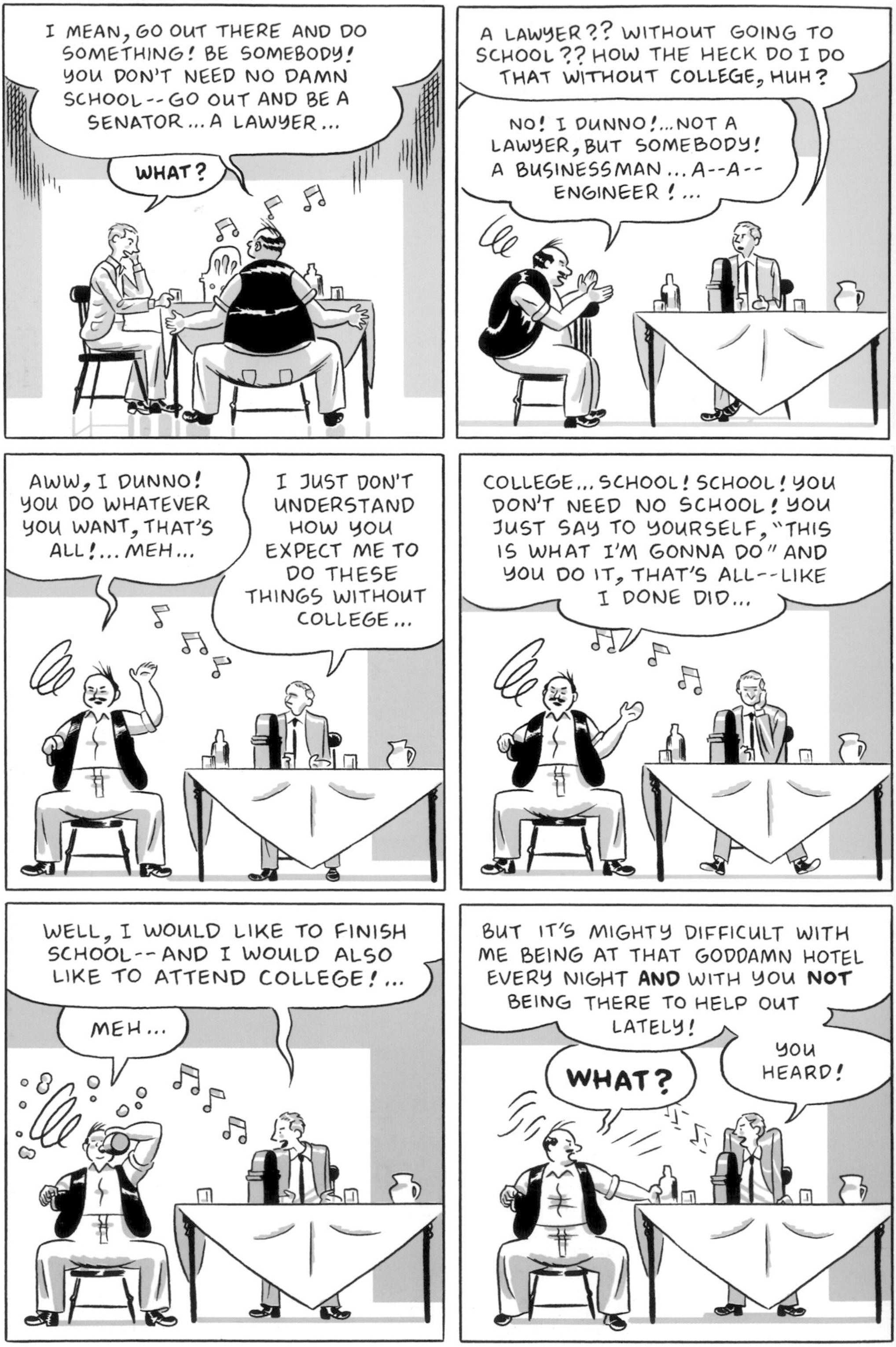

I MEAN, GO OUT THERE AND DO SOMETHING! BE SOMEBODY! YOU DON'T NEED NO DAMN SCHOOL--GO OUT AND BE A SENATOR... A LAWYER...
WHAT?
A LAWYER?? WITHOUT GOING TO SCHOOL?? HOW THE HECK DO I DO THAT WITHOUT COLLEGE, HUH?
NO! I DUNNO!... NOT A LAWYER, BUT SOMEBODY! A BUSINESSMAN... A--A--ENGINEER!...
AWW, I DUNNO! YOU DO WHATEVER YOU WANT, THAT'S ALL!... MEH...
I JUST DON'T UNDERSTAND HOW YOU EXPECT ME TO DO THESE THINGS WITHOUT COLLEGE...
COLLEGE... SCHOOL! SCHOOL! YOU DON'T NEED NO SCHOOL! YOU JUST SAY TO YOURSELF, "THIS IS WHAT I'M GONNA DO" AND YOU DO IT, THAT'S ALL--LIKE I DONE DID...
WELL, I WOULD LIKE TO FINISH SCHOOL--AND I WOULD ALSO LIKE TO ATTEND COLLEGE!...
MEH...
BUT IT'S MIGHTY DIFFICULT WITH ME BEING AT THAT GODDAMN HOTEL EVERY NIGHT **AND** WITH YOU **NOT** BEING THERE TO HELP OUT LATELY!
WHAT?
YOU HEARD!

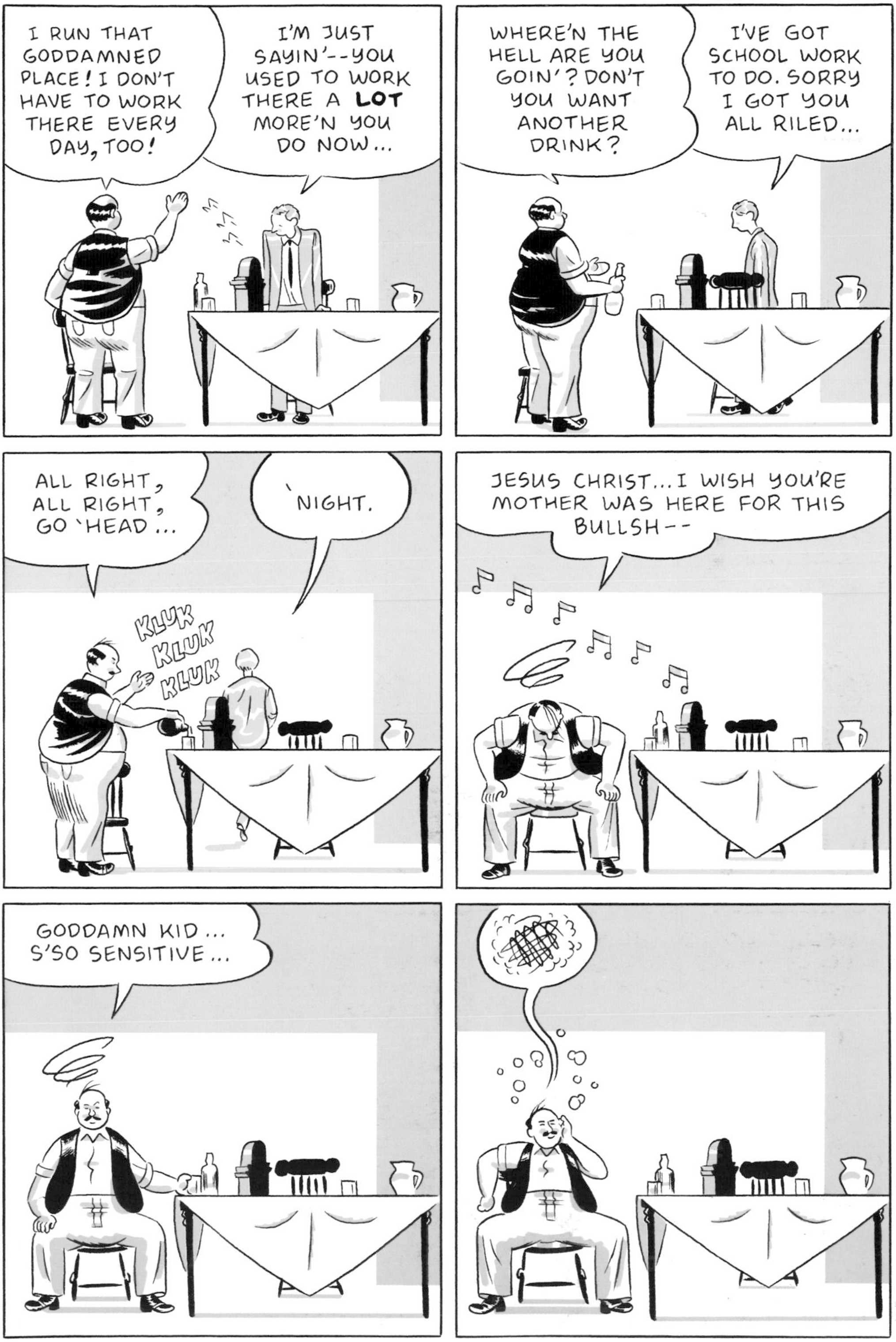

I RUN THAT GODDAMNED PLACE! I DON'T HAVE TO WORK THERE EVERY DAY, TOO!
I'M JUST SAYIN'--YOU USED TO WORK THERE A LOT MORE'N YOU DO NOW...
WHERE'N THE HELL ARE YOU GOIN'? DON'T YOU WANT ANOTHER DRINK?
I'VE GOT SCHOOL WORK TO DO. SORRY I GOT YOU ALL RILED...
ALL RIGHT, ALL RIGHT, GO 'HEAD...
'NIGHT.
KLUK KLUK KLUK
JESUS CHRIST... I WISH YOU'RE MOTHER WAS HERE FOR THIS BULLSH--
GODDAMN KID... S'SO SENSITIVE...

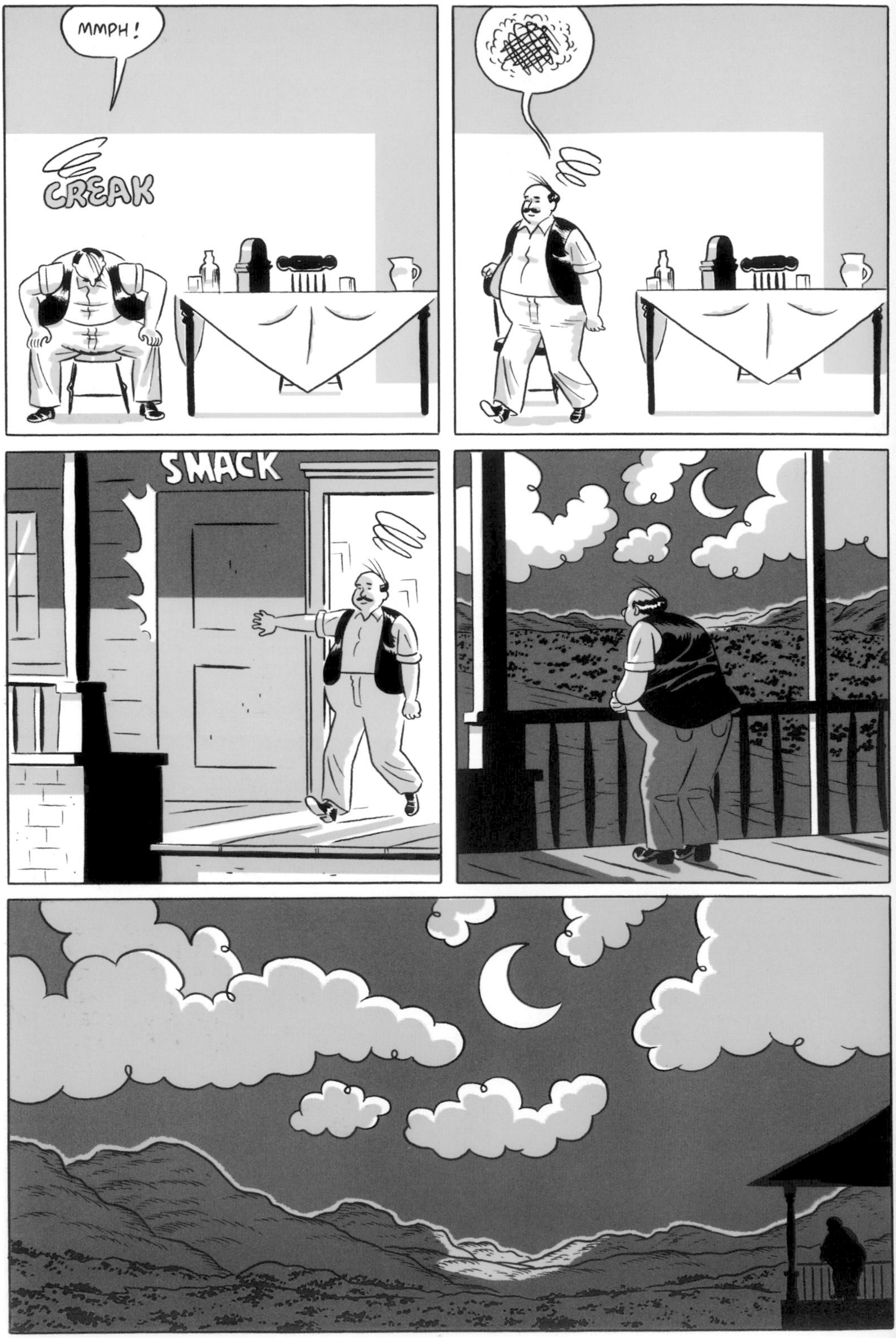
MMPH!
CREAK
SMACK

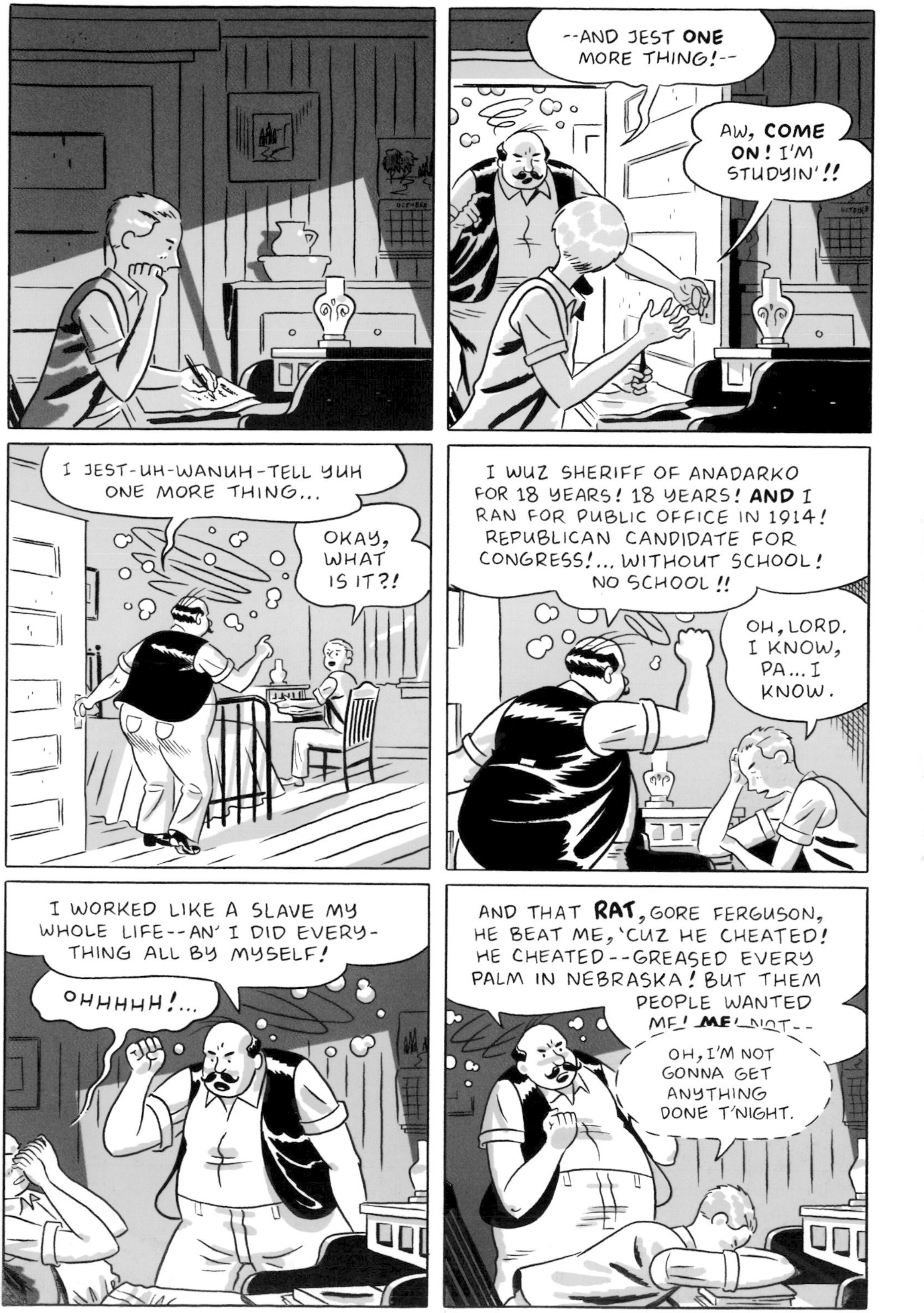
--AND JEST ONE MORE THING!--
AW, COME ON! I'M STUDYIN'!!
I JEST-UH-WANUH-TELL YUH ONE MORE THING...
OKAY, WHAT IS IT?!
I WUZ SHERIFF OF ANADARKO FOR 18 YEARS! 18 YEARS! AND I RAN FOR PUBLIC OFFICE IN 1914! REPUBLICAN CANDIDATE FOR CONGRESS!... WITHOUT SCHOOL! NO SCHOOL!!
OH, LORD. I KNOW, PA... I KNOW.
I WORKED LIKE A SLAVE MY WHOLE LIFE--AN' I DID EVERY-THING ALL BY MYSELF!
OHHHHH!...
AND THAT RAT, GORE FERGUSON, HE BEAT ME, 'CUZ HE CHEATED! HE CHEATED--GREASED EVERY PALM IN NEBRASKA! BUT THEM PEOPLE WANTED ME! ME! NOT--
OH, I'M NOT GONNA GET ANYTHING DONE T'NIGHT.

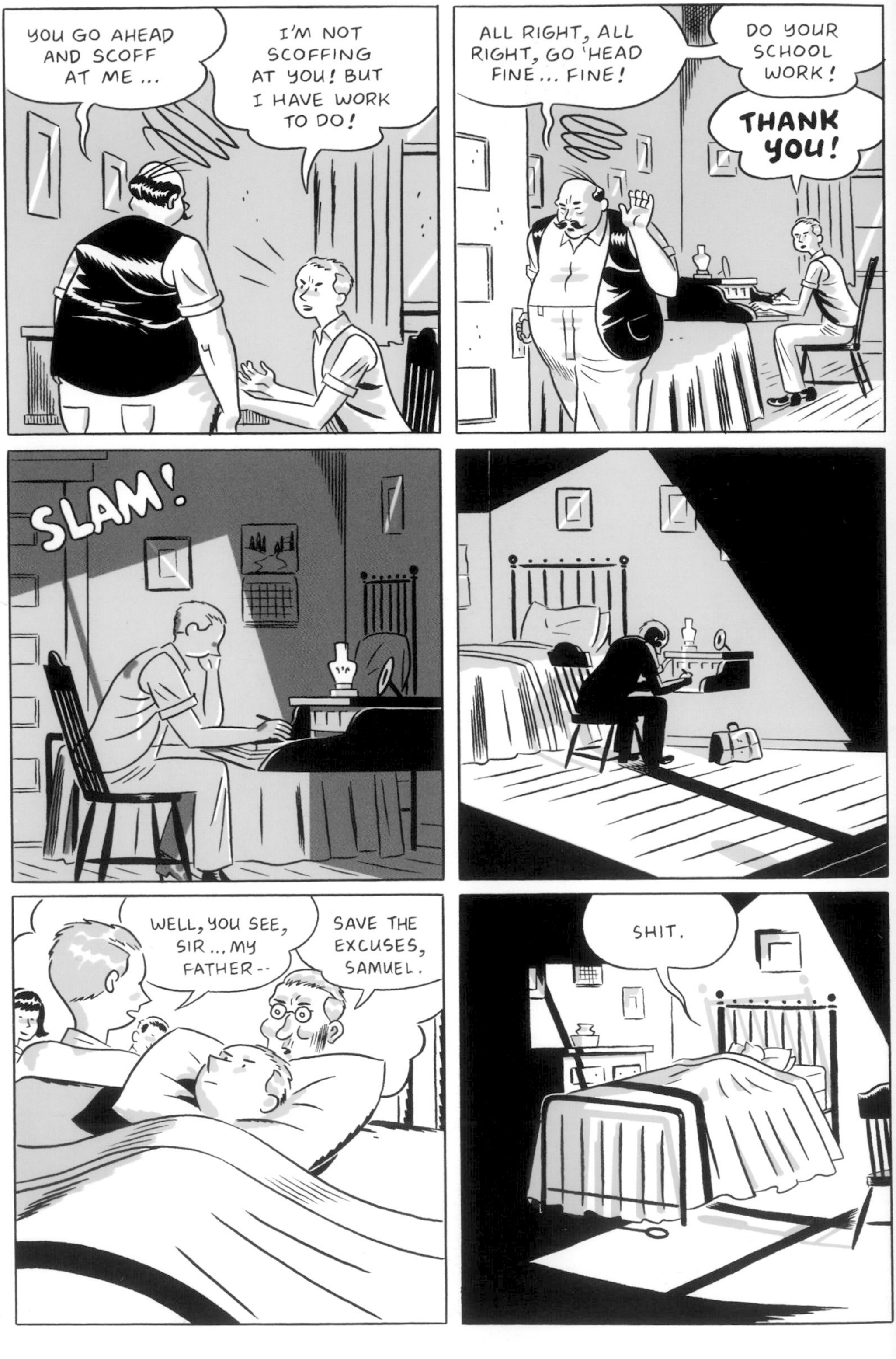
YOU GO AHEAD AND SCOFF AT ME...
I'M NOT SCOFFING AT YOU! BUT I HAVE WORK TO DO!
ALL RIGHT, ALL RIGHT, GO 'HEAD FINE... FINE!
DO YOUR SCHOOL WORK!
THANK YOU!
SLAM!
WELL, YOU SEE, SIR... MY FATHER--
SAVE THE EXCUSES, SAMUEL.
SHIT.

MURDER!

IT WAS WILLA WHO UNFORTUNATELY DISCOVERED MITCH'S BODY, LYING LIMP ON THE FLOOR OF HIS ROOM WITH A KNIFE STICKING OUT OF HIS CHEST... SHE'D LET HERSELF IN AROUND 8 A.M. TO CHANGE THE BED SHEETS...

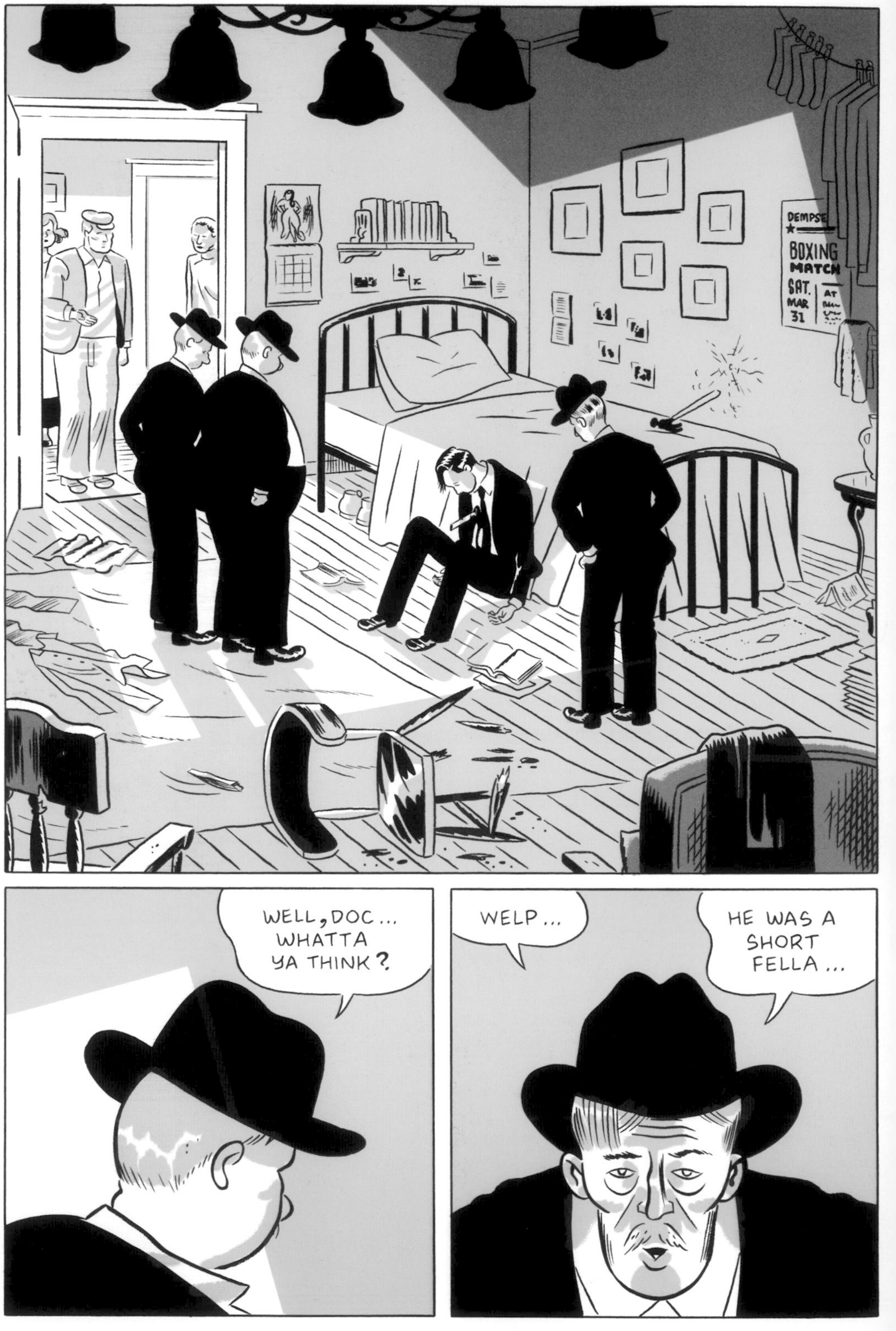
DEMPSE
BOXING MATCH
SAT. MAR 31
AT
WELL, DOC... WHATTA YA THINK?
WELP...
HE WAS A SHORT FELLA...

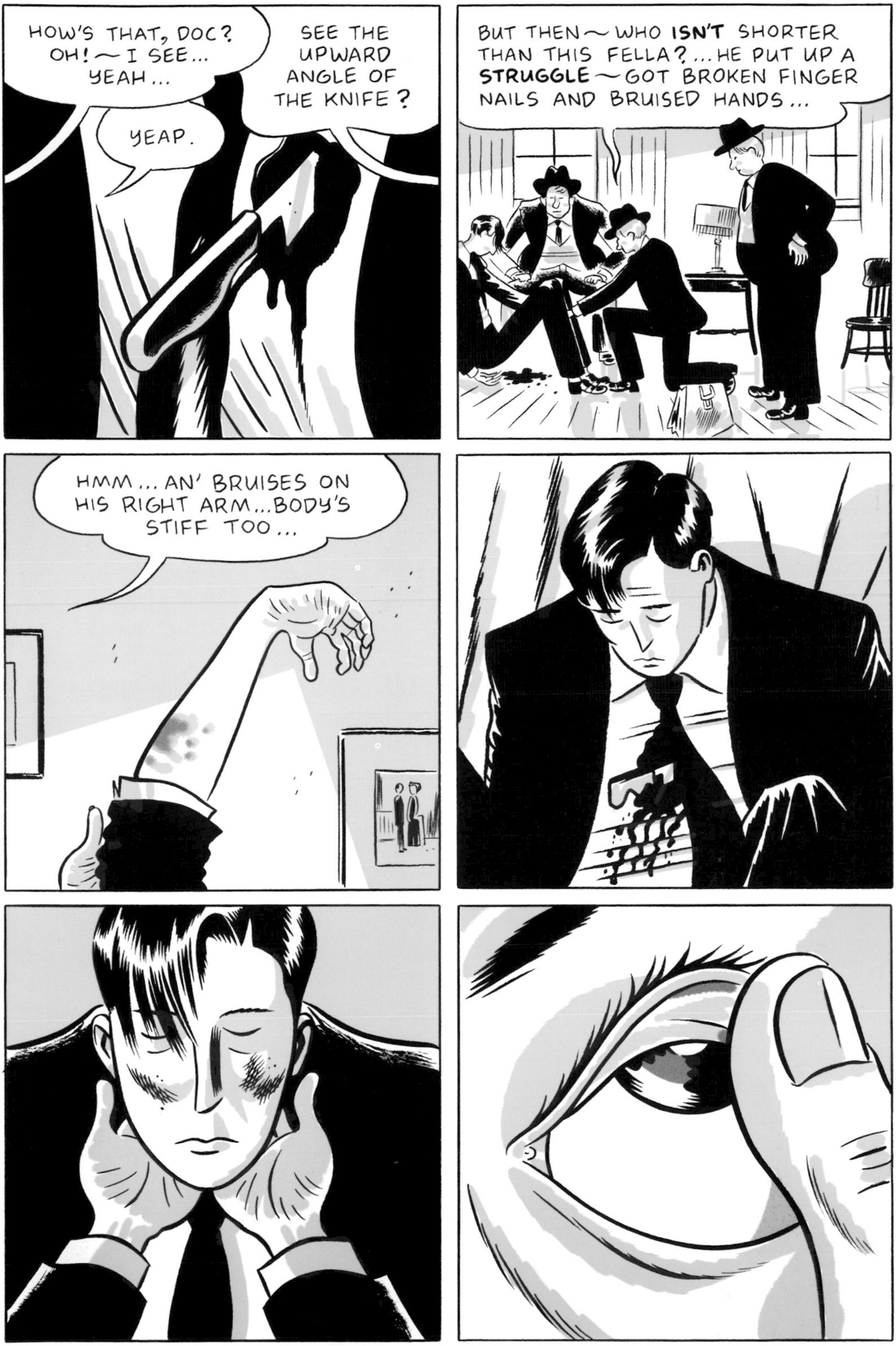
HOW'S THAT, DOC? OH! ~ I SEE... YEAH...
SEE THE UPWARD ANGLE OF THE KNIFE?
YEAP.
BUT THEN ~ WHO **ISN'T** SHORTER THAN THIS FELLA? ... HE PUT UP A **STRUGGLE** ~ GOT BROKEN FINGER NAILS AND BRUISED HANDS...
HMM... AN' BRUISES ON HIS RIGHT ARM... BODY'S STIFF TOO...

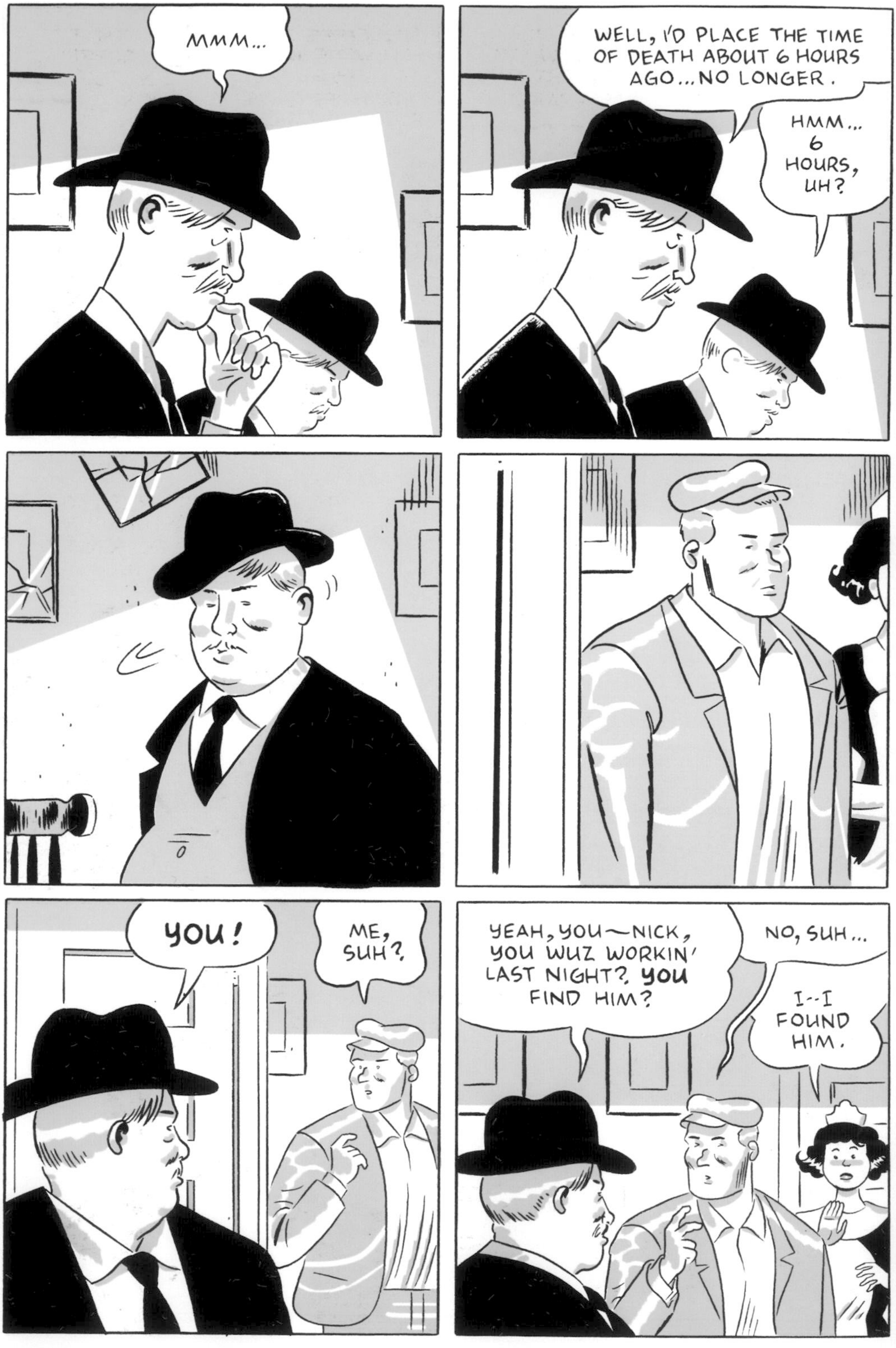
MMM...
WELL, I'D PLACE THE TIME OF DEATH ABOUT 6 HOURS AGO... NO LONGER.
HMM... 6 HOURS, UH?
YOU!
ME, SUH?
YEAH, YOU—NICK, YOU WUZ WORKIN' LAST NIGHT? YOU FIND HIM?
NO, SUH...
I--I FOUND HIM.

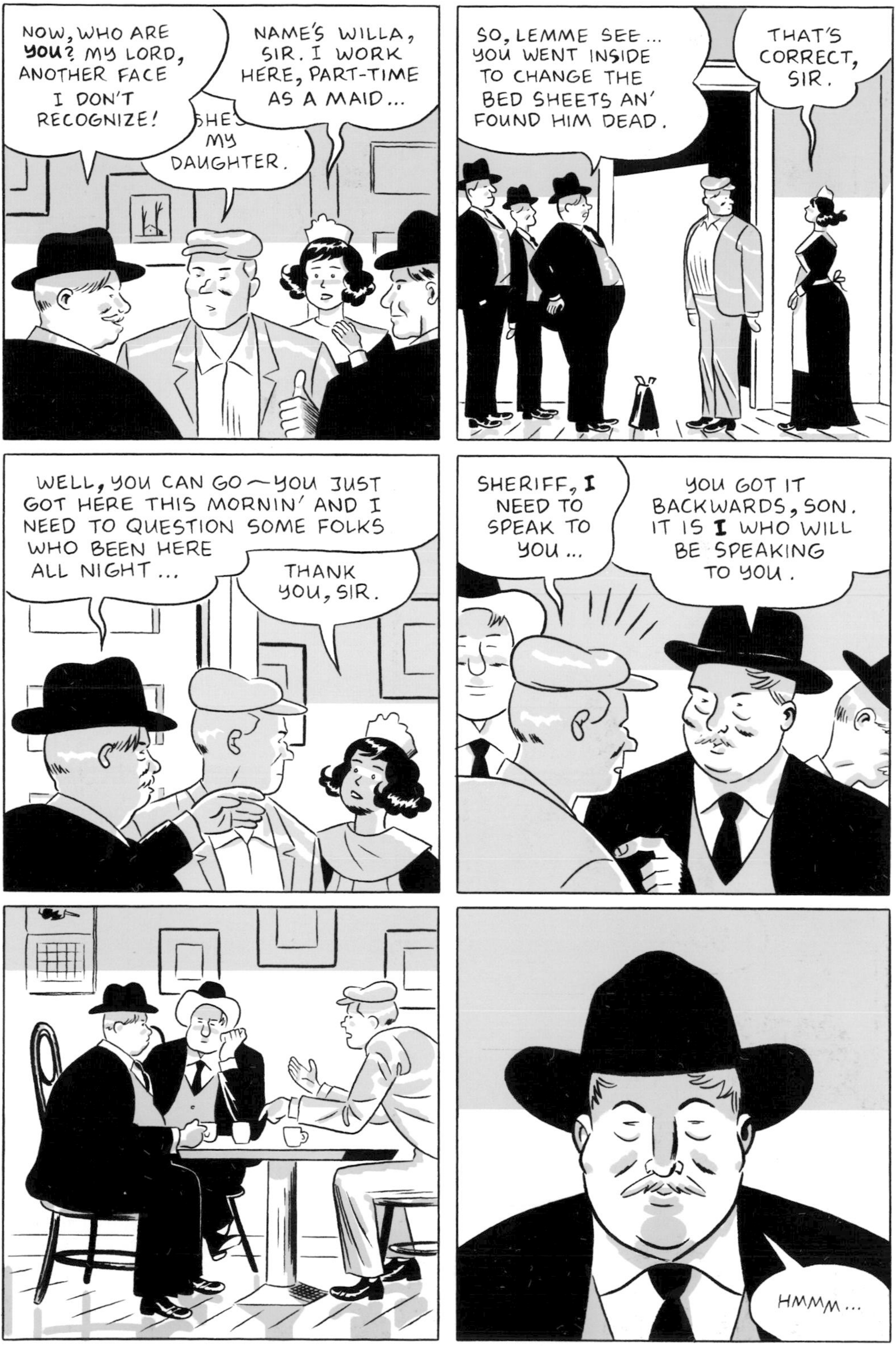
NOW, WHO ARE YOU? MY LORD, ANOTHER FACE I DON'T RECOGNIZE!
SHE'S MY DAUGHTER.
NAME'S WILLA, SIR. I WORK HERE, PART-TIME AS A MAID...
SO, LEMME SEE... YOU WENT INSIDE TO CHANGE THE BED SHEETS AN' FOUND HIM DEAD.
THAT'S CORRECT, SIR.
WELL, YOU CAN GO—YOU JUST GOT HERE THIS MORNIN' AND I NEED TO QUESTION SOME FOLKS WHO BEEN HERE ALL NIGHT...
THANK YOU, SIR.
SHERIFF, I NEED TO SPEAK TO YOU...
YOU GOT IT BACKWARDS, SON. IT IS I WHO WILL BE SPEAKING TO YOU.
HMMM...

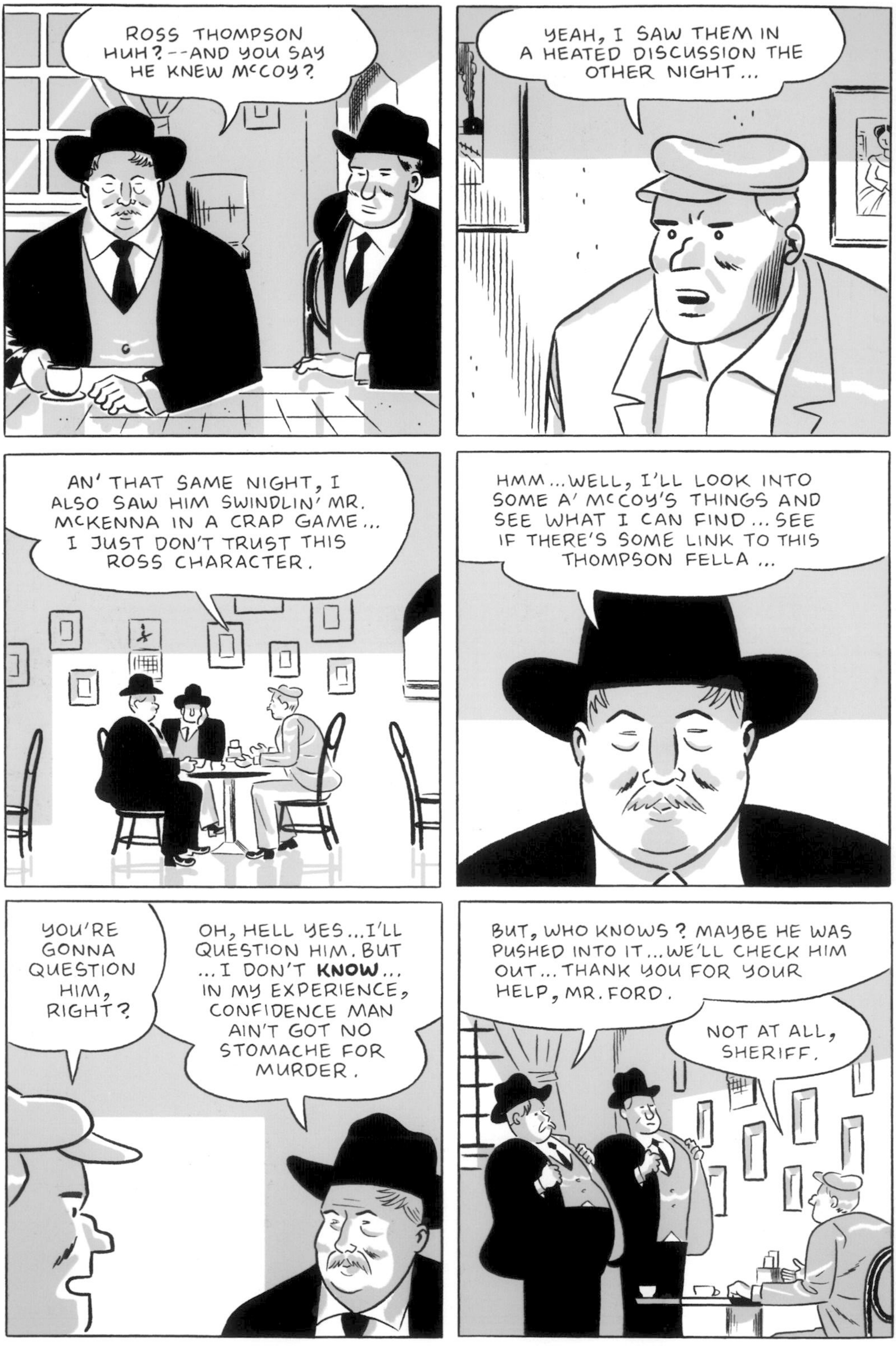

ROSS THOMPSON HUH? --AND YOU SAY HE KNEW McCOY?
YEAH, I SAW THEM IN A HEATED DISCUSSION THE OTHER NIGHT...
AN' THAT SAME NIGHT, I ALSO SAW HIM SWINDLIN' MR. McKENNA IN A CRAP GAME... I JUST DON'T TRUST THIS ROSS CHARACTER.
HMM... WELL, I'LL LOOK INTO SOME A' McCOY'S THINGS AND SEE WHAT I CAN FIND... SEE IF THERE'S SOME LINK TO THIS THOMPSON FELLA...
YOU'RE GONNA QUESTION HIM, RIGHT?
OH, HELL YES... I'LL QUESTION HIM. BUT ... I DON'T **KNOW**... IN MY EXPERIENCE, CONFIDENCE MAN AIN'T GOT NO STOMACHE FOR MURDER.
BUT, WHO KNOWS? MAYBE HE WAS PUSHED INTO IT... WE'LL CHECK HIM OUT... THANK YOU FOR YOUR HELP, MR. FORD.
NOT AT ALL, SHERIFF.

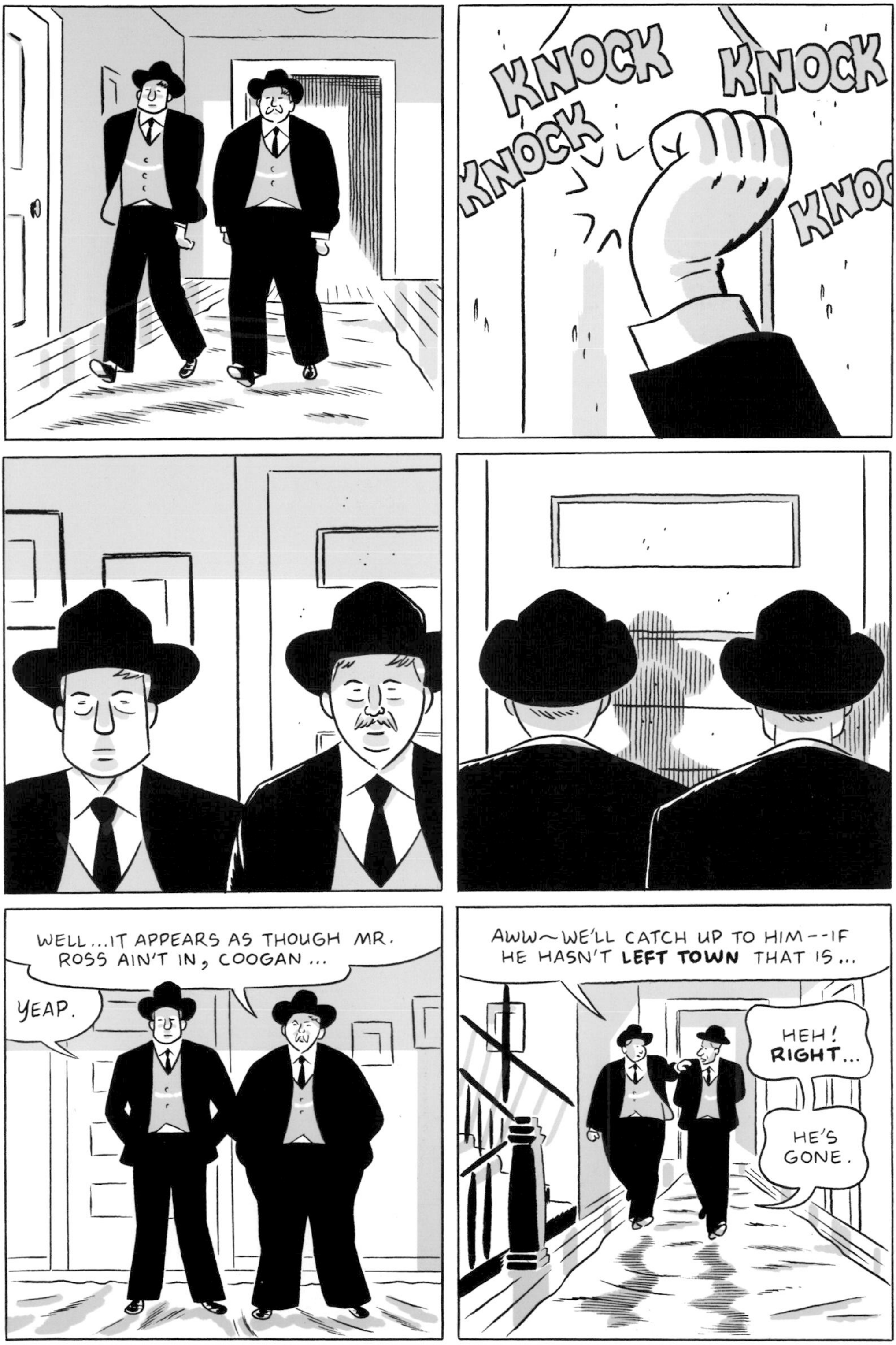
KNOCK
KNOCK
KNOCK
KNOC
WELL...IT APPEARS AS THOUGH MR. ROSS AIN'T IN, COOGAN...
YEAP.
AWW~WE'LL CATCH UP TO HIM--IF HE HASN'T **LEFT TOWN** THAT IS...
HEH! **RIGHT**...
HE'S GONE.

SNAKE EYES

WHERE IS ROSS THOMPSON? HAS HE LEFT BIG SPRING BECAUSE OF HIS INVOLVEMENT WITH McCOY? IF HE WAS **LUCKY**, HE'D HAVE LEFT TOWN TOUT SUITE ...

BUT ROSS **WASN'T** LUCKY ... HE NEEDED TO CHEAT IN ORDER TO APPEAR LUCKY ...

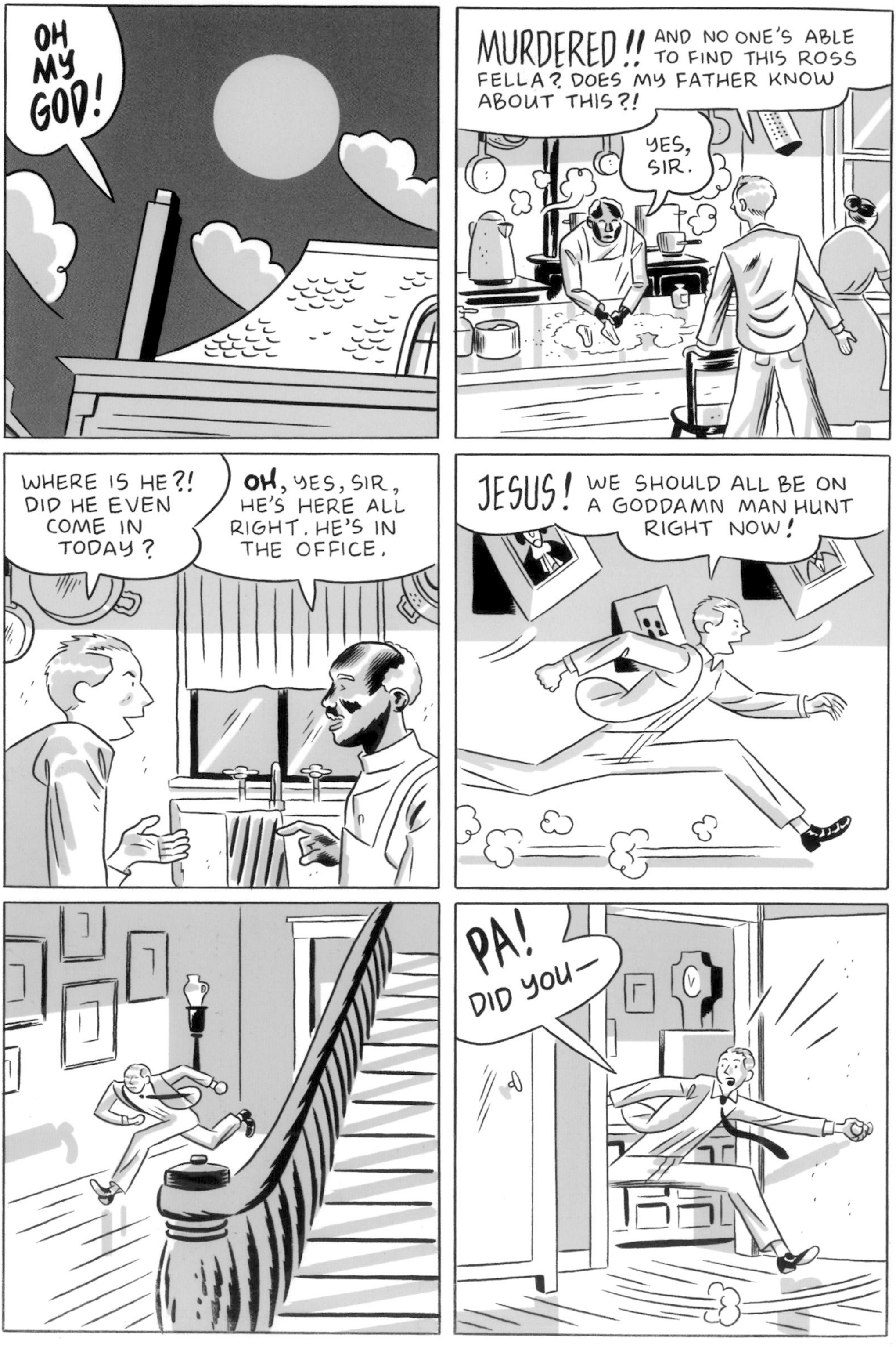
OH MY GOD!
MURDERED!! AND NO ONE'S ABLE TO FIND THIS ROSS FELLA? DOES MY FATHER KNOW ABOUT THIS?!
YES, SIR.
WHERE IS HE?! DID HE EVEN COME IN TODAY?
OH, YES, SIR, HE'S HERE ALL RIGHT. HE'S IN THE OFFICE.
JESUS! WE SHOULD ALL BE ON A GODDAMN MAN HUNT RIGHT NOW!
PA! DID YOU—

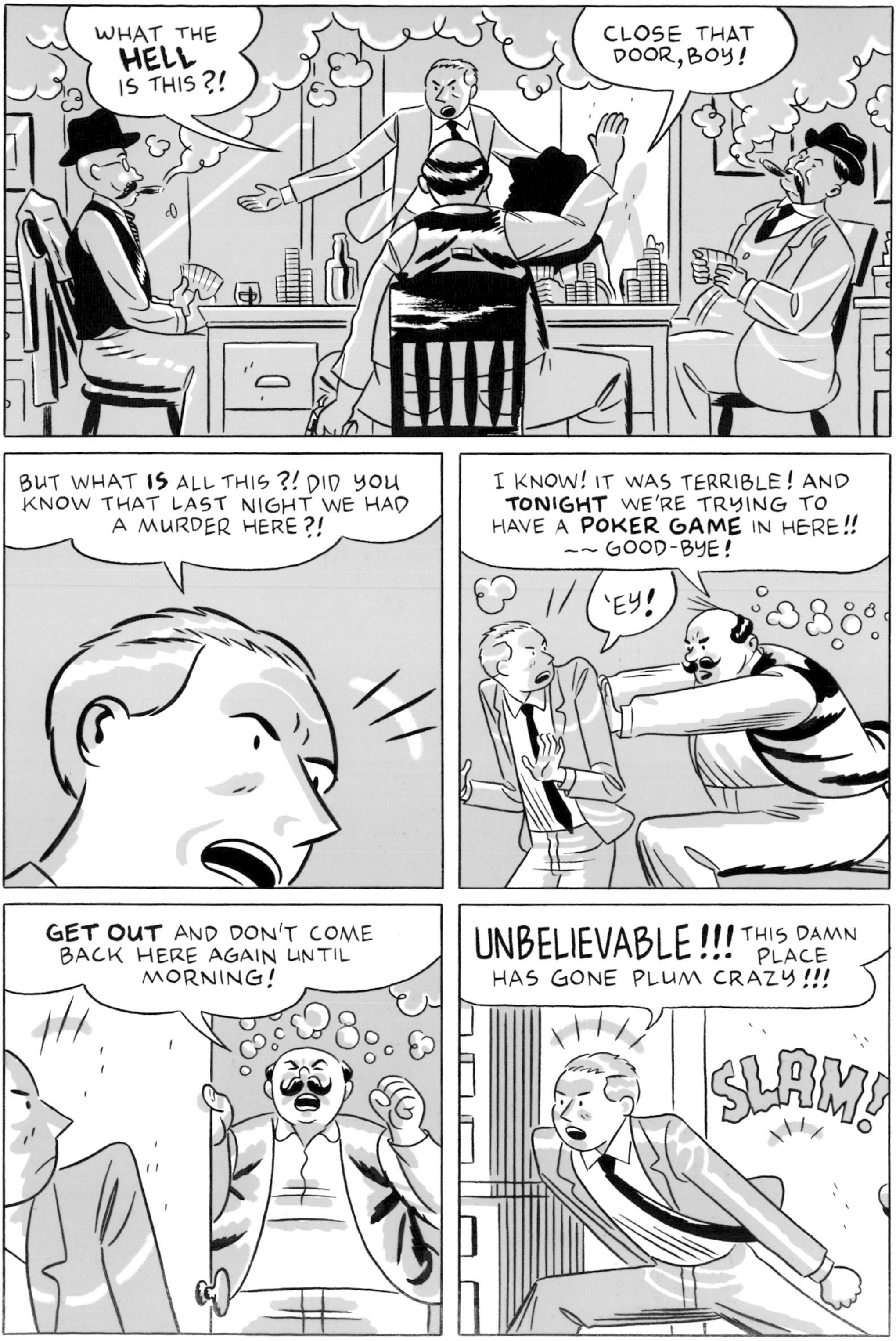
WHAT THE HELL IS THIS?!
CLOSE THAT DOOR, BOY!
BUT WHAT IS ALL THIS?! DID YOU KNOW THAT LAST NIGHT WE HAD A MURDER HERE?!
I KNOW! IT WAS TERRIBLE! AND TONIGHT WE'RE TRYING TO HAVE A POKER GAME IN HERE!! ~~ GOOD-BYE!
'EY!
GET OUT AND DON'T COME BACK HERE AGAIN UNTIL MORNING!
UNBELIEVABLE!!! THIS DAMN PLACE HAS GONE PLUM CRAZY!!!
SLAM!

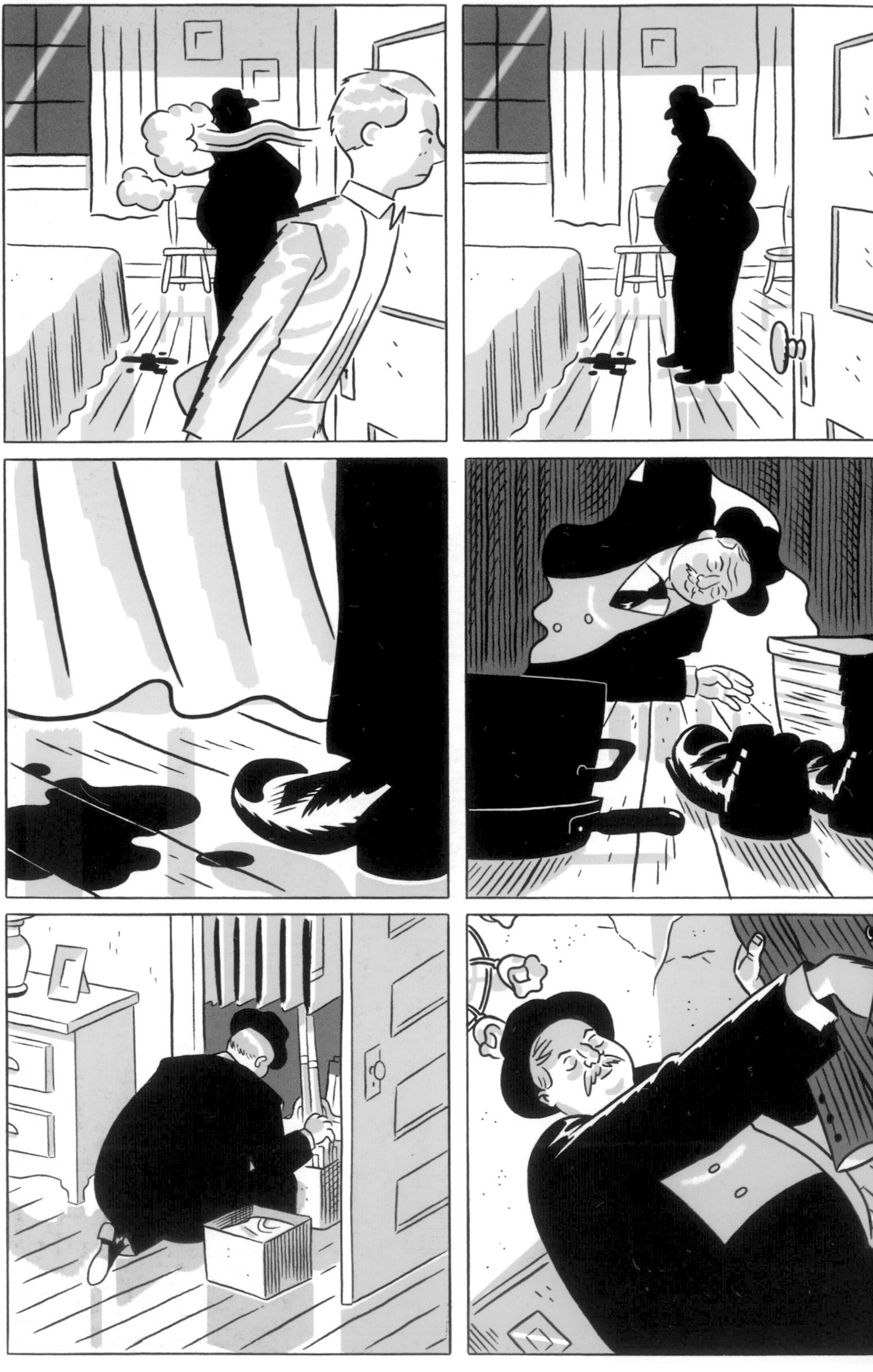

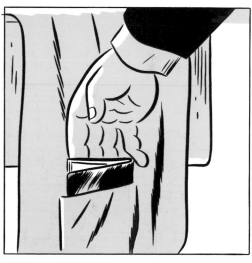

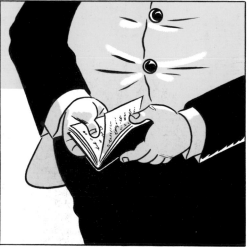

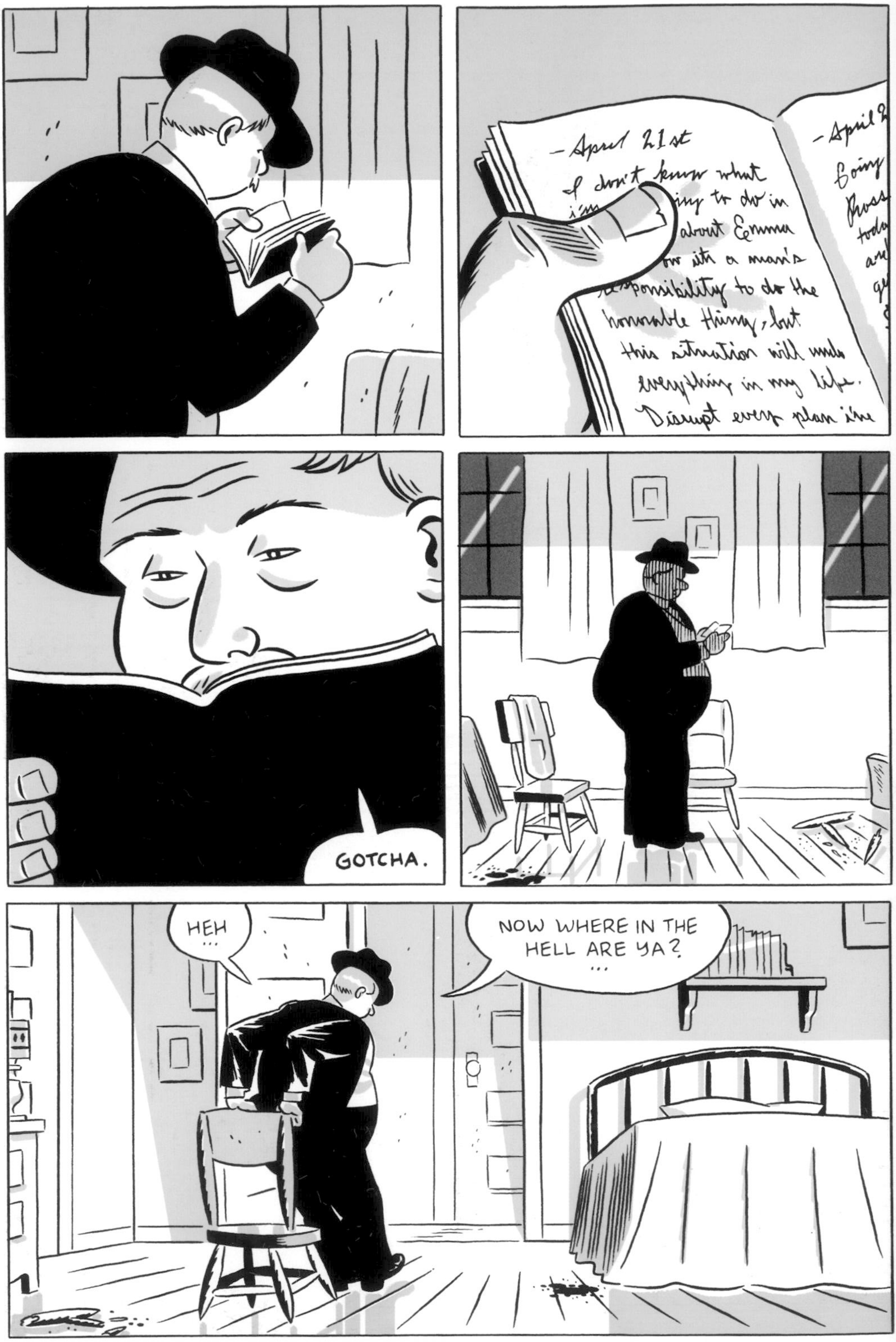
—April 21st
I don't know what
ing to do in
about Emma
it's a man's
sponsibility to do the
honorable thing, but
this situation will undo
everything in my life.
Disrupt every plan i've
—April 2
Going
GOTCHA.
HEH ...
NOW WHERE IN THE HELL ARE YA? ...

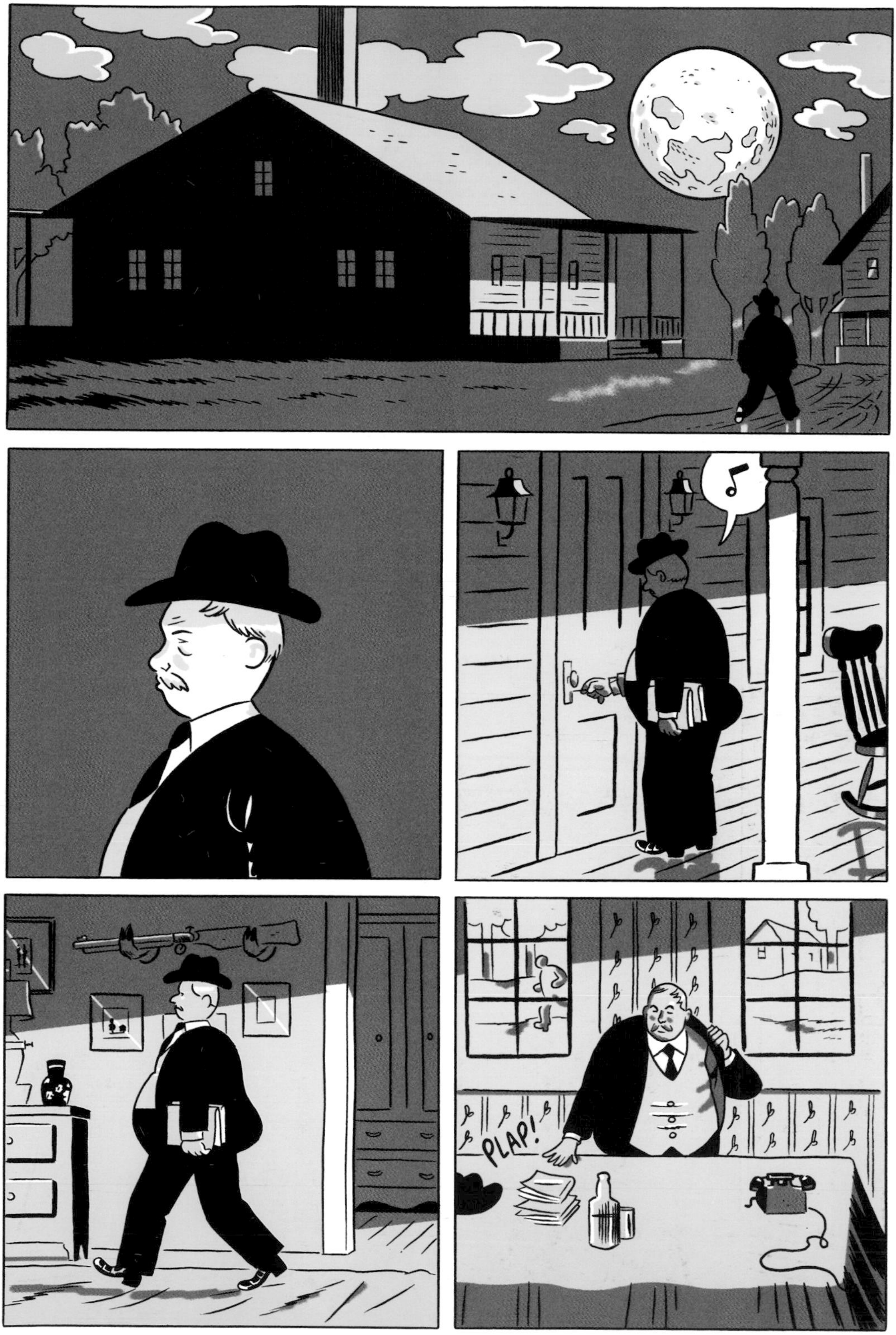
PLAP!

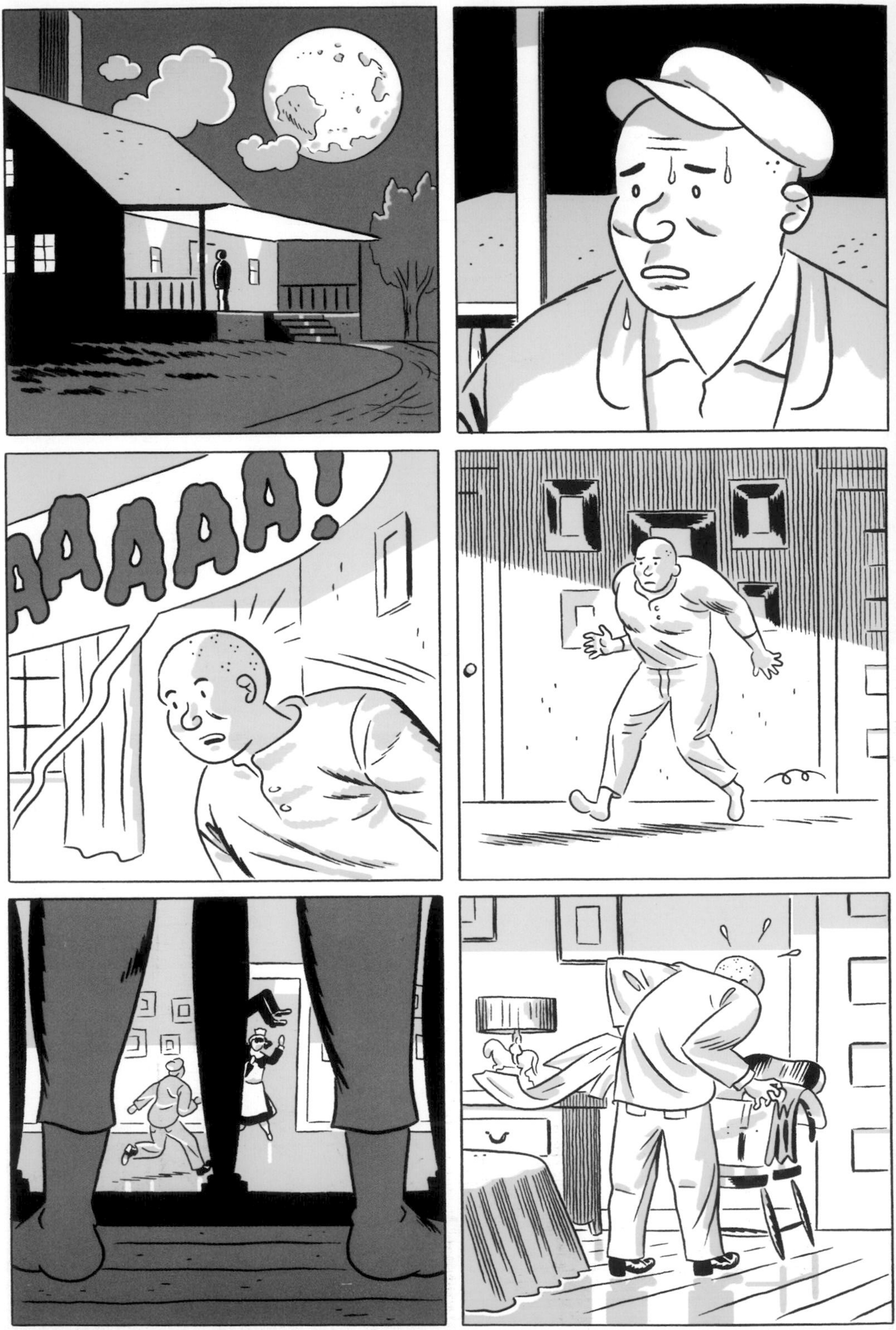
AAAAA!

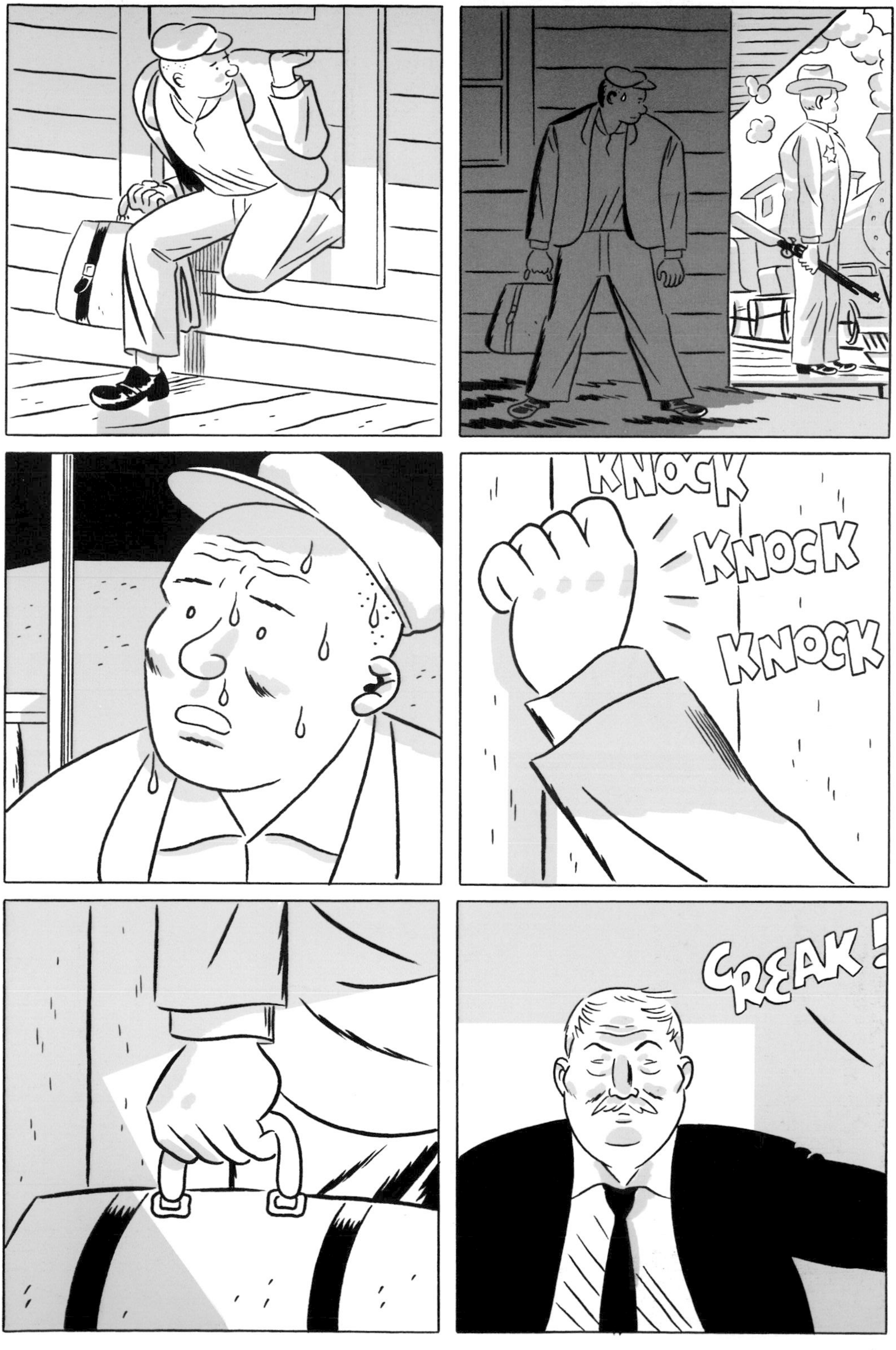
KNOCK
KNOCK
KNOCK
CREAK!

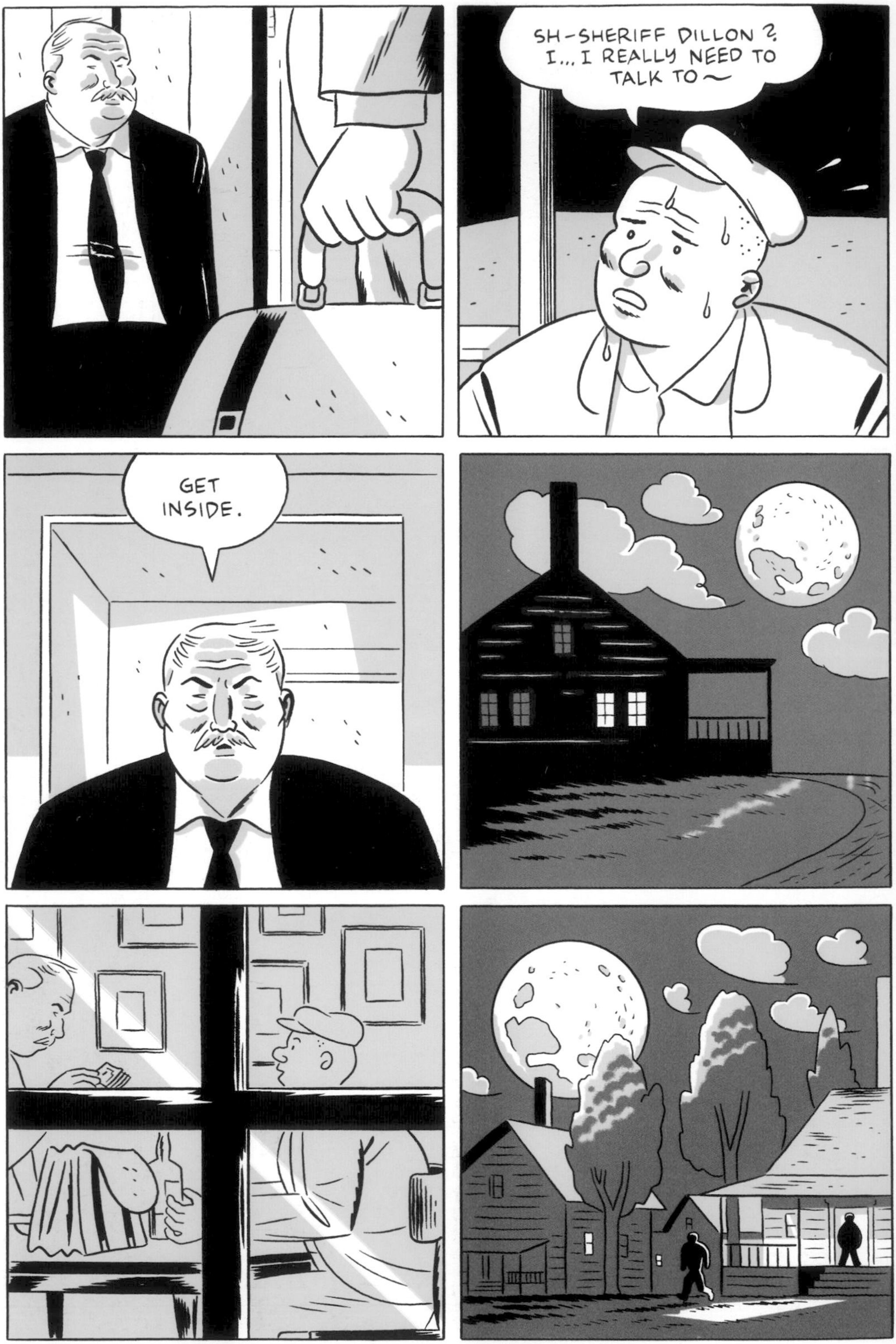
SH-SHERIFF DILLON? I... I REALLY NEED TO TALK TO~
GET INSIDE.

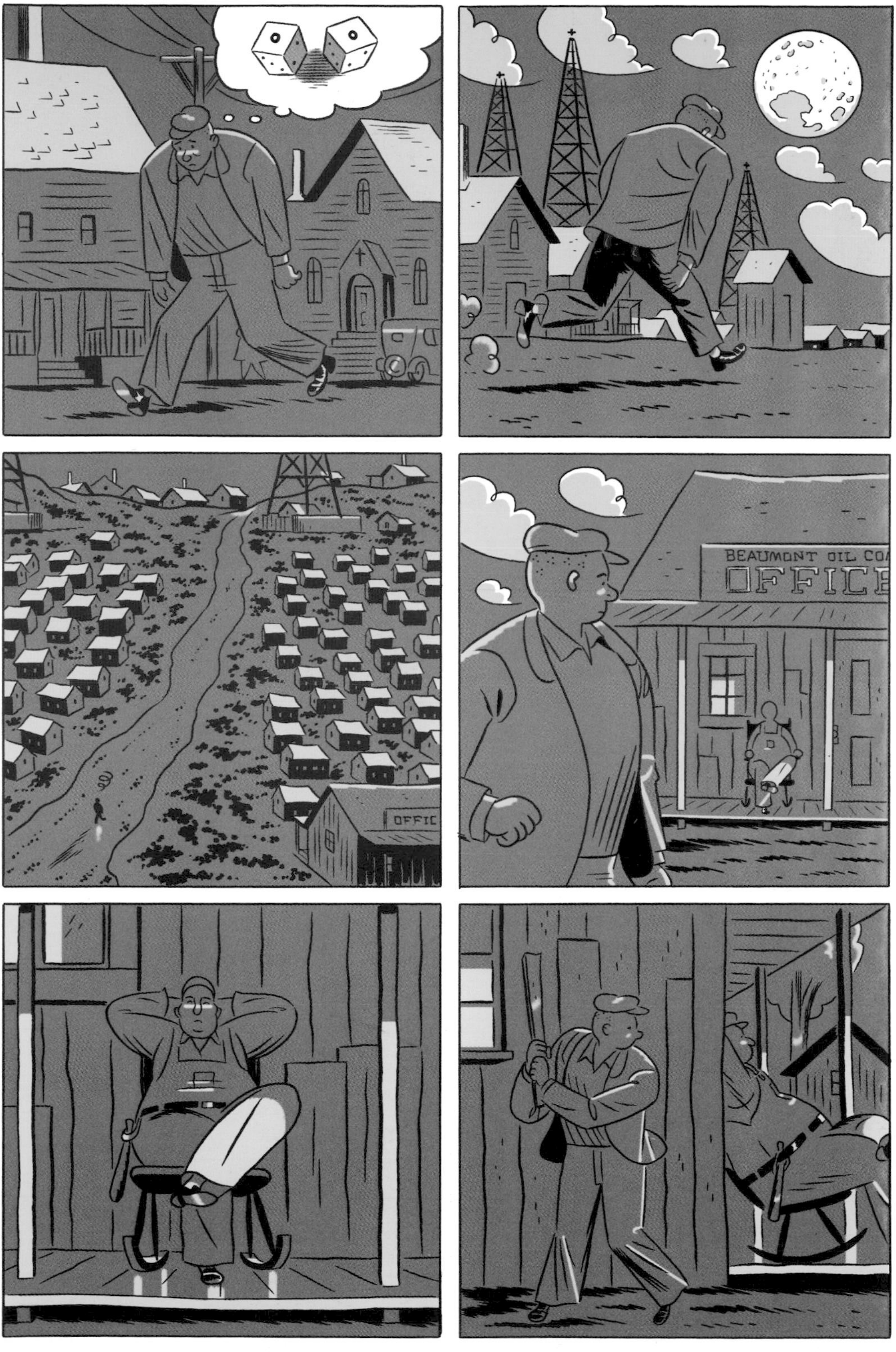
BEAUMONT OIL CO
OFFIC
OFFIC

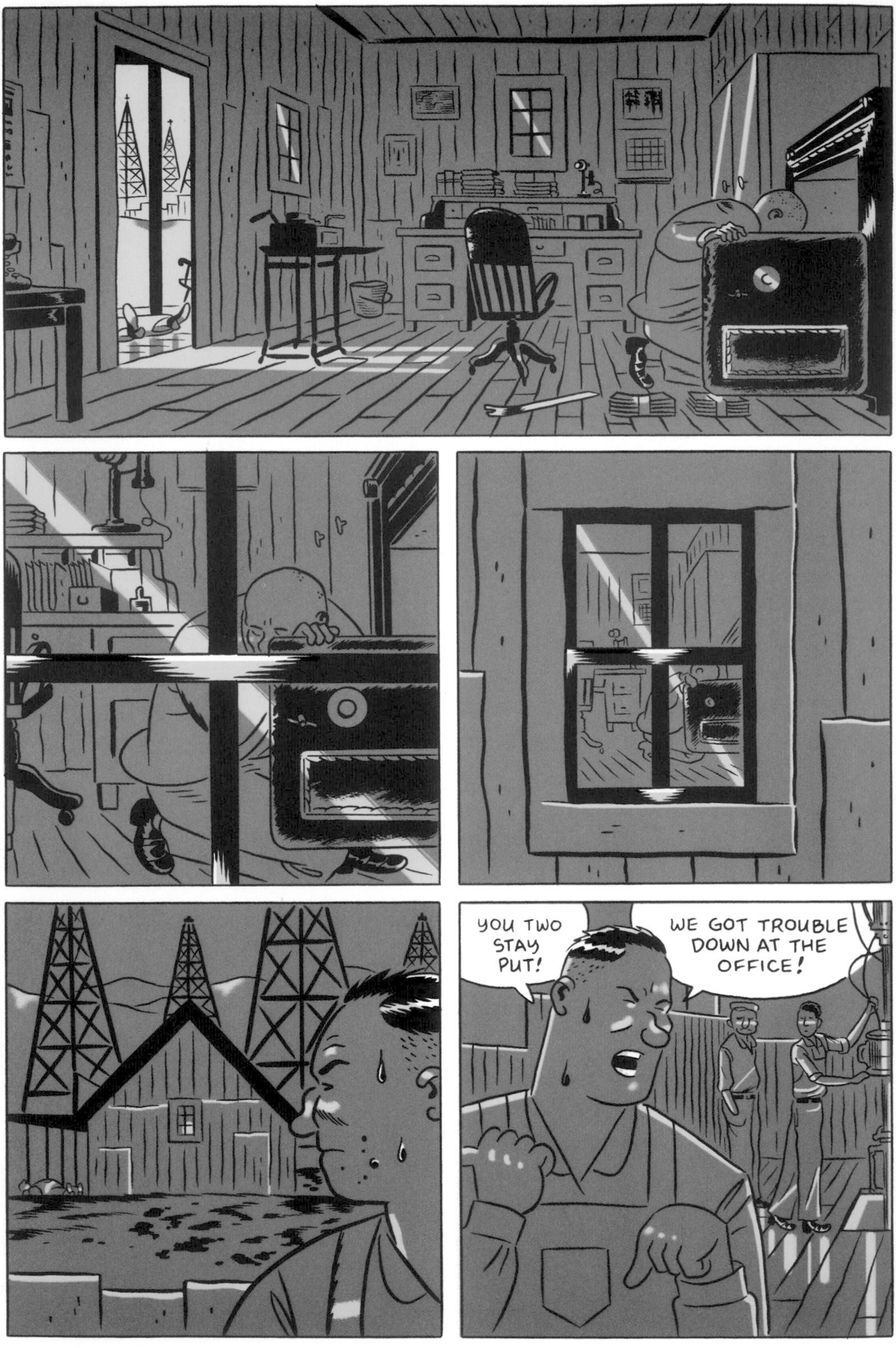
YOU TWO STAY PUT!
WE GOT TROUBLE DOWN AT THE OFFICE!

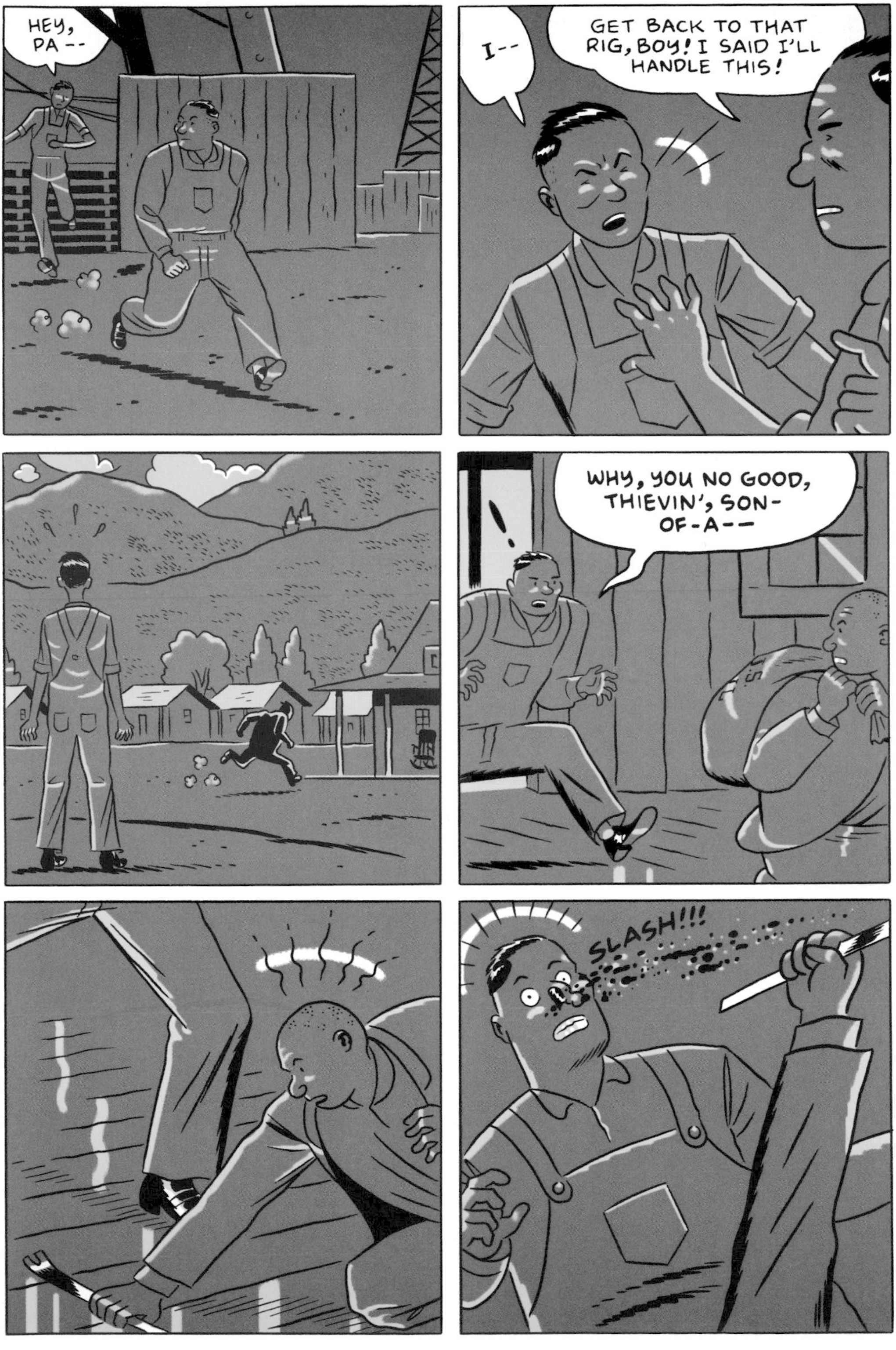
HEY, PA --
I--
GET BACK TO THAT RIG, BOY! I SAID I'LL HANDLE THIS!
WHY, YOU NO GOOD, THIEVIN', SON-OF-A--
SLASH!!!

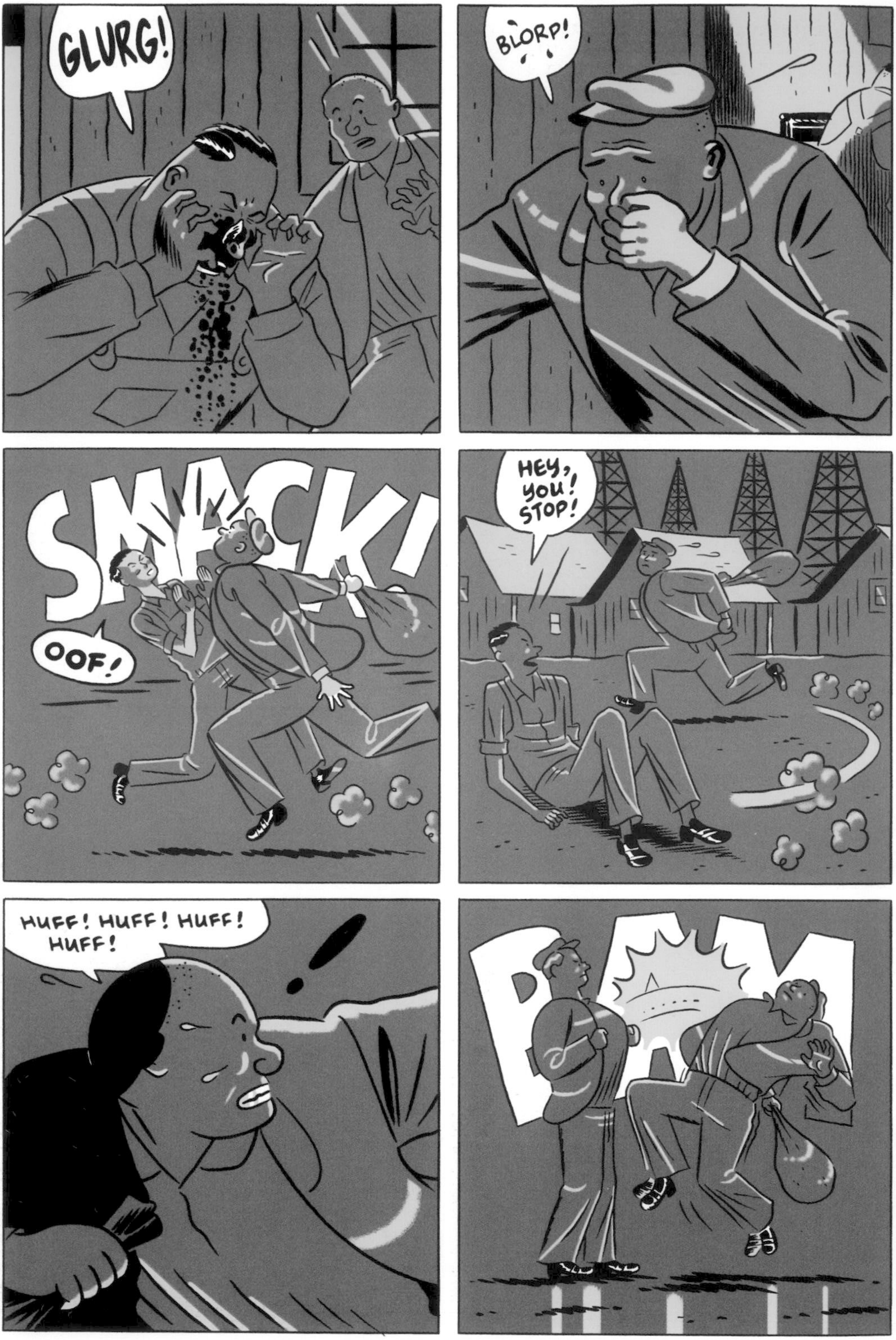
GLURG!
BLORP!
SMACK!
OOF!
HEY, YOU! STOP!
HUFF! HUFF! HUFF! HUFF!
!
BAM

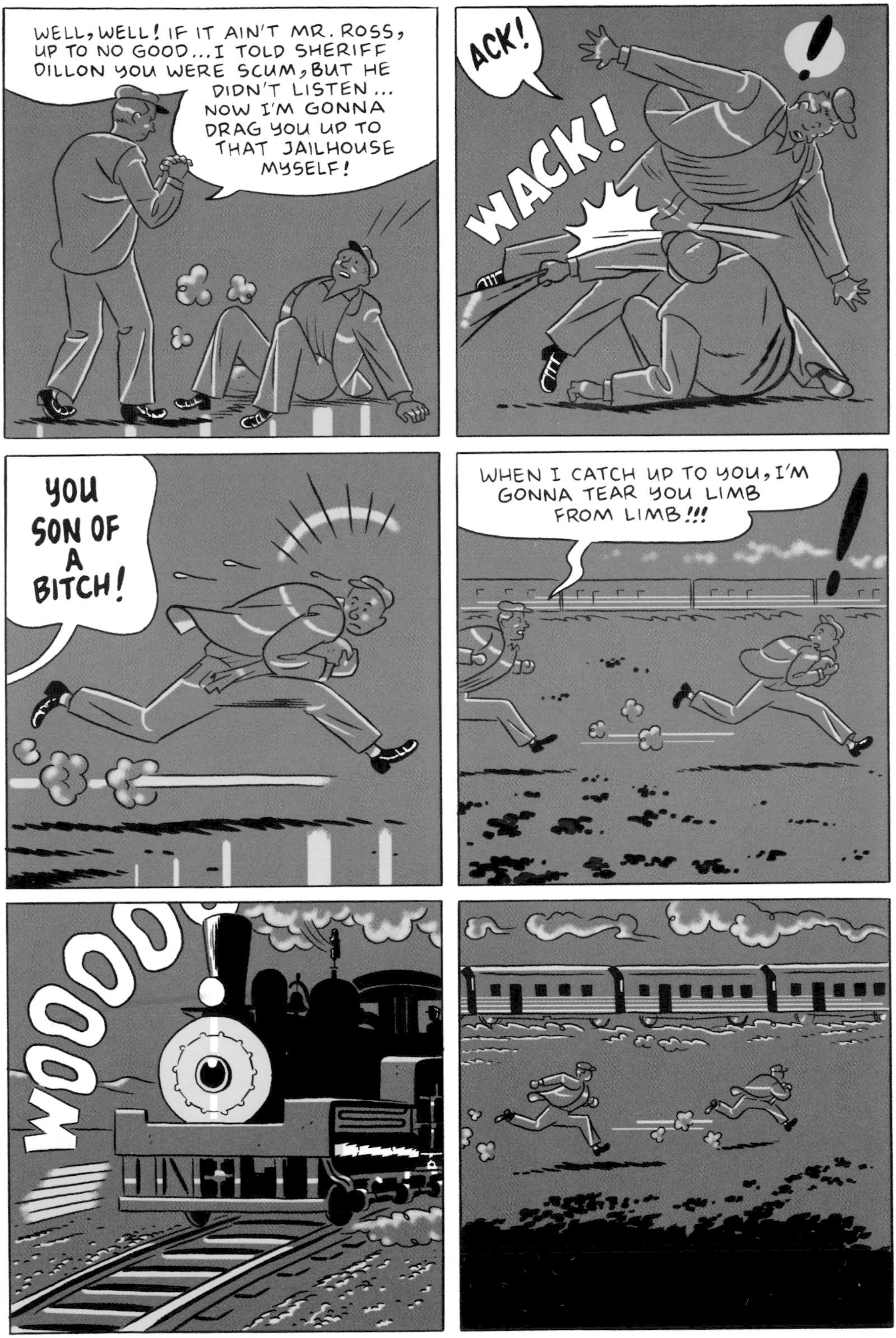
WELL, WELL! IF IT AIN'T MR. ROSS, UP TO NO GOOD... I TOLD SHERIFF DILLON YOU WERE SCUM, BUT HE DIDN'T LISTEN... NOW I'M GONNA DRAG YOU UP TO THAT JAILHOUSE MYSELF!
ACK!
!
WACK!
YOU SON OF A BITCH!
WHEN I CATCH UP TO YOU, I'M GONNA TEAR YOU LIMB FROM LIMB!!!
!
WOOOO

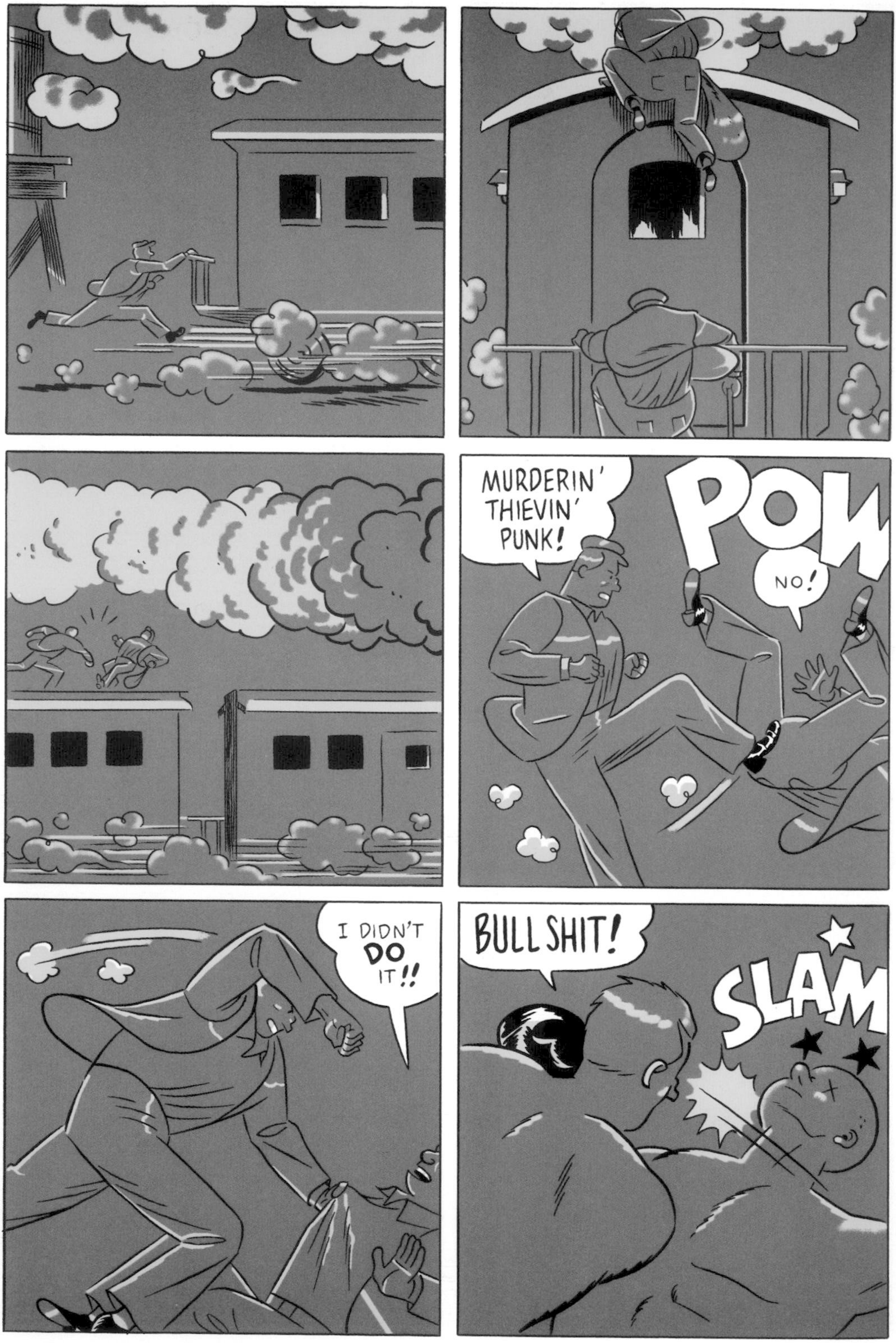
MURDERIN' THIEVIN' PUNK!
POW
NO!
I DIDN'T DO IT!!
BULLSHIT!
SLAM

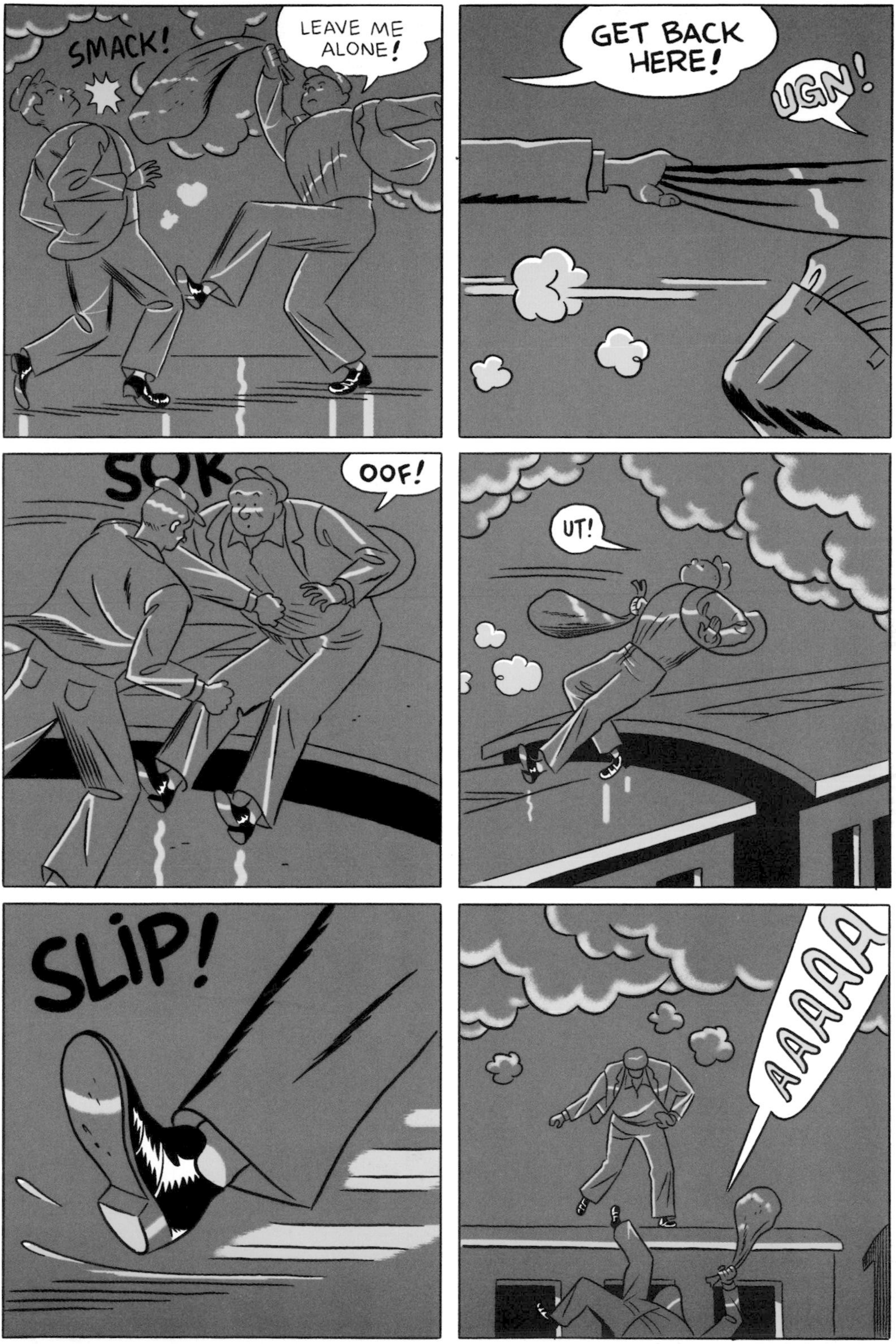
SMACK!
LEAVE ME ALONE!
GET BACK HERE!
UGN!
SOK
OOF!
UT!
SLIP!
AAAAA

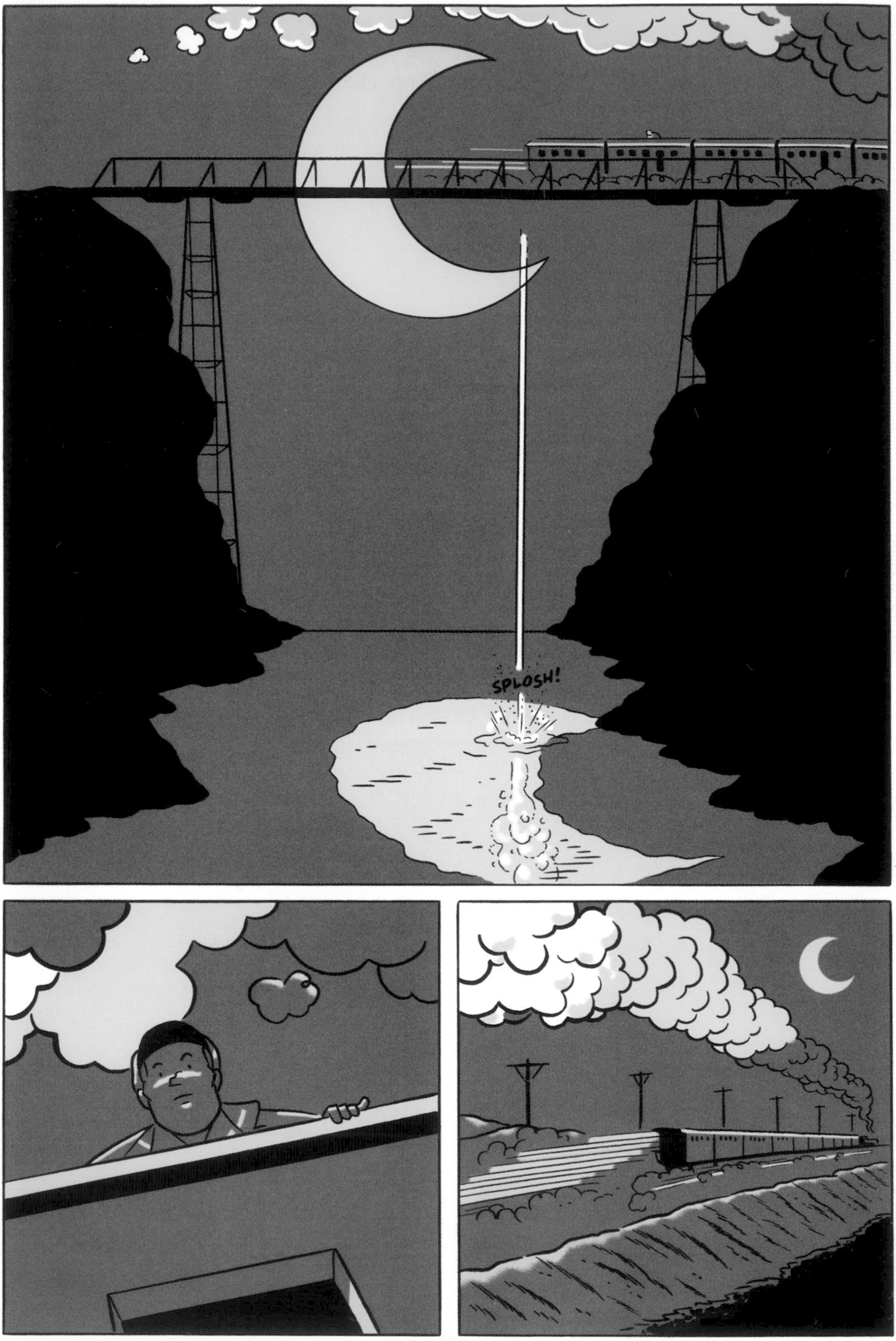
SPLOSH!

EXODUS

ALL NIGHT LONG, NICK HAD UNWITTINGLY TRAVELED BACK TO TOWN ALONG A VERY SIMILAR ROUTE TO THE ONE ROSS HAD TAKEN WHEN **HE** FIRST CAME TO BIG SPRING...

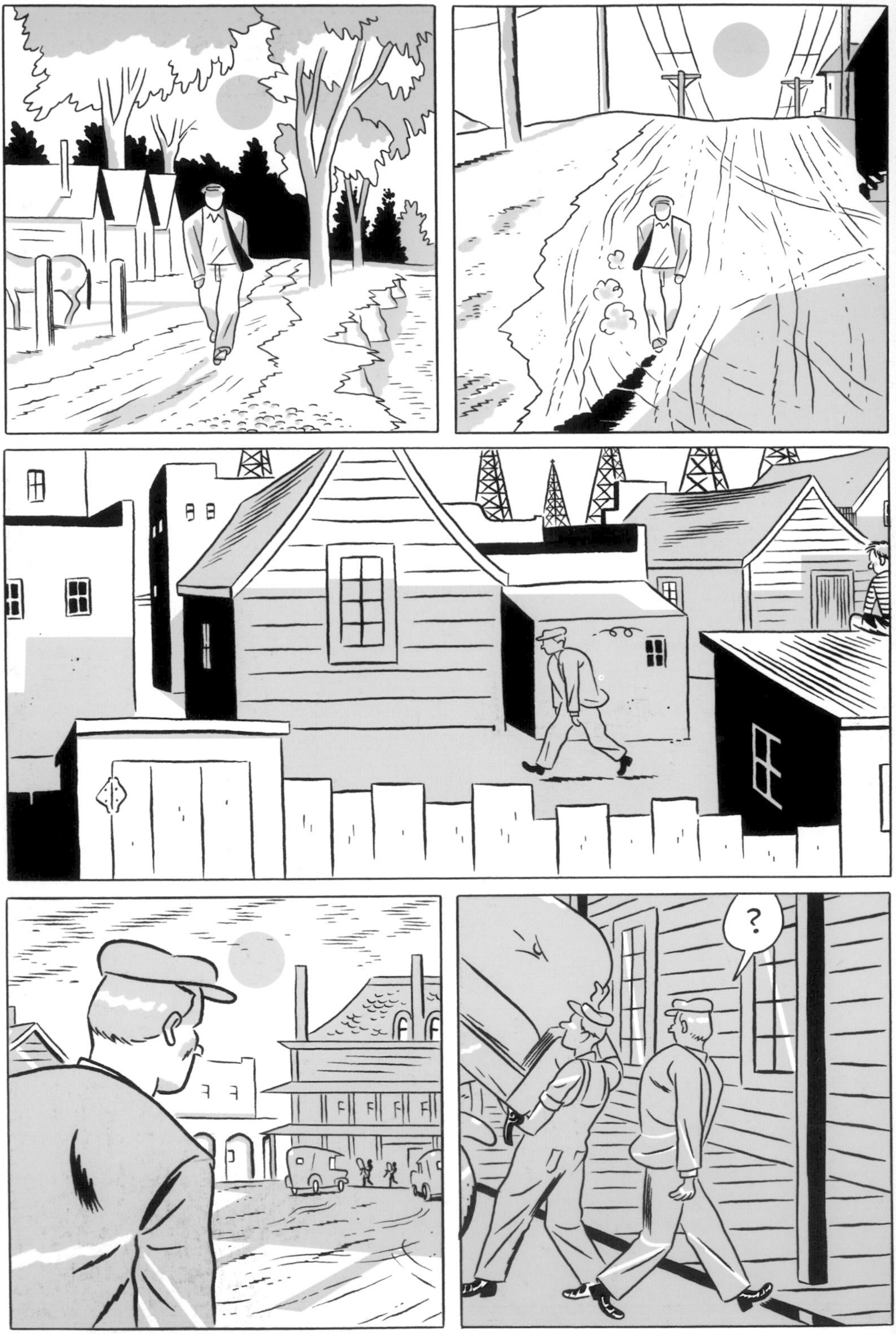
?

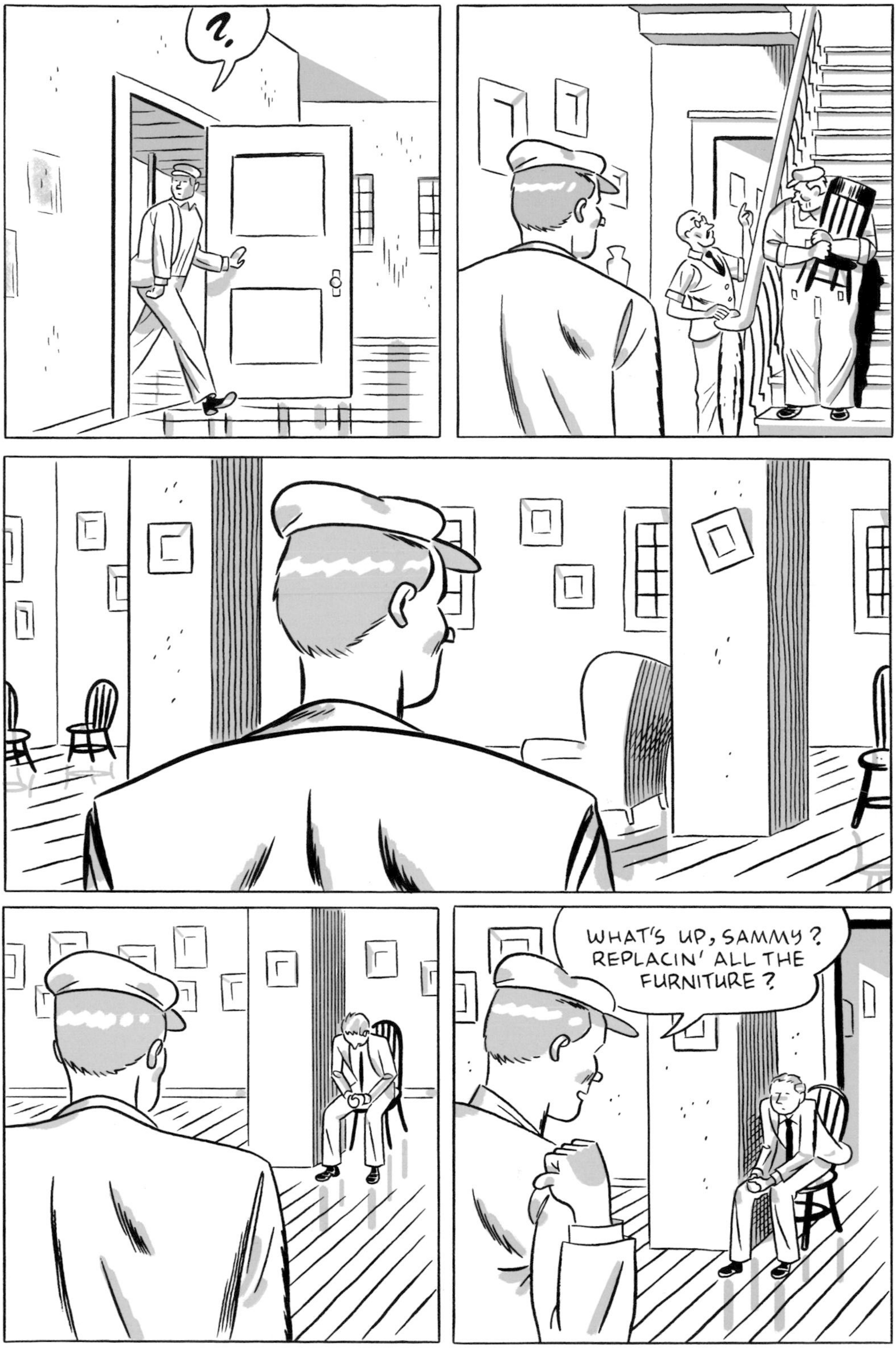
?
WHAT'S UP, SAMMY? REPLACIN' ALL THE FURNITURE?

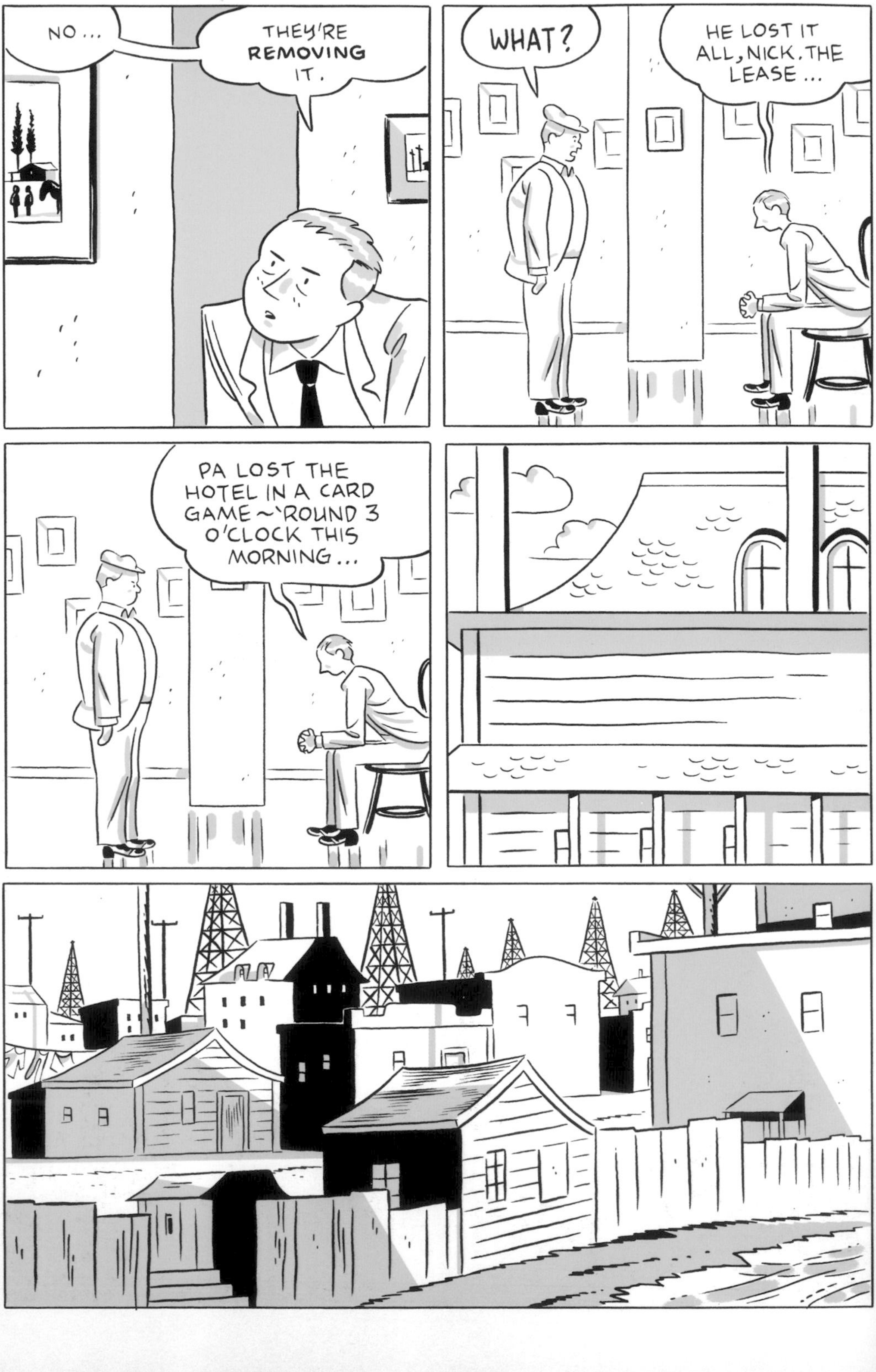
NO...
THEY'RE **REMOVING** IT.
WHAT?
HE LOST IT ALL, NICK. THE LEASE...
PA LOST THE HOTEL IN A CARD GAME ~ 'ROUND 3 O'CLOCK THIS MORNING...

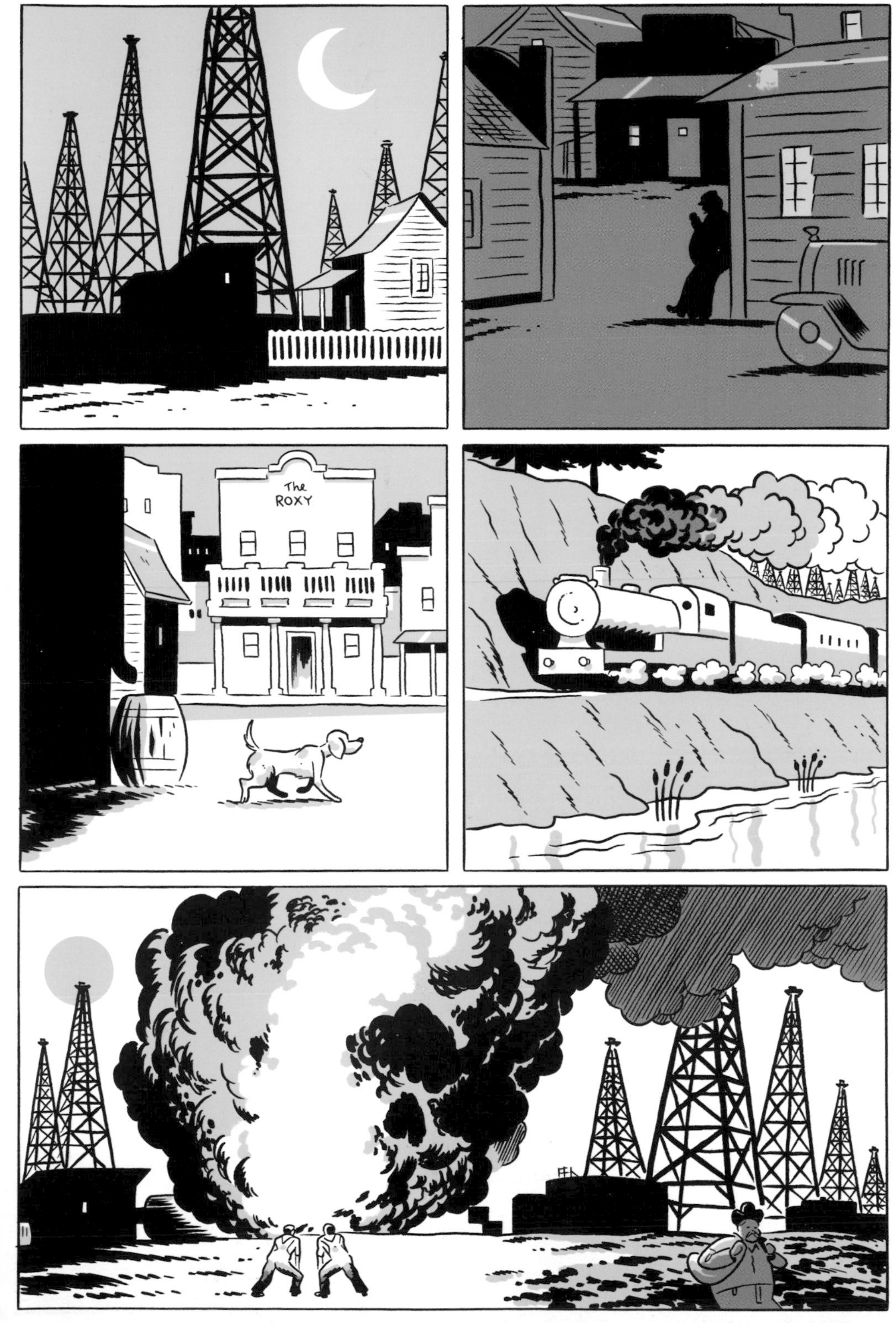
The ROXY

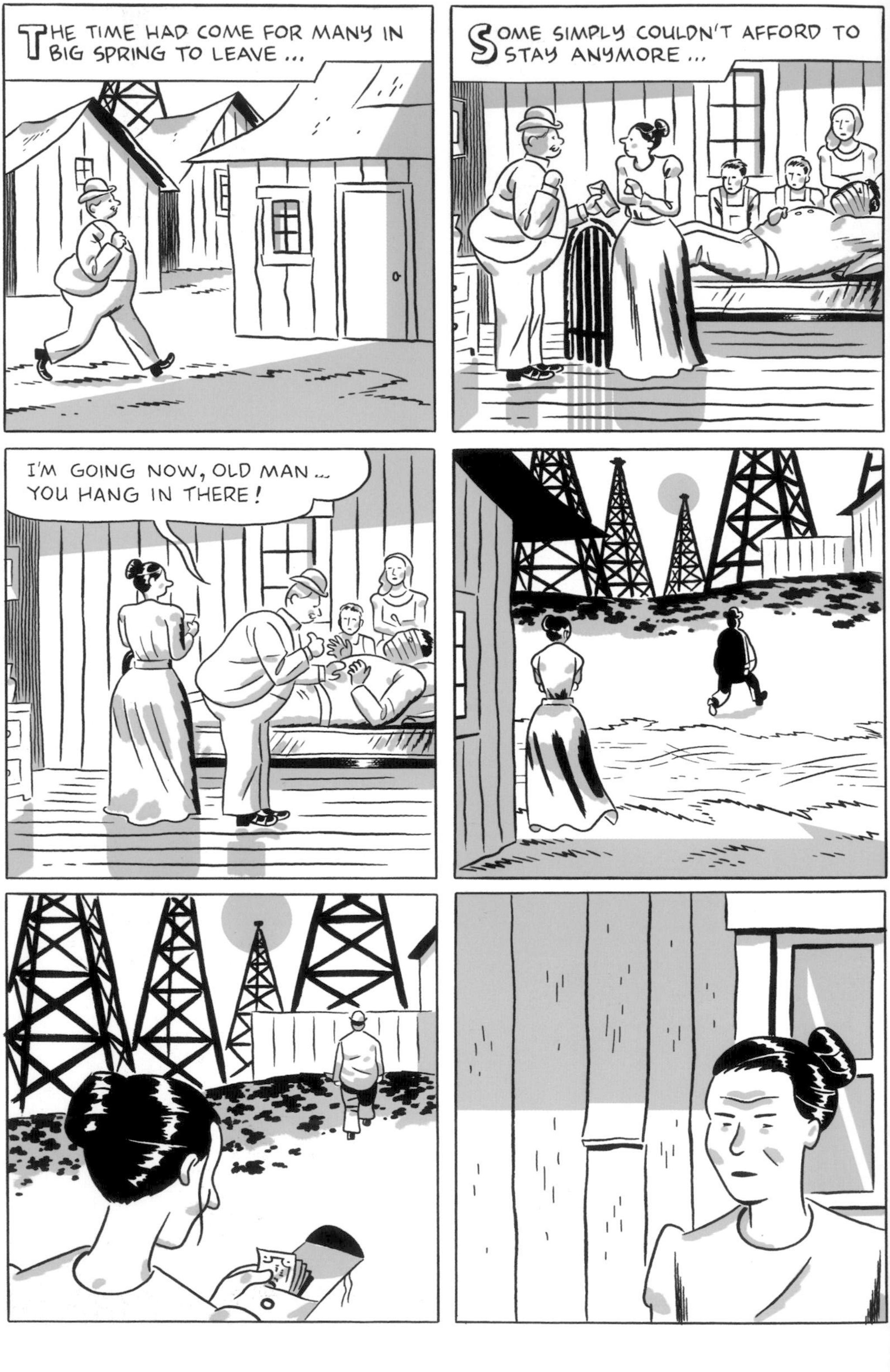
THE TIME HAD COME FOR MANY IN BIG SPRING TO LEAVE ...
SOME SIMPLY COULDN'T AFFORD TO STAY ANYMORE ...
I'M GOING NOW, OLD MAN ... YOU HANG IN THERE!

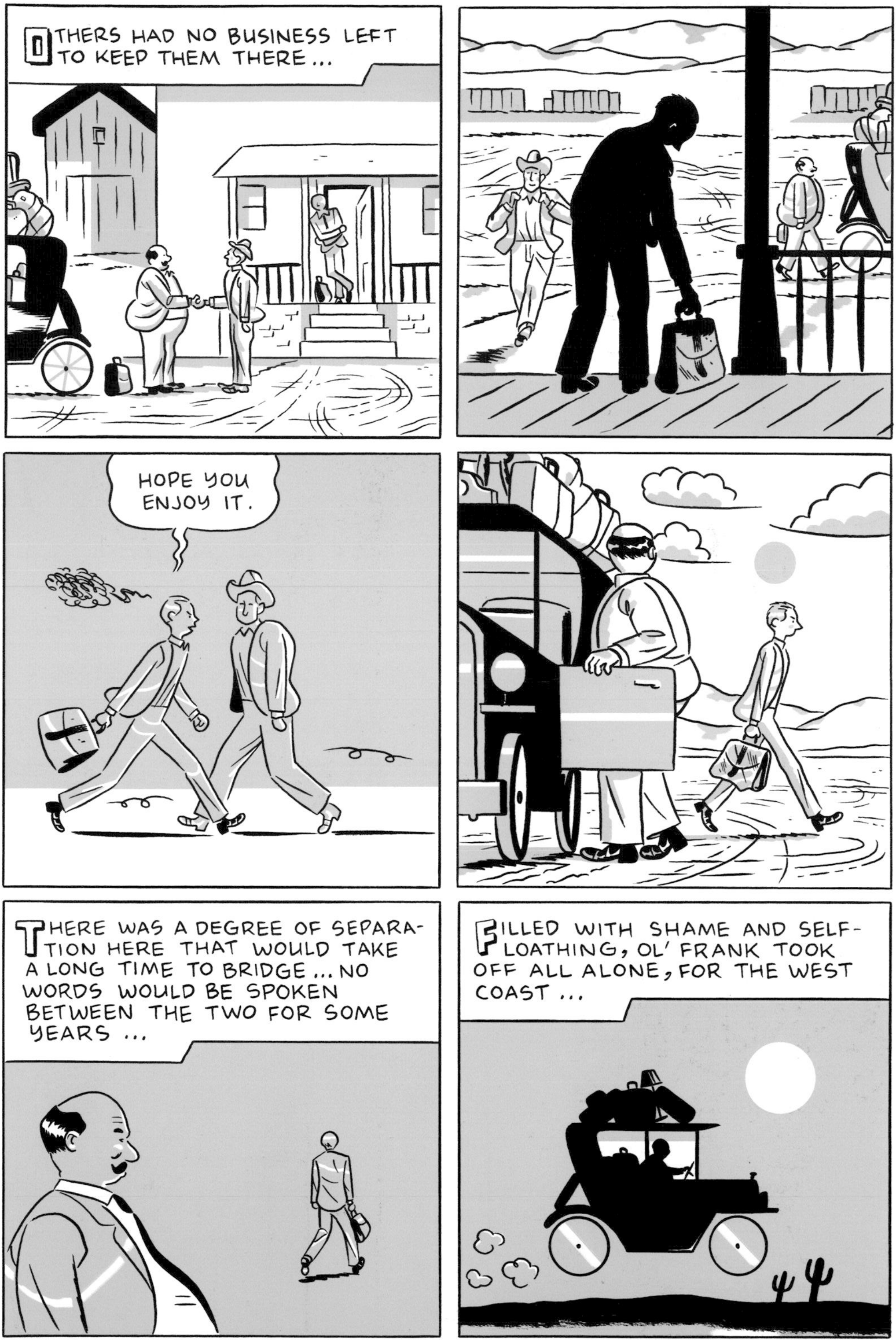
OTHERS HAD NO BUSINESS LEFT TO KEEP THEM THERE ...
HOPE YOU ENJOY IT.
THERE WAS A DEGREE OF SEPARATION HERE THAT WOULD TAKE A LONG TIME TO BRIDGE ... NO WORDS WOULD BE SPOKEN BETWEEN THE TWO FOR SOME YEARS ...
FILLED WITH SHAME AND SELF-LOATHING, OL' FRANK TOOK OFF ALL ALONE, FOR THE WEST COAST ...

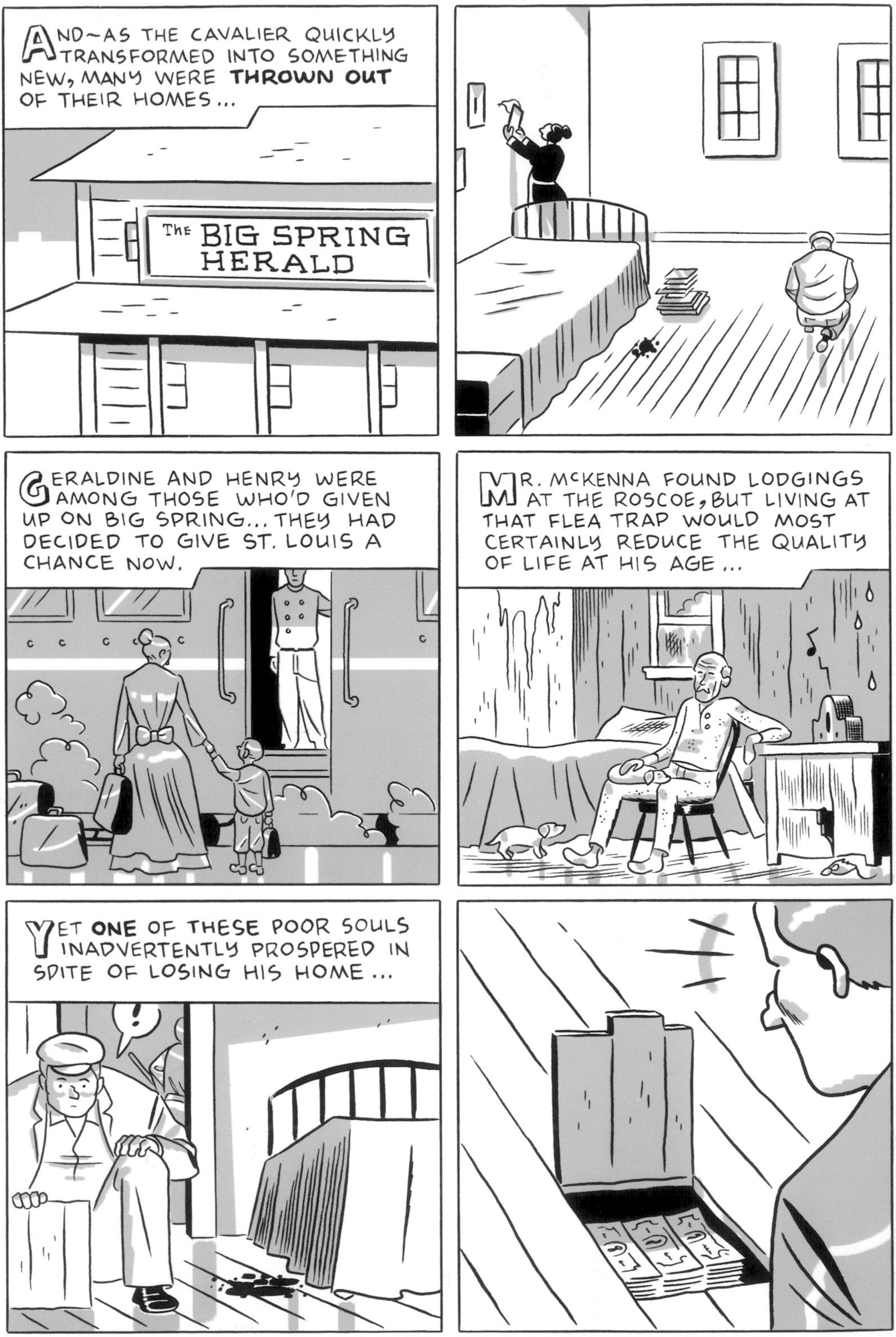
AND~AS THE CAVALIER QUICKLY TRANSFORMED INTO SOMETHING NEW, MANY WERE **THROWN OUT** OF THEIR HOMES...
The BIG SPRING HERALD
GERALDINE AND HENRY WERE AMONG THOSE WHO'D GIVEN UP ON BIG SPRING... THEY HAD DECIDED TO GIVE ST. LOUIS A CHANCE NOW.
MR. McKENNA FOUND LODGINGS AT THE ROSCOE, BUT LIVING AT THAT FLEA TRAP WOULD MOST CERTAINLY REDUCE THE QUALITY OF LIFE AT HIS AGE...
YET **ONE** OF THESE POOR SOULS INADVERTENTLY PROSPERED IN SPITE OF LOSING HIS HOME...
!

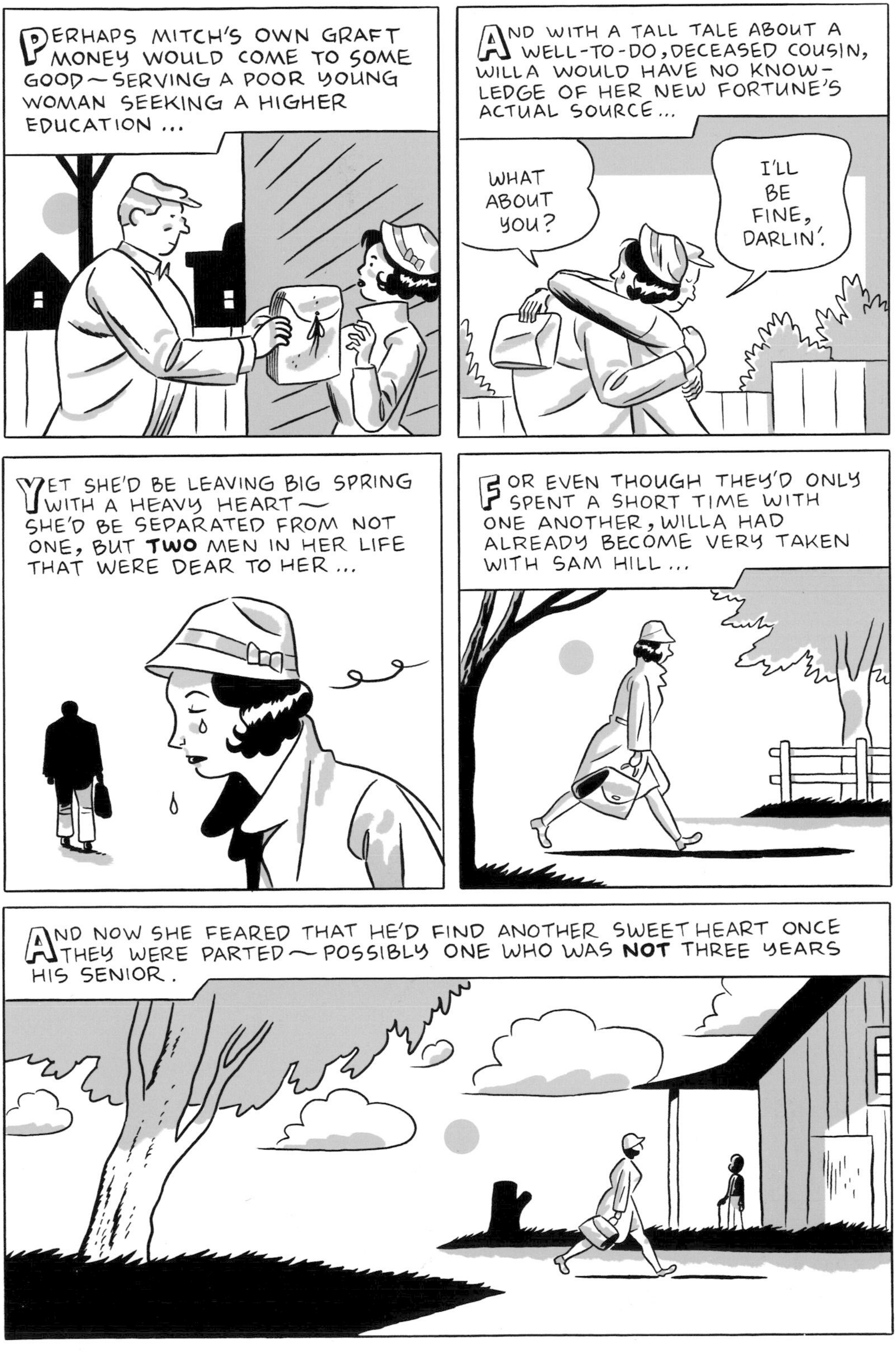
PERHAPS MITCH'S OWN GRAFT MONEY WOULD COME TO SOME GOOD — SERVING A POOR YOUNG WOMAN SEEKING A HIGHER EDUCATION ...
AND WITH A TALL TALE ABOUT A WELL-TO-DO, DECEASED COUSIN, WILLA WOULD HAVE NO KNOWLEDGE OF HER NEW FORTUNE'S ACTUAL SOURCE ...
WHAT ABOUT YOU?
I'LL BE FINE, DARLIN'.
YET SHE'D BE LEAVING BIG SPRING WITH A HEAVY HEART — SHE'D BE SEPARATED FROM NOT ONE, BUT **TWO** MEN IN HER LIFE THAT WERE DEAR TO HER ...
FOR EVEN THOUGH THEY'D ONLY SPENT A SHORT TIME WITH ONE ANOTHER, WILLA HAD ALREADY BECOME VERY TAKEN WITH SAM HILL ...
AND NOW SHE FEARED THAT HE'D FIND ANOTHER SWEETHEART ONCE THEY WERE PARTED — POSSIBLY ONE WHO WAS **NOT** THREE YEARS HIS SENIOR.

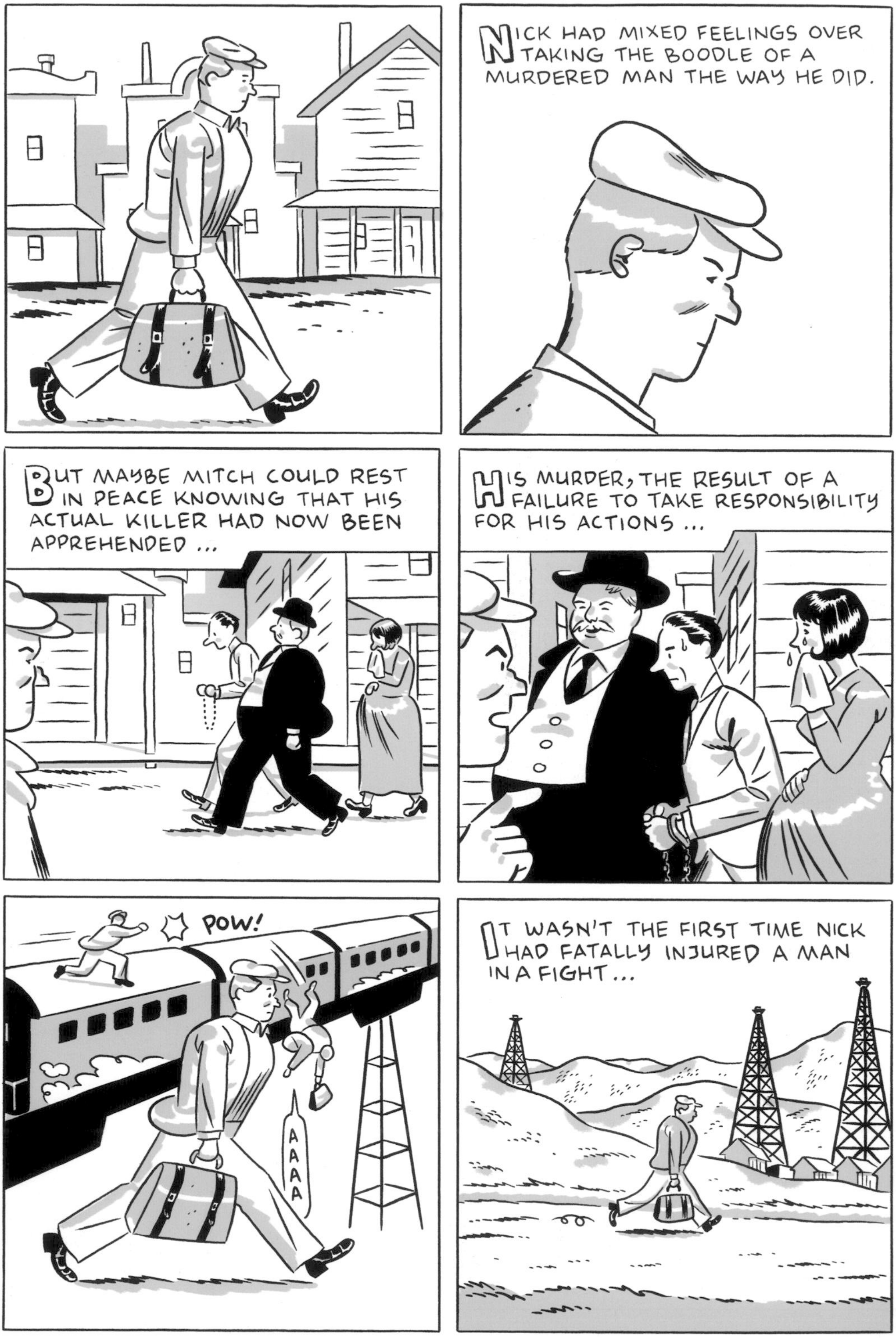
NICK HAD MIXED FEELINGS OVER TAKING THE BOODLE OF A MURDERED MAN THE WAY HE DID.
BUT MAYBE MITCH COULD REST IN PEACE KNOWING THAT HIS ACTUAL KILLER HAD NOW BEEN APPREHENDED ...
HIS MURDER, THE RESULT OF A FAILURE TO TAKE RESPONSIBILITY FOR HIS ACTIONS ...
POW!
AAAA
IT WASN'T THE FIRST TIME NICK HAD FATALLY INJURED A MAN IN A FIGHT ...

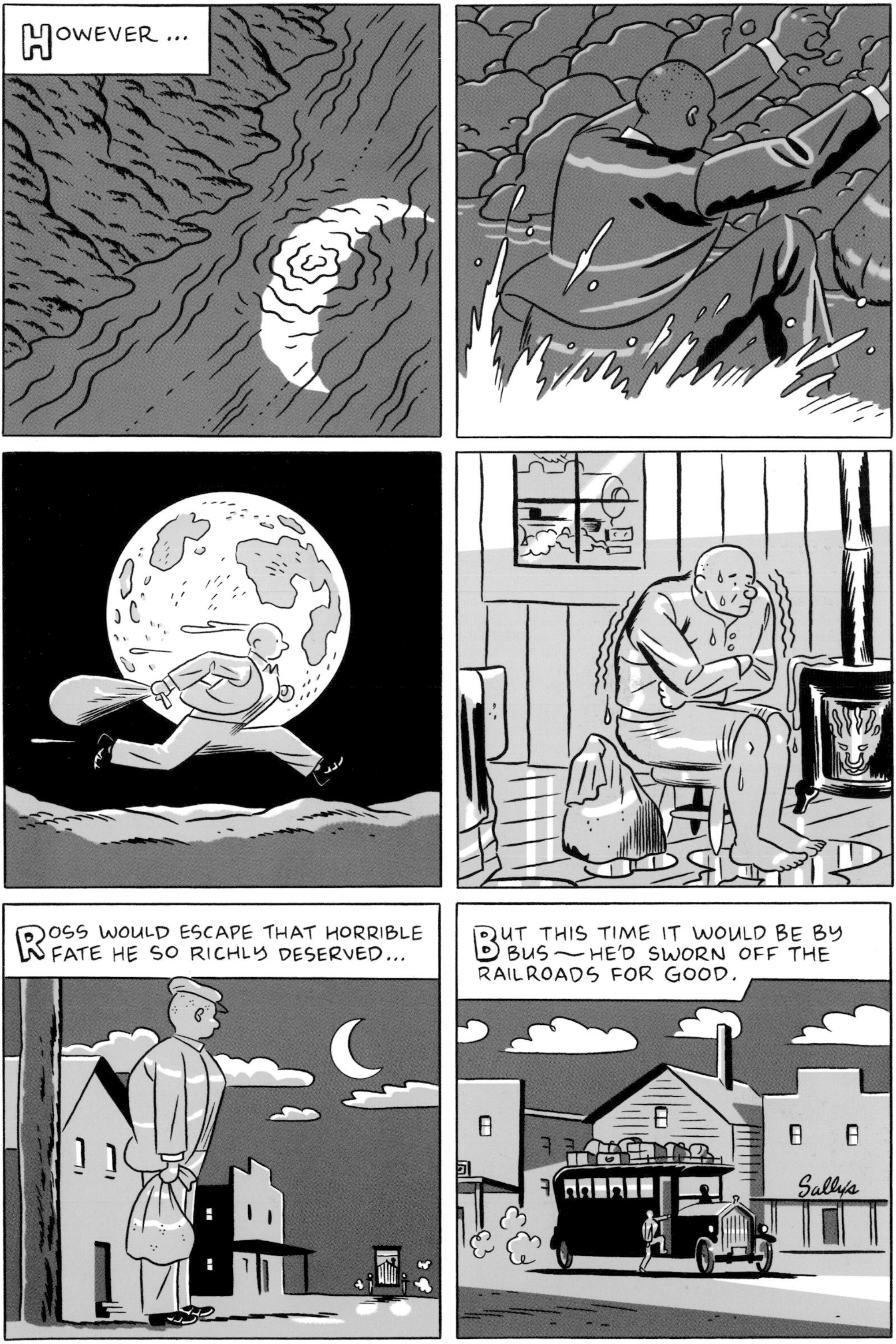
HOWEVER ...
ROSS WOULD ESCAPE THAT HORRIBLE FATE HE SO RICHLY DESERVED...
BUT THIS TIME IT WOULD BE BY BUS — HE'D SWORN OFF THE RAILROADS FOR GOOD.
Sally's

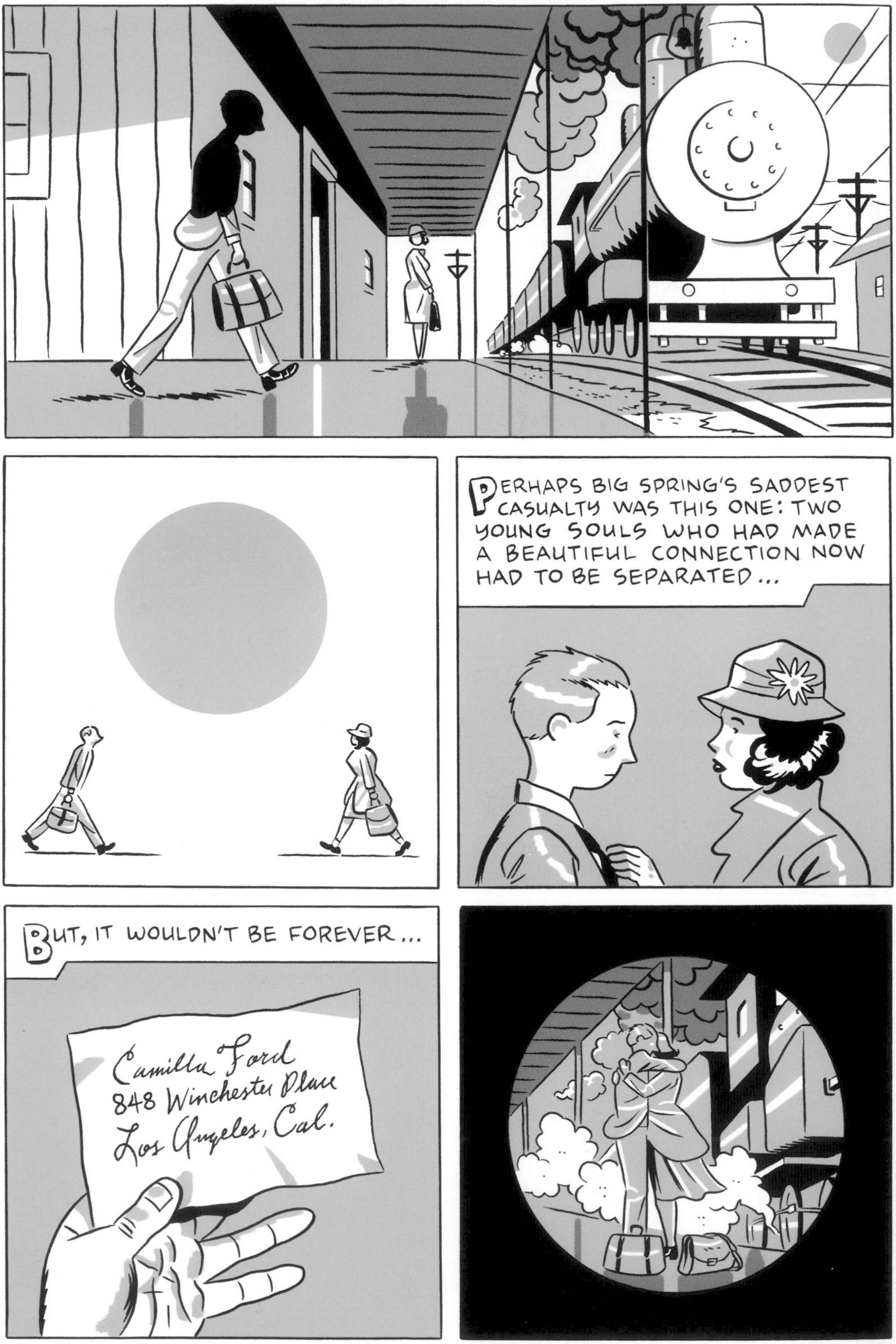
PERHAPS BIG SPRING'S SADDEST CASUALTY WAS THIS ONE: TWO YOUNG SOULS WHO HAD MADE A BEAUTIFUL CONNECTION NOW HAD TO BE SEPARATED...
BUT, IT WOULDN'T BE FOREVER...
Camilla Ford
848 Winchester Place
Los Angeles, Cal.

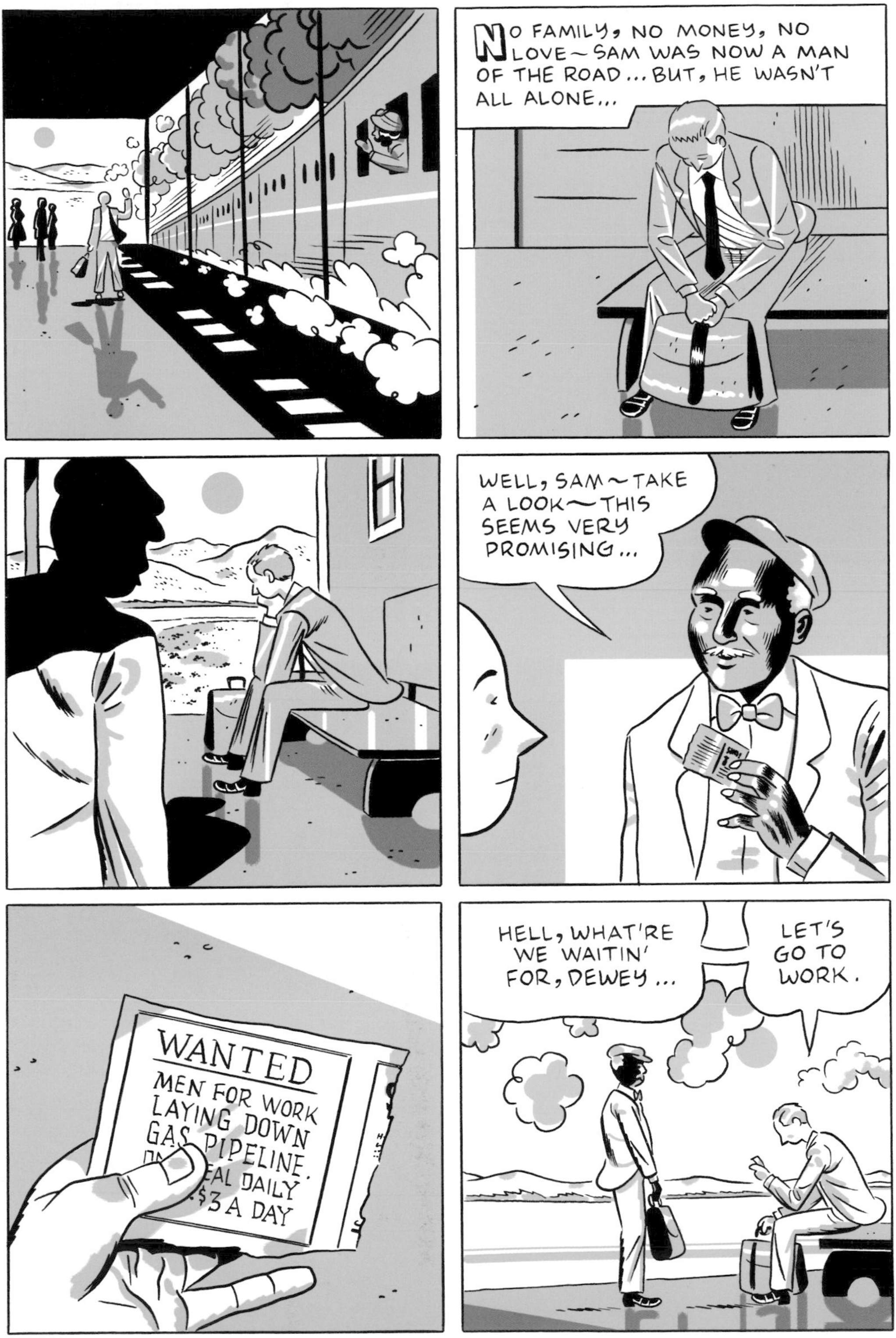
NO FAMILY, NO MONEY, NO LOVE ~ SAM WAS NOW A MAN OF THE ROAD... BUT, HE WASN'T ALL ALONE...
WELL, SAM ~ TAKE A LOOK ~ THIS SEEMS VERY PROMISING...
WANTED
MEN FOR WORK
LAYING DOWN
GAS PIPELINE.
EAL DAILY
$3 A DAY
HELL, WHAT'RE WE WAITIN' FOR, DEWEY...
LET'S GO TO WORK.

the end

Published by Rich Tommaso and Recoil Crime/Suspense
Atlanta, GA
www.richtommaso.com
richtommaso@yahoo.com

Edited by Amy Plasman

Distributed by Fantagraphics books

First edition: September 2012
Printed in China

10 9 8 7 6 5 4 3 2 1

ISBN: 978-1-60699-610-2

The publisher gratefully acknowledges the Kickstarter Foundation for its support in the
printing of this fine edition of comics.

Distributed in the U.S. by W.W. Norton and Company, Inc. (800-233-4830)

Distributed in Canada by Canadian Manda Group (800-452-6642 x862)

Distributed in the U.K. by Turnaround Distribution (44 020 8829-3002)

Distributed to comic book specialty stores by Diamond Comics Distributors (800-452-6642 x215)

Visit www.richtommaso.com
For Rich Tommaso's current on-going comics.

Thank You:

Kurt Stoskopf
Allen Mueller
Susan Johnson
John Eaton
Brian Sieveking
Leigh Smith
Miguel Alderete
David Berryman
John Lundquist
Jason Johnson
Margo Thoma
Morgane Lhote
Anne and Jacob Vagts
Mathieu Doublet
Amy Plasman
Tiffany Chatham Smith
Dean Haspiel
Eric Skillman
Igort
Christian Trimmer
Serge Ewenczyk
Gary Groth
Kim Thompson
Eric Reynolds
Joey Weiser
Joe Rice
Joe Tsambiras
Paul Karasik
Jeff Parker
Hunter Clark
Cindy Au
Chris Schweizer
Jamie S. Rich
Adam Staffaroni
Annie Koyama
Karma Savage
Alex Kim
Karl Stevens
Sara Kramer
Gerald and Cathy DeMartino
Stephen Bissette
Jessica Johnson
Keith Johnson
Lisa Healey
E Robert Wald
David Kiersh